Frommer's®

P9-COO-200

Washington, D.C.
day BY **day**™

2nd Edition

by Meredith Stanton

WILEY

Wiley Publishing, Inc.

Contents

Published by:

Wiley Publishing, Inc.

111 River St.
Hoboken, NJ 07030-5774

Copyright © 2010 Wiley Publishing, Inc., Hoboken, New Jersey. All rights reserved. No part of this publication may be reproduced, stored in a retrieval system or transmitted in any form or by any means, electronic, mechanical, photocopying, recording, scanning or otherwise, except as permitted under Sections 107 or 108 of the 1976 United States Copyright Act, without either the prior written permission of the Publisher, or authorization through payment of the appropriate per-copy fee to the Copyright Clearance Center, 222 Rosewood Drive, Danvers, MA 01923, 978/750-8400, fax 978/646-8600. Requests to the Publisher for permission should be addressed to the Permissions Department, John Wiley & Sons, Inc., 111 River Street, Hoboken, NJ 07030, 201/748-6011, fax 201/748-6008, or online at http://www.wiley.com/go/permissions.

Wiley, the Wiley Publishing logo, and Day by Day are trademarks or registered trademarks of John Wiley & Sons, Inc. and/or its affiliates. Frommer's is a trademark or registered trademark of Arthur Frommer. Used under license. All other trademarks are the property of their respective owners. Wiley Publishing, Inc. is not associated with any product or vendor mentioned in this book.

ISBN 978-0-470-49760-9

Editor: Alexia Travaglini
Production Editor: Lindsay Conner
Photo Editor: Richard Fox
Cartographer: Roberta Stockwell
Production by Wiley Indianapolis Composition Services

For information on our other products and services or to obtain technical support, please contact our Customer Care Department within the U.S. at 877/762-2974, outside the U.S. at 317/572-3993 or fax 317/572-4002.

Wiley also publishes its books in a variety of electronic formats. Some content that appears in print may not be available in electronic formats.

Manufactured in China

5   4   3   2   1

A Note from the Editorial Director

Organizing your time. That's what this guide is all about.

Other guides give you long lists of things to see and do and then expect you to fit the pieces together. The Day by Day guides are different. These guides tell you the best of everything, and then they show you how to see it *in the smartest, most time-efficient way*. Our authors have designed detailed itineraries organized by time, neighborhood, or special interest. And each tour comes with a bulleted map that takes you from stop to stop.

Hoping to relive the glory days of Washington and Jefferson, visit Butterstick (the baby panda) at the National Zoo, or tour the Smithsonian Institution's free museums? Planning a walk through Georgetown, or dinner and drinks where you can rub shoulders with lawmakers and other D.C. celebrities? Whatever your interest or schedule, the Day by Days give you the smartest routes to follow. Not only do we take you to the top attractions, hotels, and restaurants, but we also help you access those special moments that locals get to experience—those "finds" that turn tourists into travelers.

The Day by Days are also your top choice if you're looking for one complete guide for all your travel needs. The best hotels and restaurants for every budget, the greatest shopping values, the wildest nightlife—it's all here.

Why should you trust our judgment? Because our authors personally visit each place they write about. They're an independent lot who say what they think and would never include places they wouldn't recommend to their best friends. They're also open to suggestions from readers. If you'd like to contact them, please send your comments our way at feedback@frommers.com, and we'll pass them on.

Enjoy your Day by Day guide—the most helpful travel companion you can buy. And have the trip of a lifetime.

Warm regards,

Kelly Regan

Kelly Regan, Editorial Director
Frommer's Travel Guides

About the Author

A Baltimore native and resident of Washington for nearly 10 years, **Meredith Stanton** is an avid traveler, a foodie, and an art lover. Her work has profiled international travel locales, high-powered personalities, and top D.C. destinations. Stanton's writing has appeared in *USA Today, Executive Travel, Baltimore Magazine, WaterSki Magazine, WebMD, the Magazine, Washington Flyer*, and many others.

Acknowledgments

To Adam, for always keeping me grounded. And to my family, who's constant encouragement and support has been there when I needed it most.

Thank you to Lauren Kennedy for always pushing me to do better, having my back, and generally knowing which fights to fight. And thousands of thanks to my wonderful coworkers, and best friends, who help make every day worth it.

An Additional Note

Please be advised that travel information is subject to change at any time—and this is especially true of prices. We therefore suggest that you write or call ahead for confirmation when making your travel plans. The authors, editors, and publisher cannot be held responsible for the experiences of readers while traveling. Your safety is important to us, however, so we encourage you to stay alert and be aware of your surroundings.

Star Ratings, Icons & Abbreviations

Every hotel, restaurant, and attraction listing in this guide has been ranked for quality, value, service, amenities, and special features using a **star-rating system.** Hotels, restaurants, attractions, shopping, and nightlife are rated on a scale of zero stars (recommended) to three stars (exceptional). In addition to the star-rating system, we also use a **kids** icon to point out the best bets for families. Within each tour, we recommend cafes, bars, or restaurants where you can take a break. Each of these stops appears in a shaded box marked with a coffee-cup-shaped bullet ☕.

The following **abbreviations** are used for credit cards:

AE	American Express	**DISC**	Discover	**V**	Visa
DC	Diners Club	**MC**	MasterCard		

Frommers.com

Now that you have this guidebook to help you plan a great trip, visit our website at **www.frommers.com** for additional travel information on more than 4,000 destinations. We update features regularly to give you instant access to the most current trip-planning information available. At Frommers.com, you'll find scoops on the best airfares, lodging rates, and car-rental bargains. You can even book your travel online through our reliable travel booking partners. Other popular features include:

- Online updates of our most popular guidebooks
- Vacation sweepstakes and contest giveaways
- Newsletters highlighting the hottest travel trends
- Podcasts, interactive maps, and up-to-the-minute events listings
- Opinionated blog entries by Arthur Frommer himself
- Online travel message boards with featured travel discussions

A Note on Prices

In the "Take a Break" and "Best Bets" sections of this book, we have used a system of dollar signs to show a range of costs for 1 night in a hotel (the price of a double-occupancy room) or the cost of an entree at a restaurant. Use the following table to decipher the dollar signs:

Cost	Hotels	Restaurants
$	under $100	under $10
$$	$100–$200	$10–$20
$$$	$200–$300	$20–$30
$$$$	$300–$400	$30–$40
$$$$$	over $400	over $40

An Invitation to the Reader

In researching this book, we discovered many wonderful places—hotels, restaurants, shops, and more. We're sure you'll find others. Please tell us about them, so we can share the information with your fellow travelers in upcoming editions. If you were disappointed with a recommendation, we'd love to know that, too. Please write to:

Frommer's Washington, D.C. Day by Day, 2nd Edition
Wiley Publishing, Inc. • 111 River St. • Hoboken, NJ 07030-5774

12 Favorite
Moments

12 Favorite **Moments**

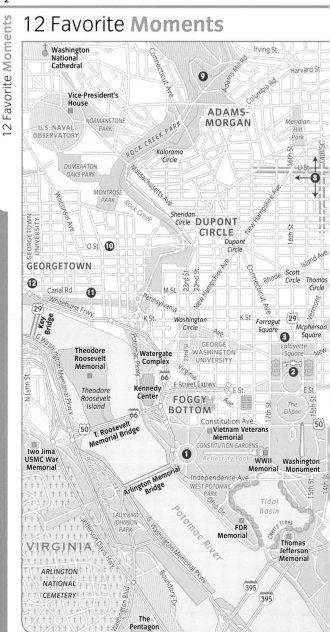

Washington National Cathedral

Vice-President's House

U.S. NAVAL OBSERVATORY

NORMANSTONE PARK

Irving St.

Harvard St.

Connecticut Ave.

Adams Mill Rd.

Columbia Rd.

9

ADAMS-MORGAN

Meridian Hill Park

ROCK CREEK PARK

Kalorama Circle

16th St.

14th St.

DUMBARTON OAKS PARK

MONTROSE PARK

Massachusetts Ave.

Rock Creek

Sheridan Circle

DUPONT CIRCLE

Dupont Circle

U St.

8

16th St.

Wisconsin Ave.

GEORGETOWN UNIVERSITY

O St. **10**

GEORGETOWN

New Hampshire Ave.

23rd St.

22nd St.

M St.

Pennsylvania

Connecticut Ave.

Rhode

Scott Circle

Thomas Circle

Island Ave.

Vermont

12

Canal Rd.

Whitehurst Frwy.

11

29

Key Bridge

G. Washington Memorial Pkwy.

N. Lynn St.

Theodore Roosevelt Memorial

Theodore Roosevelt Island

Potomac Pkwy.

Washington Circle

K St.

Ave.

K St.

Farragut Square

29

Mcpherson Square

3

GEORGE WASHINGTON UNIVERSITY

Lafayette Square

New

2

Watergate Complex

66

Kennedy Center

23rd St.

Virginia

E Street Expwy.

E St.

E St.

E St.

FOGGY BOTTOM

The Ellipse

50

66

T. Roosevelt Memorial Bridge

Constitution Ave.

Vietnam Veterans Memorial

17th St.

15th St.

14th St.

Iwo Jima USMC War Memorial

CONSTITUTION GARDENS

Reflecting Pool

1

WWII Memorial

Washington Monument

50

Arlington Memorial Bridge

Independence Ave.

WEST POTOMAC PARK

Ohio Dr.

Boundary Channel

Jefferson Davis Hwy.

LADY BIRD JOHNSON PARK

G. Washington Memorial Pkwy.

Potomac River

Tidal Basin

Cherry Trees

FDR Memorial

Thomas Jefferson Memorial

VIRGINIA

ARLINGTON NATIONAL CEMETERY

Washington Blvd.

Boundary Dr.

395

395

The Pentagon

Previous page: The U.S. Capitol in spring.

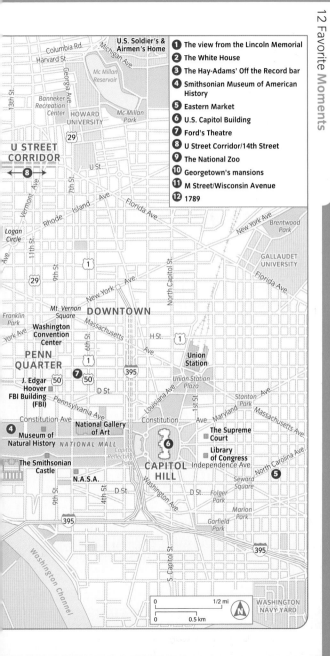

1. The view from the Lincoln Memorial
2. The White House
3. The Hay-Adams' Off the Record bar
4. Smithsonian Museum of American History
5. Eastern Market
6. U.S. Capitol Building
7. Ford's Theatre
8. U Street Corridor/14th Street
9. The National Zoo
10. Georgetown's mansions
11. M Street/Wisconsin Avenue
12. 1789

Funnyman Bob Hope once said: "I love to go to Washington—if only to be near my money." While it's true that fiscal policy and other matters of some importance are decided here, American government, with its Hollywood-like allure, is not the only attraction drawing a never-ending stream of visitors to the nation's capital. There is stunning architecture. World-class museums. Zeitgeist-changing theater. Cherry trees and great green spaces. Historic neighborhoods. An international pool of locals who call this place home. Super shopping. And, of course, the monuments that honor the brave, the fallen, and the founders of this fine country. Comedians inevitably target Washington for laughs; once you arrive in D.C., you'll be smiling, too.

① Gaze across the National Mall. From the foot of the Lincoln Memorial, the view—of the Reflecting Pool, the Vietnam and World War II memorials, the Washington Monument, and, in the distance, the Capitol Building—is monumental. It may leave a lump in the throat of even a cynical onlooker. See p 9.

② Peer through the iron fence at 1600 Pennsylvania Avenue for a glimpse of America's most famous address. Unless you reserved a tour months in advance, you can't get close, but the vision alone is enough to renew your patriotic spirit. See p 31.

③ Eavesdrop on the hushed conversations between D.C. movers and shakers at the Hay-Adams' venerable Off the Record Bar. Grab a stool and chat with longtime bartender John Boswell, confidante to ambassadors, spy masters, and presidents, and enjoy caricatures of some of the country's most powerful. See p 149.

④ Marvel at the country's cultural and historic icons at the Smithsonian's National Museum of American History, home to the Star-Spangled Banner, Dorothy's ruby slippers, Kermit the Frog, and more. See p 68.

The reflecting pool on the National Mall, with a view to the National Monument.

The Tidal Basin in spring.

⑤ Troll for treasures from Eastern Market on Capitol Hill. Savor a piping hot coffee and flaky pastry as you scavenge for unique, secondhand baubles and retro clothing, colorful flowers, organic fruits and vegetables fresh off the farm, and one-of-a-kind arts and crafts. See p 99.

⑥ Observe elected officials at work during a session of Congress. Or watch the American legal system in action, just a few blocks away, at the United States Supreme Court. See p 29.

⑦ Take in a show at the renovated Ford's Theatre. The historic site is a living memorial to President Abraham Lincoln, who was assassinated there in 1865. Along with an exhibit of collected artifacts, the theater is center stage for some of the area's most celebrated plays from Lincoln's period. See p 55.

⑧ Explore the U Street Corridor and 14th Street. The energetic, youthful, bohemian energy in these two newly regenerated

sister neighborhoods has reclaimed once-blighted streets. Now they're fairly bursting with one-off boutiques, cool cafes, and news-making art galleries. See p 82.

⑨ Roar right along with the lions, tigers, and bears at the National Zoo. Then visit the famous giant pandas, including D.C.'s beloved Tai Shan. And don't miss the sweet petting zoo or the nearby "pizza" playground for very young children. See p 47.

Think Pink

D.C. is another world in late March and April, when its ubiquitous Japanese cherry blossoms peak. Even politicians lose their pallor beneath the clouds of pink flowers along the Tidal Basin, a gift from the city of Tokyo in 1912. The **National Cherry Blossom Festival** (☎ 844/44BLOOM [442-5666]; www.nationalcherryblossom festival.org) includes a crew race, fireworks, a dinner cruise, a Japanese street fair, and more.

⓾ Bask in history amid Georgetown's massively impressive mansions. Most are at least 100 years old; many were built several centuries ago. In Georgian and Federal styles, they bear grand architectural details—such as round rooms and circular central staircases—that have all but disappeared from modern architecture. See p 90.

⓫ Rack up the charges on your credit cards in the upscale shops on M Street and

Tai Shan's birthday at the National Zoo.

Wisconsin Avenue. A legion of beautiful people, Georgetown undergrads, and D.C.'s elite are usually on parade, incurring the same fiscal damages.

⓬ Romance your significant other over a prime bottle of wine at 1789. The crackling fire and soft lighting at this tony New American restaurant has warded off many a chill in Georgetown. See p 135. ●

The White House viewed over the North Lawn.

The Best **Full-Day Tours**

8

The Best of D.C. in **One Day**

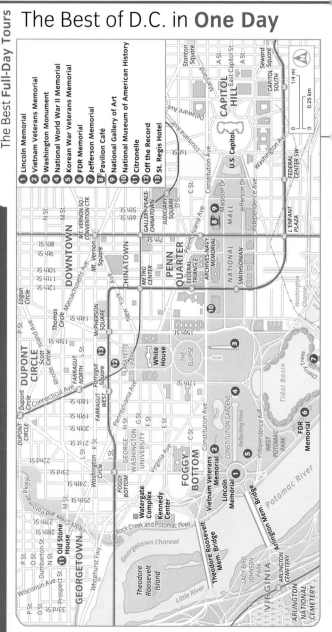

1 Lincoln Memorial
2 Vietnam Veterans Memorial
3 Washington Monument
4 National World War II Memorial
5 Korean War Veterans Memorial
6 FDR Memorial
7 Jefferson Memorial
8 Pavilion Café
9 National Gallery of Art
10 National Museum of American History
11 Citronelle
12 Off the Record
13 St. Regis Hotel

Previous page: The Library of Congress.

This full-day tour guides you through The Mall and George-town—the two parts of the District you must experience before leaving town, despite the fact that Georgetown is slightly off the public transportation grid. Both attract visitors in droves for good reason, so don't feel like a lemming if you end up following kids in matching T-shirts as you explore The Mall's free monuments and museums and then the cobblestone sidewalks of M Street in George-town. START: **Metro to Foggy Bottom, then a 30-minute walk, or take Tourmobile**

Travel Tip

I recommend exploring the monuments on foot, but those who can't might consider **Tourmobile** (☎ 888/868-7707; www.tourmobile. com). Its red, white, and blue sight-seeing trams travel in a loop around the monuments, passing by every 15 to 30 minutes. One fare is good for the day ($27 for passengers 12 and up, $13 for kids 3–11). National Park Service rangers are on duty at the following monuments daily 9:30am–11:30pm.

❶ ★★★ Lincoln Memorial.
Start your day at 8:30am, on the steps of this iconic tribute to Abraham Lincoln, the beloved 16th president of the United States. Architect Henry Bacon designed this marble, Greek temple–inspired memorial in 1914. Its 36 Doric columns reflect the states of the Union at the time of Lincoln's assassination in 1865—days after the Southern states surrendered the Civil War. Daniel Chester French designed the nearly 20-foot-tall (6m) sculpture of Lincoln, seated in solemn repose, surrounded by inscriptions of his immortal words from the Gettysburg address and his second inaugural address. You'll likely feel chills while gazing across The Mall and contemplating Lincoln's "dedication to the proposition that all men are created equal." ⏱ *30 min.*

☎ *202/426-6841. www.nps.gov/linc. Free admission. Metro: See start, above.*

❷ ★★★ Vietnam Veterans Memorial. In Constitution Gardens, "The Wall" honors the 58,000 servicemen and -women who perished or disappeared during the Vietnam War. Two black slabs of granite seem to grow from the earth toward each other, rising in height and joining to form a wide "V." Designed in 1980 by Maya Ying Lin, then an undergraduate at Yale, it has been likened to a "scar in the

The Lincoln Memorial.

The Best Full-Day Tours

The Vietnam Veterans Memorial.

earth," evoking the deep rift the war created among Americans. The names of the dead and missing are inscribed into the reflective stone. In reverent silence, mourning families make rubbings and leave flowers for their late sons, daughters, brothers, sisters, husbands, and wives. ⏱ *20 min.* ☎ *202/426-6841.*

The Washington Monument.

www.npa.gov/vive. Free admission. Metro: Foggy Bottom, then a 25-min. walk.

❸ Washington Monument. Robert Mills designed this 555-foot-tall (169m) monument to honor President George Washington. The world's tallest masonry structure when it was built in 1884, it's still visible from points throughout the city. If you can, reserve a ticket to the observatory, with its breathtaking views of the capital city. Tickets are free but required, and usually run out by 9am. You can make advance reservations for a $1.50 fee by calling ☎ 877/444-6777 or going to www.recreation.gov. ⏱ *20 min.* ☎ *202/426-6841. www.nps.gov/ wash. Daily 9am–4:45pm. Closed July 4 and Dec 25. Metro: Smithsonian, then a 10-min. walk.*

❹ National World War II Memorial. After controversy between activists demanding a tribute to "the greatest generation" that fought and died in World War II, and naysayers who didn't want The Mall altered, this serene memorial

was completed in 2004—without obstructing the views of the Lincoln Memorial or Washington Monument. Built of bronze and granite, it features 56 pillars that represent the unity of the states and territories in their decision to enter the war. The 4,000 sculpted gold stars on the Freedom Wall signify the 400,000 Americans who died fighting from 1941 to 1945. ⏱ *20 min.* ☎ *202/619-7222. www.wwiimemorial.com. Free admission. Metro: Farragut West, Federal Triangle, or Smithsonian, with a 25-min. walk.*

⑤ Korean War Veterans Memorial. The image of 19 larger-than-life ground soldiers slogging through a field, dressed in identical flowing rain capes, helmets, and battle gear, is haunting. Completed in 1986, it reminds viewers of a war forgotten by many, and honors the men and women who gave their lives for it, far from home. ⏱ *20 min.* ☎ *202/426-6841. www.nps.gov/kowa. Free admission. Metro: Foggy Bottom, then a 30-min. walk.*

⑥ FDR Memorial. This 7½-acre (3-hectare) outdoor memorial with four outdoor rooms, or galleries, celebrates the man who saw the U.S. through the Great Depression and much of World War II. Designed by Lawrence Halprin in 1978 (and completed in 1997), it tells the story of Franklin Delano Roosevelt's four-term presidency: Each gallery represents the challenges of the time and showcases FDR's most famous quotes alongside sculptures of soup

The Korean War Veterans Memorial.

lines, the president in his wheelchair, his passionately political wife Eleanor, and more. ⏱ *20 min.* ☎ *202/426-6841. www.nps.gov/frde. Free admission. Metro: Smithsonian, then a 30-min. walk.*

⑦ ★★★ Jefferson Memorial. Modeled after the Pantheon in Rome, this circular colonnaded structure fronts the picturesque Tidal Basin—which is lined with cherry trees that burst into rosy color from late March through mid-April. Architect John Russell drew from Thomas Jefferson's love of neoclassical design to celebrate the third president's contributions as a renowned architect, scientist, politician, musician, diplomat, and inventor. Dedicated in 1943, it features a 19-foot-tall (5.7m) bronze statue of Jefferson inside. ⏱ *20 min.* ☎ *202/426-6841. www.nps.gov/thje. Free admission. Metro: Smithsonian, then a 25-min. walk.*

It's tough to know where to find a quick bite to eat amid so many museums and government buildings. The **⑧ kids Pavilion Café**, in the National Gallery of Art Sculpture Garden, has a solid menu of salads, sandwiches, espresso drinks, and baked goods. Dine outdoors on warm days, or gaze out at the ice-skating rink in winter. *9th St. and Constitution Ave., NW.* ⏱ *45 min.* ☎ *202/289-3360. $. Metro: Archives, Judiciary Square, or Smithsonian.*

⑨ ★★★ National Gallery of Art. If you visit only one of the city's free art museums, make it this one, founded in 1937. Its permanent collection spans 9 centuries of masterworks: early Italian and Flemish Renaissance paintings, including the single Leonardo da Vinci painting in the U.S.; the High Renaissance works of Titian; the Dutch interiors of Vermeer; the pre-Impressionist and Impressionist works of Monet, Manet, van Gogh, Degas, Toulouse-Lautrec, Gauguin, and Cézanne; and the modern masterpieces of Picasso, O'Keeffe, Johns, and Pollock, to name a few. Art lovers may want to clear out a whole day to wander these halls. Everyone else, allot 2 hours before heading to the National Museum of American History, your next stop. ⏲ *2 hr. See p 60 for service details.*

Edgar Degas' Little Dancer Aged Fourteen, at the National Gallery.

⑩ ★★ National Museum of American History. Want to see the original Kermit the Frog hand puppet? How about Dorothy's ruby red slippers, Archie Bunker's chair, or Muhammad Ali's boxing gloves? America's history is told through its objects, art, advertising, communications, and songs at this popular museum that reopened in 2008 after extensive renovations. The Star-Spangled Banner, the flag that inspired the national anthem, has been recently restored and is now housed in a dramatic new gallery and atrium dedicated to its preservation. Julia Child's kitchen, a 1903 Winton—the first car driven across the United States—and 14 dresses from First Ladies including Laura Bush, Jackie Kennedy, and Michelle Obama are just a few more of the objects on display here. For those who wish to immerse themselves for an afternoon or a full day, see chapter 3. ⏲ *1 hr. See p 68.*

John Singer Sargent's Nonchaloir (Repose), at the National Gallery.

White Elephants

As you wander among the monuments, memorials, and museums, you can't help but notice the **U.S. Capitol Building** (see p 28), at the eastern end of The Mall; the **Federal Reserve Building,** on Constitution Avenue, almost directly across from the Vietnam Veterans Memorial (open to the public through prearranged group tours; ☎ 202/452-3324); and the **White House,** behind its imposing wrought-iron fence, at 1600 Pennsylvania Ave. The new **Capitol Visitors Center** (p 39) features an exhibit hall and detailed tour information. The **White House Visitor Center,** at 15th and E streets, offers more details and a 30-minute video. See "Political Washington" on p 28 for more information.

⓫ ★★★ **Citronelle for dinner.**
After touring The Mall, hail a cab and head for historic Georgetown, home of the wealthy, the preppy, the powerful—and some of the city's finest restaurants. Chef Michel Richard has cultivated a dining empire in D.C., and Citronelle is squarely on top with its stylish, electric atmosphere and cuisine. *See chapter 7 for service details and other dining options. 3000 M St., NW (at 30th St).* ☎ *202/625-2150. Entrees $14–$42. AE, DC, MC, V. Metro: Foggy Bottom or Roslyn.*

⓬ ★★ **Off the Record for after-dinner drinks.** No visit to D.C. would be complete without a stop at the historic Hay-Adams Hotel, across Lafayette Park from the White House, and home to this legendary drinking establishment. The bar is a well-known place to see and be seen in the District, and a frequent haunt of journalists, lobbyists, politicians, and statesmen—some of whom just might be pictured in the dozens of political caricatures on display. Ask the bartender for the lowdown.
1 Lafayette Square, NW. ☎ *202/638-6600. www.hayadams.com. Metro: McPherson Square or Farragut West. See p 149.*

⓭ ★★★ **St. Regis Hotel.** In the heart of downtown, 2 blocks from the White House, this stately hotel recently reopened after a renovation restored its original architectural details. Rooms reflect the classic Washington design, but offer high-tech amenities. Don't miss the nightly champagne sabering ritual in the lobby (6pm fall and winter, 5pm spring and summer). *See chapter 10 for other lodging options. See p 166 for service details.*

Muhammad Ali's boxing gloves, at the National Museum of American History.

The Best of D.C. in **Two Days**

1. National Zoological Park
2. National Archives
3. Eastern Market
4. Library of Congress
5. U.S. Capitol Building
6. Supreme Court
7. The Mall
8. Sonoma Restaurant and Wine Bar
9. The Shakespeare Theatre

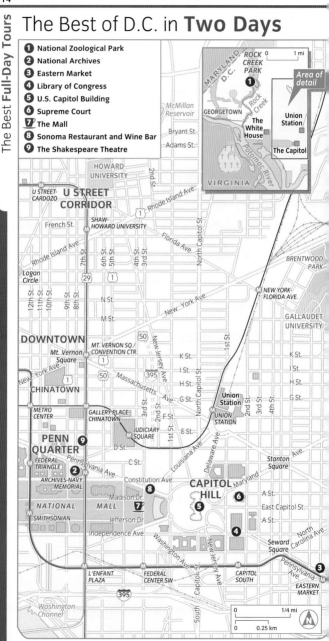

Day 2 starts at the National Zoo—home of giant pandas, lions, tigers, elephants, and more rare species. If you set out early enough (the zoo opens at 6am), you'll have time left to explore Capitol Hill—from the bustle of Eastern Market to the hustle of lawmakers and judges in the U.S. Capitol and Supreme Court buildings, both open for tours and spectators. START: **Metro to Woodley Park–Zoo**

1 ★★★ kids **National Zoological Park.** In 2005, the birth of Tai Shan, a giant panda cub, instantly captivated Washingtonians, who followed the little critter's progress every step of the way on the Zoo's online, live "pandacam." Nicknamed "Butterstick" because of his size at birth, the 3-year-old bear and his parents are still the main attraction at this 163-acre (65 hectare) park in downtown D.C. You won't need tickets to catch a glimpse of these rare creatures anymore, but crowds still regularly flock to see the pandas romp through their enclosure and eat frozen treats, so be sure to get there early. The pandas aren't the only draw here. Established in 1889, the National Zoo is home to some 500 species, many of them rare and/or endangered. You'll see cheetahs, zebras, camels, elephants, gorillas, hippos, seals, monkeys, meerkats, and, of course, lions, tigers, and (other) bears. If you have very young children, the hilly terrain can be tiring, especially on hot days. The zoo

The Panda House, at the National Zoo.

rents strollers, and the Kids' Farm provides a nice break from all that walking. Children 3 to 8 can observe farm animals up close: ducks, chickens, goats, cows, and miniature donkeys. ⏱ *60–90 min. Start: 8am (the zoo opens at 6am, so you can start earlier if you'd like more time) and allow 20 min. for Metro to next tour stop. 3001 Connecticut Ave. NW, adjacent to Rock Creek Park.*

Big cats at the National Zoo.

☎ 202/673-4800 or 673-4717. www. natzoo.si.edu. Free admission. Daily Apr–Oct (weather permitting): grounds 6am–8pm; animal buildings 10am–6pm. Daily Oct–Apr: grounds 6am–6pm; animal buildings 10am–4:30pm. Metro: Woodley Park–Zoo/ Adams Morgan or Cleveland Park.

Need a quick coffee or snack? Look for one of the three year-round eateries on zoo grounds: the **Mane Restaurant** on Lion/Tiger Hill, **Panda Café** near the Fujifilm Panda Habitat, or **Express Grill** at Panda Plaza. **PopStop,** across from the Small Mammal House, is seasonal. Vending machines are positioned near restroom and information facilities throughout the park.

❷ ★★ **National Archives.** After the Zoo, return to the Metro and head for the National Mall where you'll find, among the Smithsonian museums, some of the most important historic documents in U.S. history. The original Declaration of Independence, signed by members of Congress; the Constitution; the

Bill of Rights; and other fascinating glimpses into America's past are on display in the Rotunda of the National Archives Building. The Emancipation Proclamation, Articles of Confederation, Edison's light bulb patent, and letters from Abraham Lincoln can also be ogled at this monument to history. 🕐 1 hr: Start 9:45am. One-hour guided tours are available Mon–Fri, 9:45am. Reservations for self-guided tours are encouraged. 700 Pennsylvania Ave, NW. www.archives.gov. Mar 15 to Labor Day Mon–Fri 10:15am–5:30pm, Day after Labor Day to Mar 14, Mon–Fri 10:15am–4pm. Closed Thanksgiving and Dec 25. Metro: Archives/Navy Memorial.

❸ ★★ **Eastern Market.** Built in 1873, this city institution is a flea market, farmer's market, and crafts fair all rolled into one. A fire in 2007 destroyed its historic South Hall, but while it's being rebuilt you can still catch farmers' merchants selling their wares in the East Hall directly across the street. Recharge over lattes, pancakes, muffins, omelets, or even ham sandwiches and salt-and-vinegar chips here before you

The original Declaration of Independence, at the Library of Congress.

Interior of the Library of Congress.

shop. The outdoor lot fills on weekends (Mar–Dec) with farmers and fresh produce, artisans and ceramics, and bargain-hunters haggling over a mishmash of antiques. 🕐 *1 hr. See p 99 for service details.*

4 Library of Congress. Want to see the original "rough draft" of the Declaration of Independence written in Thomas Jefferson's own hand? This American treasure is here, along with the papers of other presidents, historic maps, revolving exhibitions, and multimedia resources. 🕐 *1 hr.; arrive 30 min. before tour begins. Docent-led, scheduled public tours depart Mon–Sat, in the Great Hall of the Thomas Jefferson Building, at 10:30, 11:30am, 1:30, 2:30, and 3:30pm. No 3:30pm tour on Saturdays. 101 Independence Ave. SE. www.loc.gov. Mon–Sat. 8:30am–4:30pm, except for federal holidays. Metro: Capitol South or Union Station.*

5 ★★★ U.S. Capitol Building. This majestic, 19th-century neoclassical landmark has served as the seat of American lawmaking since the first Congress in 1800. In 1793, George Washington laid the cornerstone of Dr. William Thornton's original design, and various architects saw to the building's completion in 1819. A museum of American art and history, as well as its principal civic forum, the Capitol is worth a stop just to see its architecture and hundreds of paintings, sculptures, and other artworks throughout its 17-acre (6.8-hectare) floor area. Tours can be arranged at the new Capitol Visitor Center (☎ **202/226-8000;** Mon–Sat 8:30am–4:30pm except Thanksgiving, Dec 25, and Jan 1), whose exhibition hall features the original plaster cast of the *Statue of Freedom,* the bronze statue that stands atop the Capitol dome, as well as 24 sculptures from the Capitol's Statuary Hall depicting each state's favorite sons and daughters. Visiting the CVC and the Capitol are free, and you can preorder Capitol tour tickets online. All food, beverages, large bags, and pointed objects are prohibited. 🕐 *1 hr. Entrance at the Capitol Visitors Center on E. Capitol St. at 1st St. NW. ☎ 202/225-6827. www.visitthecapitol.gov. Metro: Capitol South or Union Station.*

The Library of Congress reading room.

The Supreme Court of the United States.

Tip

You can find complete coverage of how to view the House or Senate galleries in session in "Political Washington" (see p 28).

6 ★★ **Supreme Court.** The chamber of the U.S. Supreme Court, the highest tribunal in the land, has been restored to its mid-19th-century appearance. Its nine justices, appointed for life terms, decide our collective fate—whether they're

The interior of the Supreme Court.

weighing in on federal laws or, more rarely, sealing a contested presidential election. The court convenes the first Monday in October and stays in session until it has heard all its cases and handed down decisions. The Court hears oral arguments the first 2 weeks of each month on Monday, Tuesday, and Wednesday. Visitors can listen to the arguments on short tours, or they can watch the day's entire proceedings. ⏱ *1–2 hr.; lines can be long, so be prepared to wait for up to 1 hr. If you're a legal eagle or Court TV fanatic and absolutely must see the day's full proceedings, arrive by 8:30am and get in line early, for first-come, first-served seating. Everyone else can start at 2pm or 3pm and gain entry with time to spare. 1 1st St. NE (between E. Capitol St. and Maryland Ave. NE).* ☎ *202/479-3211. www.supremecourtus.gov. Free admission. Mon–Fri 9am–4:30pm, except for federal holidays. Metro: Capitol South or Union Station.*

You have an hour or two before dinner and don't want to spoil it. If the weather is warm, grab a soda and snack at any of the many vendor carts stationed on **7** **The Mall.** Then, either relax on the grass and people-watch, admire the sights, check out a monument, or take in one of the dozens of events held on The Mall through the year—from kite-flying festivals to international dance performances. (Visit www.nps.gov/mall for a schedule.) Otherwise, take shelter at **Union Station** (Columbus Circle at Massachusetts Ave. and 1st St.), just a few blocks north, where you'll find snacks, coffee, shopping, and stunning architecture—plus a Metro station for transportation to your next stop.

8 ★ **Sonoma Restaurant and Wine Bar.** Oenophiles and fans of simply prepared, New American fare will adore Sonoma. With 40-plus wines by the glass, plus a lovingly edited wine list of some 200 Italian and French bottles, this upscale but casual bistro is the perfect place to sit and unwind after a long day of sightseeing. Airy and elegant, Sonoma serves "small plates" in four food groupings: cheeses and charcuterie, handmade pasta and pizzas, wood-grilled meats and fish, and organic salads and produce. Book your table in advance to be guaranteed an evening at this ever-popular hotspot. *If you plan to see a show after dinner, reserve for 5:30 or 6pm and tell your server you need the check by 7:30pm. See chapter 7 for other dining options. 223 Pennsylvania Ave. SE.* ☎ *202/544-8088. www.sonomadc.com. Lunch Mon–Fri; dinner daily. Metro: Capitol South.*

9 ★★ **The Shakespeare Theatre.** Catch the Bard's best, from A Midsummer's Night's Dream to Othello, in productions with astounding sets and nationally known actors. *450 7th St. NW (between D and E sts.).* ☎ *202/547-1122. www.shakespearedc.org. Tickets $23–$68. Metro: Gallery Place/Chinatown or Archives/Navy Memorial.*

Sonoma Restaurant and Wine Bar, with more than 40 vintages by the glass.

The Best of D.C. in **Three Days**

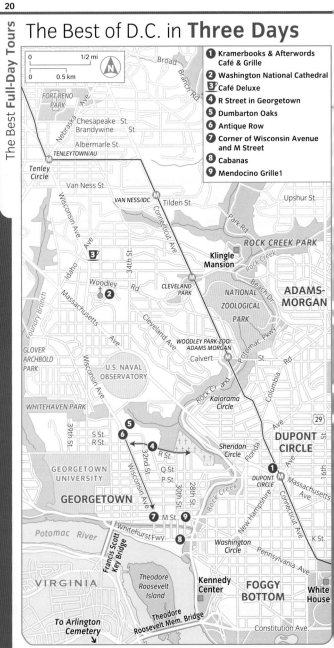

1. Kramerbooks & Afterwords Café & Grille
2. Washington National Cathedral
3. Café Deluxe
4. R Street in Georgetown
5. Dumbarton Oaks
6. Antique Row
7. Corner of Wisconsin Avenue and M Street
8. Cabanas
9. Mendocino Grille1

The Day 3 itinerary spirits you away from the crowds, past the highlights of Dupont Circle to the National Cathedral. Then you'll spend a leisurely afternoon browsing, spending some dosh, and sipping espressos in Georgetown. By the end of Day 3, you'll feel as though you know Washington—and we bet you won't want to leave. START: **Metro to Dupont Circle**

❶ ★★ Kramerbooks & Afterwords Café & Grill. This bookstore, grill, and coffee shop is the nerve center of Dupont Circle. A legendary gathering place, it's always packed with cool college kids, stylish gay men, voracious readers, debating politicians, and curious tourists who feel the urge to pick up Walt Whitman's *Leaves of Grass.* Open early in the morning and late at night, it's the perfect spot to start the day, over breakfast and the *Washington Post.* ⏱ *1 hr. Start: 8:30am. 1517 Connecticut Ave. NW (between Dupont Circle and Q St.).* ☎ *202/387-1400. www.kramers. com. $6.25–$9.75; lunch $8.25–$13; dinner $11–$18. Daily 7:30am–1am. Metro: See start, above.*

Kramerbooks & Afterwords Café & Grill, Dupont Circle.

❷ ★★★ Washington National Cathedral. This glorious cathedral, the world's sixth largest, is where presidents are eulogized and sometimes interred, and where many a member of high society is wed. With vaulted ceilings and rich stone carvings, the English Gothic architecture incorporates stones from shrines and historic buildings around the

Dumbarton Oaks, former home of Mildred and Robert Woods Bliss.

Washington National Cathedral.

universe—including outer space. That's right: A piece of lunar rock from the Apollo XI mission is embedded in the stained-glass Space Window. It's a big hit with kids, as is the Darth Vader gargoyle hidden among the spires. Episcopalian, the church has no local congregation; rather, it has functioned as a national house of prayer for various denominations, including Jewish and Serbian Orthodox citizens. (Download your own self-guided tour at www.cathedral.org.) ⏰ *1 hr. Start: 11am. Massachusetts and Wisconsin aves. NW.* ☎ *202/537-6200. tours@cathedral.org for tour information. Free admission. Mon–Fri 10am–5:30pm; Sat 10am–4:30pm; Sun 8am–6:30pm. No direct Metro access.*

Airy, light, and warm, **3** ★★ kids **Café Deluxe** is a bustling neighborhood bistro that serves New American classics such as roasted chicken, tuna steaks, and burgers. With small portions and crayons for kids. ⏰ *1 hr. 3228 Wisconsin Ave. NW (at Macomb St.).* ☎ *202/628-2233. $$. No direct Metro access.*

In pleasant weather, walkers will enjoy the roughly 20-minute downhill stroll to R Street, our next stop. Everyone else can take the 30, 32, 34, 35, or 36 bus lines in front of the Russian Embassy at 2650 Wisconsin Ave. NW, about a block north of the intersection of Wisconsin and Calvert. Taxis are also always plentiful on this main drag.

❹ **R Street in Georgetown.** With its four- and five-story brick Federal and Georgian-style mansions, painted in robins-egg blue and sunny yellow; its private gardens rife with red tulips and pale pink hydrangeas; and its uniform row houses and manicured lawns, this street epitomizes residential Georgetown. Simply put, R Street between Wisconsin Avenue and 28th Street NW is where most Washingtonians would choose to live if money were no object. It is also home to a spectacular botanical garden, a historic park, meandering trails with romantic benches and weeping willow trees, and a grand, private cemetery. ⏰ *2 hr. Start: 1:30pm.*

Samuel Francis Dupont Memorial.

Antique stores on Wisconsin Avenue, in Georgetown.

5 Dumbarton Oaks. Once a private residence, this 19th-century mansion is a research center for studies in Byzantine and pre-Columbian art and history, as well as landscape architecture. A former cow pasture, the grounds of Dumbarton Oaks were fashioned into staggeringly beautiful traditional European gardens—with an orangery, crocus, scilla, narcissus, magnolia, and cherry blossoms. Walkways are lined with bubbling fountains, stone archways, romantic hideaways, tiled pools, and a Roman-style amphitheater. The mansion reopened in 2008 after renovations, and the gardens remain open year-round, weather permitting (Apr–May are peak months). 🕐 *30 min. 1703 32nd St. NW (garden entrance at 31st and R sts.).* 📷 *202/339-6401. www.doaks. org. Gardens: $8 adults; $5 kids & seniors. Tues–Sun year-round; Mar 15–Oct 31 2–6pm, Nov 1–Mar 14 2–5pm (except national holidays and Dec 24). No Metro access.*

6 Antique Row. Depending which way you're walking, Antique Row is either a cool cruise downhill or a steep upgrade. In either case, antiques lovers won't care—they'll be too busy gaping at the storefronts with mint condition 18th-century divans, beautifully painted Persian consoles, weathered ceramic water jugs, and all sorts of one-of-a-kind finds. The best of the lot: Carling Nichols, Cherry, Gore-Dean, and for early-20th-century fans, Random Harvest. Bring your black AmEx card for this shopping stroll—prices are that steep. 🕐 *45 min. Start: 3:45pm. Wisconsin Ave., from S to N sts.*

7 ★★ Corner of Wisconsin Avenue and M Street. Look down M Street and you'll spy Intermix, Coach, Lacoste, Sephora, Kate Spade, and the new design district, Cady's Alley. Look up Wisconsin and see Benetton, Ralph Lauren, the Apple Store, Baby Gap, Sugar, Urban Chic, and a slew of antiques stores. It could be an expensive afternoon. When you're all shopped out, walk south, downhill, on Wisconsin Avenue. It will deliver you to the Washington Harbor and the Potomac River. 🕐 *1½ hr. Start: 4:30pm.*

Detour to Arlington National Cemetery

Arlington National Cemetery's 612 acres (248 hectares) honors national heroes and more than 260,000 war dead, veterans, and dependents. Many famous Arlington graves bear nothing more than simple markers, such as five-star General John J. Pershing's tomb. Highlights include the **Tomb of the Unknowns,** containing the unidentified remains of service members from World Wars I and II, and the Korean War. **Arlington House** (☎ 703/235-1530; www.nps.gov/arho), built by Martha and George Washington's grandson, George Washington Parke Custis, is a 20-minute walk from the Visitor Center. **Pierre Charles L'Enfant's grave,** near Arlington House, is believed to afford the best view of Washington, the city he designed. Below Arlington House is the **gravesite of John Fitzgerald Kennedy.**

Jacqueline Kennedy Onassis rests next to her husband, and Robert Kennedy is buried close by. Arrive close to 8am to contemplate the site quietly. The **Visitor Center** offers a detailed map, restrooms, and **Tour-mobile tickets** (p 9).

Tombstones at Arlington.

❽ Cabanas for cocktails. Stroll the promenade, gaze at the boats slicing through the Potomac waves, and then order a cocktail—you deserve to sit down and relax. The Washington Harbor has loads of restaurants, but most are better for their outdoor seating and views of the river than for their culinary inventiveness. So we suggest you stop by Cabanas, or any of its neighboring restaurant/bars (they're right on top of each other), for a dirty martini or cold beer. And don't snack: Save room for a great meal, back on M Street. 🕐 *Head back to M St. by 7:15pm. 3050 K St. NW (waterfront).* ☎ *202/944-4242. Cocktails $7–$10. Lunch & dinner daily. Metro: Foggy Bottom.*

❾ ★★ Mendocino Grille for dinner. On a beautiful night, nothing beats a garden table at this stylish restaurant, which fuses the flavors of California and the Mediterranean. The interior is open and airy, the wine list is great, and lovely small touches abound. Bowls of zesty warm olives, for example, help stave off hunger while chef Drew Trautmann works his magic in the kitchen. It's casual enough that you won't need to change or fuss for dinner, but elegant enough that you shouldn't wear shorts. Book your table in advance, especially on weekend nights. See chapter 7 for other options. *2917 M St. NW (at 29th St.).* ☎ *202/333-2912. www.mendocinodc.com. Entrees $18–$27. Metro: Foggy Bottom.* ●

Africa

Political Washington

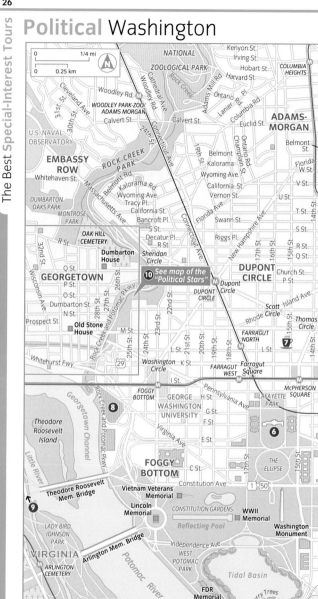

Previous page: The Smithsonian National Museum of Natural History.

D.C. Area

1 The U.S. Capitol Building
2 The Supreme Court
3 The FBI
4 International Spy Museum
5 Charlie Palmer Steak
6 The White House
7 Post Pub
8 The Watergate
9 The CIA
10 Map of the Political Stars
11 The Pentagon

Oh, the intrigue . . . the drama . . . the repressed yawns among members of Congress as they fight to stay awake during marathon legislative sessions on Capitol Hill. Exciting or not, Washington is pure politics, 24/7. If you live here, there's no escape from the maneuverings of our elected officials, and the (sometimes biting, sometimes toothless) press corps that hounds them. As they say, when in Rome . . . wear a toga. In Washington, don a (decent if not great) business suit, tuck The Economist into your bag, and wear your most winning (if not most sincere) grin. Work the crowds, shake hands, lobby for action, and forget the promises you made moments ago. You'll fit right in. START: **Metro to Capitol South or Union Station**

A legislator ascends the Capitol steps.

1 ★★★ The U.S. Capitol Building. Viewed from the wide avenues that radiate toward and away from it, the Capitol is almost palatial in its grandeur, atop the highest point between the Potomac and Anacostia rivers. Connected to the White House by a grand diagonal avenue (Pennsylvania Ave.), the Capitol was part of architect Pierre L'Enfant's plan to embody the separation of powers in the capital grid and architecture, when he laid out the city in 1791. The Capitol complex includes the Capitol, the House and Senate Office Buildings, the U.S. Botanic Garden, the Capitol Grounds, the Library of Congress buildings, and the Supreme Court Building. Among the Capitol's most impressive features are the cast-iron dome, the rotunda, the old Senate and Supreme Court chambers, the Brumidi Corridors, and the National Statuary Hall. When you tour the building, you'll see interior embellishments that include richly patterned and colored floor tiles, the vaulted and ornately decorated corridors on the first floor of the Senate wing, and the fluted white marble pillars lining the Hall of Columns, plus hundreds of paintings, sculptures, and other artworks, including the 4,664-square-foot (433 sq. m) fresco *The Apotheosis of Washington*. In late 2008, visiting the Capitol changed monumentally with the opening of the Capitol Visitor Center. This half billion–dollar complex, located beneath the Capitol itself, has an exhibition hall featuring the Statue of Freedom, amendments to the Constitution, and an 11-foot (3.4m) tall model of the Capitol Dome. Hands-on exhibits include virtual tours of the building and touchable reproductions of famous Capitol artworks. Remember—food, beverages, large bags, and pointed objects are prohibited on these tours. *East end of The Mall (entrance on E. Capitol and 1st sts. NW).*

Legislative Sessions Live

If you wish to visit the House and/or Senate galleries while they are in session, you'll need a pass from your congressional representative, or from your sergeant-at-arms if you live in the District (and suffer "taxation without representation"). The House gallery is open weekdays from 9am to 4pm when the House is not in session; the line for entry is on the south side of the U.S. Capitol Building. The Senate gallery is closed when not in session; the line for entry is on the north side of the **U.S. Capitol Building** (☎ **202/224-3121;** www.house.gov or www.senate.gov).

☎ *202/226-8000. www.aoc.gov, www.house.gov, or www.senate. gov. Mon–Sat, 1st tour at 8:50am and last at 3:20pm. Closed Jan 1, Thanksgiving, and Dec 25. Metro: See Start, above.*

❷ ★★ The Supreme Court. Whether they're voting over dimpled chads, overriding the popular vote in a presidential election, or walking a social tightrope over controversial federal laws, the nation's nine Supreme Court justices, who

are appointed for life terms, cast their votes here. Where the buck stops when it comes to determining the liberties of Americans, the chamber of the highest court in the land has been restored to its mid-19th-century appearance. It's worth visiting, if only to see for yourself how justice prevails—or sometimes doesn't.

The Court convenes on the first Monday in October and stays in session until it has heard all of its cases

The Senate Chamber of the U.S. Capitol.

The Guardian of Law, outside the U.S. Supreme Court.

and handed down its decisions. It hears oral arguments the Monday, Tuesday, and Wednesday of the first 2 weeks of each month. Visitors can listen to the arguments on short tours, or they can watch the entire day's proceedings. **Note:** If you are a legal eagle or Court TV fanatic bent on spending the whole day here, arrive by 8:30am to get in line early; seating is first-come, first-served. *1st and E. Capitol sts. NW.*

The Spy Museum.

202/479-3211. www.supreme courtus.gov. Free admission. Mon–Fri 9am–4:30pm, except federal holidays. Lines can be long; be prepared to wait for up to 1 hr. Metro: Capitol South or Union Station.

❸ The FBI. The highest level of American law enforcement, the Federal Bureau of Investigation is headquartered on Pennsylvania Avenue, between 9th and 10th streets, in the J. Edgar Hoover Building. While it once offered public tours, they have recently been suspended until further notice, due to "extensive renovations." But that shouldn't stop you from buying an FBI sweatshirt from a street vendor, and telling the kids back home you toured it anyway. *For more info on the FBI, check out www.fbi.gov.*

The official seal of the Federal Bureau of Investigation.

A model of the White House made by Jan and Zweifel.

④ ★★ International Spy Museum.

James Bond, eat your heart out. This place makes your "high-tech" gadgetry seem, well, quaint. Come tour the real deal, the first American museum dedicated to the art of espionage. Learn about Soviet double agents, attend a revolving itinerary of expert lectures, view the spy treasures from Hollywood films, play spy games, and do other supercool, supersneaky stuff. *800 F St. NW.* ☎ *866/SPY-MUSEUM (779-687386). www.spymuseum.org. Admission $18 adults, $17 seniors, $15 kids 5–11, free for kids under 5. Hours change monthly; see website for details. Metro: Gallery Place/Chinatown.*

An authentic shoe camera from the International Spy Museum.

Hungry Hill staffers and powerful politicos congregate in the sleek ⑤ ★★ **Charlie Palmer Steak** to enjoy prime steaks and crab cakes, among other seafood classics. *101 Constitution Ave, NW.* ☎ *202/547-8100. www.charliepalmersteak.com. $$$–$$$$$. Metro: Capitol South or Union Station.*

⑥ ★★★ The White House.

President John Adams and his wife, Abigail, were the first tenants, back in 1800, and every subsequent U.S. president and his wife have lived here since. President Barack Obama and his wife, Michelle, are the newest to call the House home, planting an organic garden on its lawn and even building a play set for daughters Malia and Sasha on the south grounds. But the White House has seen its share of drama over the years: It endured a fire set by invading British troops in 1812; survived another blaze in 1929 during Herbert Hoover's presidency; lived down President Clinton's Oval Office shenanigans in the late 1990s; and even served as a backdrop for the Aaron Sorkin series, *The West Wing,* taking drama to an Emmy-winning level. If you wish to tour its legendary rooms—from the elegant reception area of the Blue Room to the Yellow Oval Room, where state guests are entertained before or after official luncheons—you must do so in a group of 10 people or more. You also need

The Best Special-Interest Tours

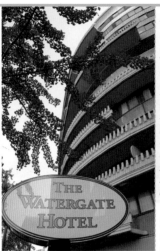

The infamous Watergate Hotel.

The Washington Post—immortalized by Bob Woodward and Carl Bernstein's dogged reporting on the Watergate scandal—at once exposes and greases the political machinery of the capital. Stop by the **7** ★★ **Post Pub,** where legions of ink-stained scribes come to slam a beer after a hard day fact-checking the latest innuendo, accusation, or blatant lie issued by one of the U.S.' fearless leaders. *1422 L St. NW (15th St.).* ☎ *202/628-2111. $. Metro: McPherson Sq. or Farragut North.*

to make an official request and submit it through your member of Congress. These self-guided tours are scheduled on a first-come, first-served basis and need to be made at least 1 month in advance of your visit. To enhance your experience, stop by the White House Visitor Center to view exhibitions on the architecture, furnishings, events, and social history of America's First Address. *1600 Pennsylvania Ave. NW.* ☎ *202/456-7041 (24-hr. information hot line). www.whitehouse. gov. Free admission. Tours: Tues–Sat 7:30am–12:30pm; visitor center: daily 7:30am–4pm. Closed on federal holidays. Metro: Federal Triangle and McPherson Sq.*

President Richard Nixon, who made the Watergate infamous.

8 The Watergate. Remember when the Watergate Hotel was synonymous only with Nixon, botched burglaries, and Woodward and Bernstein? Now, when you walk by this Washington legend, you can't help but think of another salacious scandal that found its orbit here: The adjacent Watergate condo complex is where Monica Lewinsky hid for 9 months from a stalking press corps after news broke of her affair with President Bill Clinton. She left the residence in October 1998, leaving a note of apology to her neighbors. *Hotel: 2650 Virginia Ave. NW. Condo complex: 700 New Hampshire Ave. NW. Metro: Foggy Bottom.*

9 The CIA. Created in 1947, the Central Intelligence Agency is shrouded in mystery and speculation. This is another Washington institution that lives as much in our imaginations as it does in its dual headquarters, in McLean and Langley, Virginia. Its agents are involved in everything from nuclear proliferation to counter-terrorism to organized crime

Where Politicos Drink & Dine

For breakfast, lunch, and dinner on Capitol Hill, ★★ Bistro Bis (15 E St. NW; ☎ 202/661-2700), in the St. George Hotel, is a haunt among the power-tie/pumps-and-pearls-set. Also on the Hill: Lounge 201 (201 Massachusetts Ave. NE; ☎ 202/544-5201). Where else can you shoot pool, sip a cocktail, and eavesdrop on the scuttlebutt of young Hill staffers, who flock here after work? In Penn Quarter, The Capital Grille (601 Pennsylvania Ave. NW; ☎ 202/737-6200) is ground zero for cigars, Scotch, steaks, suspenders, and high-level lobbying. Look for the sideshow of 20-something interns duking it out with 40-something power mavens for the attentions of married congressmen on the make. Catch prominent members of Congress wheeling and dealing at The Monocle (107 D St. NE; ☎ 202/546-4488), a tasty mainstay for lunchtime steaks and crab cakes. Steps from the White House, in the Hay-Adams Hotel, Off the Record Bar (800 16th St. NW; ☎ 202/638-6600) serves stiff drinks to power mongers. And John Boswell—four-time *Washingtonian* magazine "Best Bartender" winner—pretends not to overhear state secrets. When *Prep* author Curtis Sittenfeld held a book party, Smith Point (1338 Wisconsin Ave. NW; ☎ 202/333-9003) was the very preppy place where she held it. A hotspot among SUV-driving Young Republicans, it's where to head for Nantucket-style entrees—and the latest looks in Lacoste wear. The Bush twins were regulars at Town Hall (2218 Wisconsin Ave. NW; ☎ 202/333-5641) during their going-out days. Both levels of this New American restaurant are still constantly packed with Georgetown undergrads, but it's unlikely you'll see the Obama girls, ages 10 and 7, there anytime soon.

(and, some may wonder and worry, who knows what else?). Tours are not offered to the public due to security concerns. You can take either a virtual tour of the CIA Museum, which holds a declassified, permanent collection of artifacts and photographs of historic espionage tools; or a virtual tour of the CIA itself—what they'll show you, anyway—at the official website. *www.cia.gov.*

⓾ Map of the Political Stars. If you've ever cruised around Beverly Hills, California, you've seen the signs selling "Star Maps" that pinpoint the gated entrances to your favorite celebrities' private dwellings. Because Washington has famously been described as "Hollywood for Ugly People," I thought a map to the political stars was appropriate. Politicos set up house all around the District, but Georgetown is like the North Star when it comes to finding government types, past and present, so I focused the tour on this enclave for the rich and powerful—the Beverly Hills of the nation's capital.

Map of the Political Stars

A **Old Stone House** Pre-Revolutionary house preserved in its original condition (3051 M St. NW). **B** **John Kerry** A residence of the senator and former presidential candidate (3322 O St. NW). **C** **John and Jackie Kennedy** Their home before moving into the White House (3307 N St. NW). **D** **The *Exorcist* House** Right next to it are those famous steps (3600 Prospect St. NW). **E** **Alexander Graham Bell** Home of the inventor of the telephone (1527 35th St. NW). **F** **John Edwards** The former senator and his family live here. Also the former home of CIA head Frank Wisner. Legend has it that many CIA agents lived along Q Street during the Agency's founding years (3327 P St. NW). **G** **John Warner and Elizabeth Taylor** Home—once upon a time (3240 S St. NW). **H** **John F. Kennedy** He lived here after first being elected to Congress from Massachusetts's 11th District (1528 31st St. NW). **I** **Bob Woodward** Home of the Watergate reporter (3027 Q. St. NW). **J** **Tudor Place** Once home to six generations of

Martha Washington's descendants, it's now a museum (1644 31st St. NW). **K** **Katharine Graham** Former home of the woman who guided the *Washington Post* for decades (2920 R St. NW). **L** **Dumbarton House** Originally belonged to Joseph Nourse, register of the Treasury for six presidents (2715 Q St. NW). **M** **Henry Kissinger** Home of the superdiplomat (3026 P St. NW). **N** **Miss Lydia English's Georgetown Female Seminary** Visited by Martin Van Buren, James Buchanan, and Daniel Webster (1311 30th St. NW). Later served as a Union Army hospital. **O** **Jackie Kennedy** She lived here briefly following JFK's assassination (3017 N St. NW). **P** **Beall Mansion** A portion of it is the oldest remaining brick structure in Georgetown, dating from 1780 (3033 N St. NW). **Q** **Pamela and Averil Harriman Home** (3038 N St. NW). **R** **Foxhall House** Residence of Henry Foxhall, whose foundry provided guns for the War of 1812 (2908 N St. NW). ⏱ *90 min.*

Aerial view of the Pentagon from the northeast.

11 ★★★ **The Pentagon.** The headquarters for the Department of Defense is one of the world's largest office buildings, holding approximately 23,000 government workers, both military and civilian. Perhaps only the White House figures as much into the collective consciousness. Popularized in Hollywood movies, it was scarred on the tragic day of September 11, 2001, when a hijacked airliner ripped into its west side, killing 125 workers and 59 passengers. The building smoldered for days. But, incredibly, the gash in its wall was rebuilt within 6 months and new offices were constructed by the 1-year anniversary of the attack. In dedication to the lives lost in the attack, the Pentagon 9/11 Memorial was constructed and unveiled on September 11, 2008. It consists of 184 benches—one for each victim—that range in height to represent the youngest and oldest persons killed in the attack. It's free and open to the public every day. For visitors who want to tour the building and pay their respects, you'll need to reserve a group tour at least 2 weeks (and a maximum of 3 months) in advance of your visit. *Off I-395.* ☎ *703/697-1776. http:// pentagon.afis.osd.mil. To submit your tour request, go to the web site and click "Tours." Free admission. Metro: Pentagon.*

Off the Record Bar in the Hay-Adams Hotel—deemed "one of the world's best hotel bars" by Forbes.

D.C. for **Architecture Lovers**

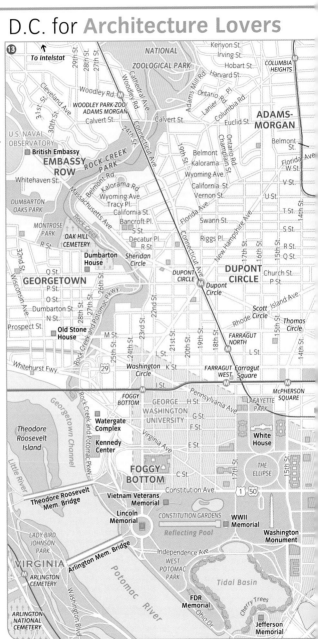

To Intelstat

NATIONAL ZOOLOGICAL PARK

Kenyon St.
Irving St.
Hobart St.
Harvard St.

COLUMBIA HEIGHTS

26th St.
28th St.
27th St.

Woodley Rd.
Woodley Rd.
WOODLEY PARK-ZOO/
ADAMS MORGAN

Cleveland Ave.

31st St.
30th St.

Cathedral Ave.
Connecticut Ave.
24th St.

Calvert St.
Calvert St.

Adams Mill Rd.
19th St.

Ontario Rd. Pl.
Lanier Pl.
Columbia Rd.
Euclid St.

ADAMS-MORGAN

U.S. NAVAL OBSERVATORY
British Embassy
EMBASSY ROW

Whitehaven St.

DUMBARTON OAKS PARK

MONTROSE PARK

ROCK CREEK PARK

Belmont Rd.
Kalorama Rd.
Wyoming Ave.
Tracy Pl.
California St.
Bancroft Pl.
S St.
Decatur Pl.
R St.

Massachusetts Ave.
Rock Creek

Belmont
Kalorama
Wyoming Ave.
California Ave.
Vernon St.

Ontario Rd.
Champlain St.

Belmont St.
Florida Ave.
W St.
V St.
U St.

Florida Ave.

Swann St.

Riggs Pl.

New Hampshire Ave.

17th St.
16th St.
15th St.
14th St.

T St.
S St.
R St.
Q St.

Connecticut Ave.

OAK HILL CEMETERY

Dumbarton House

Sheridan Circle

DUPONT CIRCLE
Dupont Circle

DUPONT CIRCLE

Church St.
P St.

32nd St.

Wisconsin Ave.

Q St.
GEORGETOWN
P St.
O St.
Dumbarton St.
N St.

32nd St.
28th St.
27th St.
26th St.

23rd St.

Scott Circle
Rhode Island Ave.

Island Ave.
15th St.

Thomas Circle

Prospect St.
Old Stone House

M St.

25th St.
24th St.
23rd St.
21st St.
20th St.
19th St.

L St.

FARRAGUT NORTH

17th St.
16th St.
15th St.
14th St.

Rock Creek and Potomac Pkwy.

Whitehurst Fwy.

29

Washington Circle

K St.

L St.

FARRAGUT WEST Farragut Square

McPHERSON SQUARE

I St.

Pennsylvania Ave.

LAFAYETTE PARK

Theodore Roosevelt Island

Georgetown

Rock Creek and Potomac Pkwy.

FOGGY BOTTOM
Watergate Complex
Kennedy Center

GEORGE WASHINGTON UNIVERSITY

Virginia Ave.

H St.
G St.
F St.
E St.

White House

THE ELLIPSE

17th St.

15th St.

FOGGY BOTTOM

C St.

Constitution Ave.

1 50

Theodore Roosevelt Mem. Bridge

Vietnam Veterans Memorial
Lincoln Memorial

CONSTITUTION GARDENS
Reflecting Pool

WWII Memorial

Washington Monument

LADY BIRD JOHNSON PARK

Arlington Mem. Bridge

Independence Ave.
WEST POTOMAC PARK

Tidal Basin

Cherry Trees

VIRGINIA
ARLINGTON CEMETERY

Potomac River

Washington Blvd.

FDR Memorial

Ohio Dr.

Jefferson Memorial

ARLINGTON NATIONAL CEMETERY

Little River

Theodore Roosevelt Channel

1 L'Enfant's Grid
2 The U.S. Capitol Building
3 Capitol Visitor Center
4 Folger Shakespeare Library
5 The Jefferson Building of the Library of Congress
6 National Museum of the American Indian
7 Smithsonian Castle
8 The National Gallery of Art
9 National Portrait Gallery
10 National Building Museum
11 Union Station
12 Center Café
13 National Cathedral

L'Enfant's Grid

A few years ago, Italian journalist Beppe Severgnini wrote *Ciao, America: An Italian Discovers the U.S.*—which hilariously details his experience living in an historic Georgetown row house. He echoes the sentiments I've heard among many expat Europeans in Washington: that despite the stark foreignness of America, despite the fast-food, techno-obsessed, impatient, kid-worshipping culture of this country, at least in D.C. there is the architecture. The state, international, and museum buildings here evoke the grand structures of Paris and the historically wrought designs of London, with the neoclassical embellishments of both—Roman-style pillars, carved flourishes, and weathered stone lions sitting on guard before public entrances. START: **Metro to Capitol South or Union Station**

The realization of Pierre L'Enfant's grid plan for the U.S. Capitol.

① L'Enfant's Grid. Designed in 1791 by French engineer Pierre L'Enfant, the District's street plan—a conventional city grid overlaid with grand, diagonal avenues—mimics the reverberating circular system of many great European cities. Designed to embody the separation of powers, and the balance between state and federal government, the grid links the Capitol and the White House via the grand Pennsylvania Avenue. Diagonal avenues are named for the states. The 2½-mile-long (4km), 400-foot-wide (120m) esplanade known as the National Mall links the White House with the Washington Monument.

Washington fired L'Enfant, whose grand scheme prevailed but took more than a century to build, with major snafus along the way (the British torched the Executive Mansion, the Capitol Building, and the Library of Congress in 1814). But D.C.'s centennial in 1900 brought renewed interest and commitment to L'Enfant's idea, attracting the likes of Frederick Law Olmstead, Daniel Burnham, and Charles McKim to realize its genius. *See the Library of Congress on p 57, which houses L'Enfant's original drawings.*

② ★★★ The U.S. Capitol Building. If New York's buildings are about height and might, and L.A.'s about low-level sprawl, Washington's are about neoclassical harmony and a fierce reverence for the era that birthed the nation's capital. No building better exemplifies these values than the Capitol. Amateur architect George Washington praised the original plans, drafted by Dr. William Thornton, for their "grandeur, simplicity, and convenience." Construction, however, was anything but simple. When Congress first met here in November 1800, it was still under construction. The project would take 34 years and six architects to complete, in 1826. It ended up being too small for its occupants, and so a second round of construction took place, finished by 1851. Lincoln insisted the expansion continue during the Civil War. The neoclassical structure now covers 4 acres (1.6 hectares); from the baseline of the east front to its pinnacle at the Statue of Freedom, the building is 288 feet (86m) tall. *Entrance at the Capitol Visitors Center on E. Capitol St. at 1st St. NW.* ☎ *202/225-6827. www.aoc.gov, www.visitthecapitol.gov, www.house. gov, www.senate.gov. Mon–Sat, 8:30am–4:30pm. Closed Jan 1, Thanksgiving, and Dec. 25. Metro: Capitol South or Union Station.*

❸ ★★★ Capitol Visitor Center. After 8 years and some highly contested arguments among Congress

The Capitol dome interior.

Folger Shakespeare Library reading room.

members, the largest addition to the 215-year-old U.S. Capitol building was unveiled in 2008. From the outside, it may not look like much—but that's the point. The Center was built underground on three levels, so as not to distract from the historic plan of the U.S. Capitol. At 580,000 square feet (5.4 hectares), it's three-quarters the size of the famous monument to American government and features skylights offering unique perspectives on the Dome and structures above. *First Street and East Capitol St. NE;* ☎ *202/226-8000. Free admission. Mon–Sat 8:30am–4:30pm except for Thanksgiving Day, Dec. 25, and Jan. 1. Metro: Capitol South or Union Station*

❹ Folger Shakespeare Library. The marble exterior of this neoclassical building blends harmoniously with the nearby Library of Congress and Supreme Court, but the interior is pure Tudor England, complete with oak paneling and plaster ceilings. The building was designed by Paul Philippe Cret, but the Shakespeare bas-reliefs on the exterior were designed by John Gregory. Masks of Comedy and Tragedy hang above the doors. *201 E. Capitol St. NE.* ☎ *202/ 544-7077. www.folger.edu. Free*

Curbing Vertical Sprawl

In 1899, Congress passed the Heights of Building Act, which stipulated that no private structure could rise higher than the Capitol Building or other important government edifice—meaning the skyscrapers of other towns would never stand a chance. (A later act amended this height restriction to 130 ft./39m, and made exceptions for spires, towers, and domes.) This merely challenged contemporary architects to soar to new "heights"; modern design here is concise but nonetheless stunning.

admission. Mon–Sat 10am–4pm; free walk-in tours daily at 11am. Closed federal holidays. Metro: Capitol South or Union Station.

❺ ★ The Jefferson Building of the Library of Congress. Originally, a much smaller version of the Library of Congress sat inside the new Capitol, until the British destroyed it upon sacking the city during the War of 1812. In its place, Thomas Jefferson offered his personal library. In 1886, Congress finally authorized construction of a larger Italian Renaissance–style library, designed by local architects John L. Smithmeyer and Paul J. Pelz. In the coming years, an equally impressive interior was added, courtesy of architect Edward Pearce Casey, who added decoration by more than 50 American artists. In the Main Reading Room, crane your neck to see the dome 160 feet (48m) above; the cupola is a female figure painted by artist Edwin Blashfield, representing "Human Understanding." *101 Independence Ave. SE (at 1st St.).* ☎ *202/707-8000. www.loc.gov. Free admission.*

The I. M. Pei wing of the National Gallery.

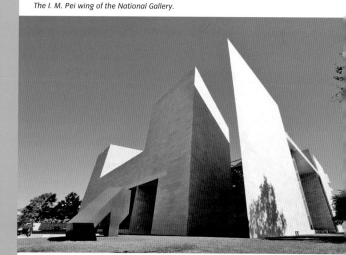

The National Gallery's East Building atrium.

Obtain same-day free tickets to tour the library inside the west entrance on 1st St. Mon–Sat 8:30am–4:30pm. Closed federal holidays. Metro: Capitol South.

6 ★★ **The National Museum of the American Indian.** A team of Native architects and consultants designed this pueblo-looking museum constructed of Kasota stone on the National Mall. With its curved façade and angled placement, the building aligns with Native American beliefs in the cardinal points. The grounds include cascading water, as well as wetlands of wild rice, marsh marigolds, corn, native tree species, and indigenous plants to honor local Native people. *4th St. & Independence Ave. SW. ☎ 202/633-1000. Free admission. Daily 10am–5:30pm, except Dec. 25. www.nmai.si.edu. Metro: L'Enfant Plaza*

7 **Smithsonian Castle.** From museums to monuments, marble is de rigueur for buildings along the National Mall. So no wonder this gothic Castle, placed squarely in the middle of the lot, sticks out. Architect James Renwick, Jr., of St. Patrick's Cathedral in New York, designed the original Smithsonian Institution Building in 1855, and constructed it of red sandstone from nearby Seneca Creek, MD. The classic structure is now home base for the Smithsonian Information Center and its own gallery. *1000 Jefferson Dr. SW. ☎ 202/633-1000. www.si.edu. Free admission. Daily, 8:30am–5:30pm. Metro: Smithsonian.*

8 **The National Gallery of Art.** The museum's triangular-shaped East Building—with its acute-angled stone corners, designed in 1978 by I. M. Pei—may look worlds apart from the neoclassical West Building across the plaza, but its marble was cut from the same quarry in Tennessee. The West Building, a design match with the nearby Natural History museum, was designed by John Russell Pope in 1941. *Constitution Ave. NW (3rd and 7th sts.). ☎ 202/737-4215. www.nga.gov. Free admission. Mon–Sat 10am–5pm; Sun 11am–6pm. Closed Jan 1 and Dec 25. Metro: Archives, Judiciary Sq., or Smithsonian.*

⑨ ★★★ The National Portrait Gallery. Designed by a number of prominent architects, including Robert Mills (designer of the Washington Monument), this museum was the third public building constructed in the city, after the Capitol and the White House. During the Civil War, it served as the site of Lincoln's second inaugural ball as well as a hospital for soldiers. Although it's a notable example of Greek Revival architecture, it was almost demolished in the 1950s before the Smithsonian Institution took over its control. It closed in 2001 for a 5-year renovation project that added more exhibition space, an auditorium, and an enclosed courtyard featuring a dramatic glass-and-steel roof. *8th and F sts. NW (in the U.S. Patent Office Building).* ☎ *202/ 275-1738. www.npg.si.edu. Free admission. Call for hours. Metro: Gallery Place/Chinatown.*

⑩ National Building Museum. This palatial brick museum took roughly 5 years to build, and was modeled after Italy's monumental Palazzo Farnese that Michelangelo

The interior dome of Union Station.

commissioned in 1589. The massive Great Hall of the building holds colossal Corinthian columns—among the tallest in the world—and extends 116 x 316 feet (35 x 96m). A fountain bisects the hall, stretching 28 feet (8.5m) across. Strategically placed windows, vents, and archways are part of a unique ventilation system that whisks a continuous flow of fresh air through the building. *401 F St. NW.* ☎ *202/272-2448. Free admission. Mon–Sat, 10am–5pm, Sun 11am–5pm. www. nbm.org. Metro: Judiciary Square.*

⑪ Union Station. When master architect Daniel Burnham designed this Beaux Arts–style building, which opened in 1907, he was determined to make it a grand gateway for a magnificent city, complete with 96-foot (29m) ceilings inlaid with 70 pounds (32 kilograms) of 22-karat gold leaf. Upon its completion in 1908, Union Station was the largest train station in the world; if laid on its side, the Washington Monument would fit into its concourse. Its original area, along with the terminal zone, totaled 200 acres (80 hectares) and included 75 miles (121km) of track. It was also enormously expensive, costing roughly $125 million. *50 Massachusetts Ave. NE.* ☎ *202/371-9441. www.union stationdc.com. Free admission. Daily 24 hr. Metro: Union Station.*

Linger over the view of Union Station's opulent atrium while enjoying a few quick bites of American fare at the **⑫ Center Café.** *Union Station, 50 Massachusetts Ave. NW;* ☎ *202/682-0143; arkrestaurants. com. $. Metro: Union Station.*

⑬ ★★★ National Cathedral. More than 200 stained-glass windows adorn this classic Gothic-style cathedral, the second largest in the United States and sixth largest in

the world; one of them has a rock from the moon embedded in its center. The building, made largely of gray Indiana limestone and finally completed in 1990 after more than 80 years of work and 2 centuries of planning, contains a number of magnificent wood-carvings, metal work, and other artworks. Frederick Bodley, an Anglican Church architect, originally oversaw the project (with additional supervision by architect Henry Vaughan), but Philip Hubert Frohman took over after World War I. The top of the cathedral tower is the highest point in the city. *Massachusetts and Wisconsin aves. NW (entrance Wisconsin).* ☎ *202/537-6200. www.national cathedral.org. Free admission. Mon–Fri 10am–5:30pm; Sat 10am–4:30pm; Sun 8am–6:30pm. Gardens daily until dusk. Metro: Cleveland Park, with a 20-min. walk. Also see "The Best of D.C. in Three Days" on p 14.*

A circular staircase inside the Intelsat building.

Strong Foundations

While not open for public tours, these architectural sites around D.C. are still known for their cutting-edge design and landmark looks. Graham Gund Architects of Cambridge, Massachusetts, designed the 12-story **National Realtors Association** headquarters (500 New Jersey Ave. NW; ☎ 202/383-1000; free tours by appointment only; Metro: Judiciary Sq.) to be environmentally sustainable, with recycled building materials, permeability to natural daylight to reduce energy costs, and a carbon dioxide monitoring system to introduce more fresh air into highly populated areas. Sir Edwin Lutyens—an architect of the late 19th and early 20th centuries, renowned for his English country houses and remodeled castles—designed **The British Embassy** (100 Massachusetts Ave. NW; Metro: Cleveland Park) in 1928. This prominent Embassy Row structure is notable for its tall chimneys and high roofs, suggestive of the Queen Anne period. Built in 1987, the **Intelsat** building (3400 International Dr. NW; ☎ 202/944-6800; www.intelsat.com; free tours by appointment only; Metro: Van Ness/UDC) comes with a space-age design, courtesy of John Andrews International. Its unique facade provides natural lighting to the "office pods" inside, as well as conserves energy.

Washington for Kids

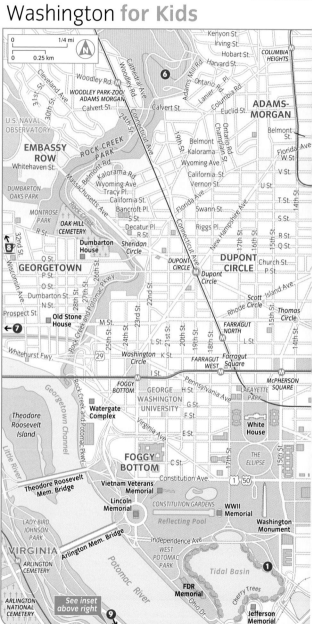

Kenyon St.
Irving St.
Hobart St.
Harvard St.
COLUMBIA HEIGHTS

Woodley Rd.
Cleveland Ave.
31st St.
30th St.
WOODLEY PARK-ZOO/ADAMS MORGAN
Calvert St.
Woodley Rd.
Cathedral Ave.
Calvert St.
Connecticut Ave.
24th St.
Adams Mill Rd.
Ontario Rd.
Lanier Pl.
Columbia Rd.
Euclid St.
ADAMS-MORGAN

U.S. NAVAL OBSERVATORY
EMBASSY ROW
Whitehaven St.
ROCK CREEK PARK
Massachusetts Ave.
Belmont Rd.
Kalorama Rd.
Wyoming Ave.
Tracy Pl.
California St.
19th St.
Belmont
Kalorama
Champlain St.
Ontario Rd.
Wyoming Ave.
California St.
Vernon St.
Belmont St.
Florida Ave.
W St.
V St.
U St.

DUMBARTON OAKS PARK
MONTROSE PARK
OAK HILL CEMETERY
R St.
Rock Creek
Bancroft Pl.
S St.
Decatur Pl.
R St.
Florida Ave.
Swann St.
Riggs Pl.
New Hampshire Ave.
17th St.
16th St.
15th St.
14th St.
T St.
S St.
R St.
Q St.

32nd St.
8
Wisconsin Ave.
GEORGETOWN
P St.
O St.
Dumbarton St.
N St.
Dumbarton House
27th St.
26th St.
Sheridan Circle
DUPONT CIRCLE
Dupont Circle
DUPONT CIRCLE
Church St.
P St.

Prospect St.
7
Old Stone House
28th St.
Rock Creek and Potomac Pkwy.
25th St.
24th St.
23rd St.
M St.
22nd St.
L St.
21st St.
20th St.
19th St.
Connecticut Ave.
Rhode Island Ave.
Scott Circle
18th St.
FARRAGUT NORTH
L St.
Thomas Circle
14th St.

Whitehurst Fwy.
29
Washington Circle
K St.
Pennsylvania Ave.
FARRAGUT WEST
Farragut Square
McPHERSON SQUARE
I St.

FOGGY BOTTOM
GEORGE WASHINGTON UNIVERSITY
Watergate Complex
Virginia Ave.
H St.
G St.
F St.
E St.
LAFAYETTE PARK
White House

Georgetown Channel
Rock Creek and Potomac Pkwy.
Theodore Roosevelt Island
Little River
FOGGY BOTTOM
C St.
Constitution Ave.
17th St.
THE ELLIPSE
15th St.
1 50

Theodore Roosevelt Mem. Bridge
LADY BIRD JOHNSON PARK
Vietnam Veterans Memorial
Lincoln Memorial
CONSTITUTION GARDENS
Reflecting Pool
WWII Memorial
Washington Monument

VIRGINIA
ARLINGTON CEMETERY
Arlington Mem. Bridge
Independence Ave.
WEST POTOMAC PARK
Potomac River
FDR Memorial
Ohio Dr.
Tidal Basin
Cherry Trees
Jefferson Memorial

ARLINGTON NATIONAL CEMETERY
See inset above right
9

0   1/4 mi
0   0.25 km
N

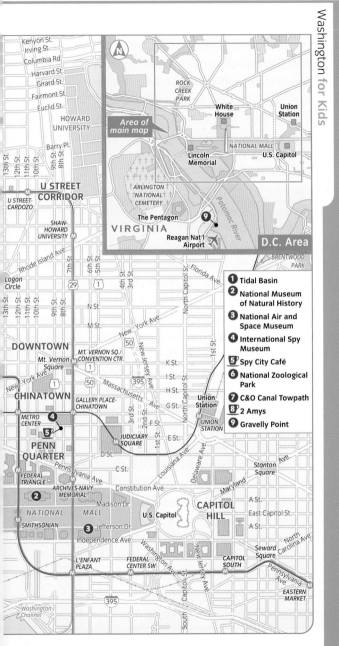

1 Tidal Basin
2 National Museum of Natural History
3 National Air and Space Museum
4 International Spy Museum
5 Spy City Café
6 National Zoological Park
7 C&O Canal Towpath
8 2 Amys
9 Gravelly Point

Here's a bold statement: Disney World included, there is no better place to take the kids on vacation than Washington, D.C. The District is overflowing with the stuff of great field trips: pandas, dinosaur bones, spy gadgets, rocket ships, insect gardens, historic monuments—and many are free. There's even a park, adjacent to Ronald Reagan National Airport, that is so close to the runways, you feel as though planes are landing on top of you. Ask any kid—nothing is cooler than this. START: **Metro to Smithsonian**

❶ ★★★ Paddling the Tidal Basin. The Jefferson Memorial overlooks the serene waters of the Tidal Basin, dotted with paddle boats on sunny days. Marry a history lesson with great exercise— and see the monuments and cherry blossoms from a beautiful, unique vantage point. *1501 Maine Ave. SW (15th St.).* ☎ *202/479-2426. 2-passenger boat $8 per hr.; 4-passenger boat $16 per hr. Mar 15 to mid-Oct daily 10am–6pm. Metro: Smithsonian.*

❷ ★★ National Museum of Natural History. Founded in 1846, this enormous repository for animal and plant specimens, many long extinct, includes the remains of 46 dinosaurs—guaranteed to wow

even the most Nintendo-obsessed kids. Look for the stegosaurus in the Hall of Dinosaurs on the first floor. The outdoor Butterfly Habitat Garden, on the 9th Street side of the building, is another crowd-pleaser: 11,000 square feet (1,022 sq. m) of winding trails and lush vegetation that supports an estimated 26 species of butterflies, the area cultivates interaction between these winged creatures and the plants and flowers that attract them, while educating and delighting visitors. *10th St. and Constitution Ave.* ☎ *202/633-1000. www.mnh.si.edu. Free admission. Daily 10am–5:30pm (Fri–Sat, and in summer, until 7:30pm). Closed Dec 25. Metro: Smithsonian or Federal Triangle.*

The National Museum of Natural History.

Tiger at the National Zoo.

③ ★★★ National Air and Space Museum. Containing the largest historic collection of air- and spacecraft in the world, this is the place to explore rocket ships that have shot to the stars, see real Russian and American spacesuits, view the Wright Brothers' plane and World War II bombers, even inspect the earliest passenger planes (kids can walk through the fuselage of one). The number of crafts suspended from the sky-high ceiling, to simulate flight, inspires lots of upturned heads and dropped jaws. The Lockheed Martin IMAX Theater will transport your little ones to Mars or the moon with awesome 3-D effects; look for revolving films and times. *Independence Ave. between 4th and 7th sts. ☎ 202/633-1000. www.nasm.si.edu. Free admission. Daily 10am–5:30pm (until 7:30pm in summer), except Dec 25. Metro: Smithsonian or L'Enfant Plaza (Smithsonian Museums/Maryland Ave. exit).*

④ ★★ International Spy Museum. Older kids who think the zoo is for babies will love this place,

the sole public museum in the world dedicated to espionage. They'll learn about Soviet double agents, view the spy treasures from Hollywood films, play spy games, and take part in other supersneaky stuff. *See p 31, bullet 4.*

The ⑤ **Spy City Café** is the perfect lunch spot for spy museum visitors. Salads, soups, sandwiches, and pizzas are offered, plus photos of spy sites in Washington—the spying capital of the world. *9th and F sts., ☎ 202/654-0995. www. zoladc.com/spycity.html. $. Metro: Gallery Place/Chinatown.*

⑥ ★★★ National Zoological Park. Established in 1889, the National Zoo is home to some 500 species, many of them rare and/or endangered. It also occupies 163 acres (65 hectares) of beautifully landscaped and wooded land, wonderful for strolling and enjoying the sunshine. Start your tour with the famous pandas. *See p 15, bullet 1.*

The National Zoo

ROCK CREEK PARK

Kangaroos
Panda Pavilion
6B
Giraffes
6D
Elephant House
6C
Panda Café
6A
Hippopotamus
Small Mammal House
WETLANDS
Golden Lion Tamarins *(Summer)*
Mexican Wolves
Great Ape House
6E
Reptile Discovery Center
Great Flight Exhibit
Bird House
Bald Eagles
GREAT MEADOW
Think Tank
Seals
Sloth Bears
Lions
Tigers
6F
Amazonia
Lion/Tiger Hill
6G
Picnic Pavilion
Kid's Farm
6H

🍴 Food & Drink
🎁 Gift Shop
ⓘ Information
⛱ Picnic Area
🚻 Rest Rooms

Beach Dr.
Rock Creek
Rock Creek

Since his birth in 2005, **Tai Shan** (aka Butterstick) and his family take center stage at the zoo's **6A FujiFilm Giant Panda Habitat.** Follow **6B Olmsted Walk** and you'll spot several natural habitats holding cheetahs, zebras, and kangaroos. A new and improved Elephant House should be unveiled in 2011, but for now, look for the **6C Asian elephants** next door to the **6D Giraffe House.** Off the main drag, you'll find natural wetlands, bald eagles, and seals. Farther south, at the

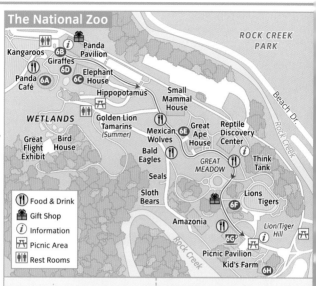

Examining a tusk near a T-Rex replica at the zoo's Elephant House.

6E Great Ape House, you can look through large glass walls as six orangutans exhibit some very human-like grooming, wrestling, and even hugging. **6F The Great Cats** are in a circular habitat south of the Great Ape House. Lions and tigers sun themselves, their tails batting as they gaze at you. **6G Mane Restaurant.** This cafeteria-style restaurant offers burgers, fries, chicken sandwiches, and other fast-food fare. Dine in, or enjoy the nearby Picnic Pavilion. At the **6H Kids' Farm,** children 3 to 8 can meet and greet ducks, chickens, goats, cows, and miniature donkeys up close. Toddlers love the nearby "pizza" playground.

7 C&O Canal Towpath. Have rambunctious little ones? Rent a bike at any nearby outfitter (see p 121 for specifics) and hit the C&O Canal Towpath. The gravelly trail follows a 19th-century canal that begins in Georgetown and heads west, ending 184 miles (296km) later in Cumberland, Maryland. It's a favorite of hikers, joggers, and bicyclists; and if you're looking to blow off steam after museum touring, you'll love it too. *See p 120 for service details.*

Mom and Dad need a drink, and the kids are ravenous. Take them to **8 ★ 2 Amys** for authentic Neapolitan pizza while you savor lovely Italian red wine by the glass. *3715 Macomb St. NW.* ☎ *202/885-5700.* www.2amyspizza.com. $$–$$$. No Metro access (a taxi is advised).

9 Gravelly Point. If your kids are thrill-seekers, drive to this park that borders Reagan National Airport, minutes outside the District. (You'll need a car because no return taxis are available.) On any given day, you'll find teenagers, toddlers, and grandparents parked or picnicking on the grass, just feet from the airport runways. As they gaze upward, jet after jet descends and flies directly overhead, so close you can read the markings on the underbelly of the plane—ZSHOOOMMMM—and then lands safely a short distance away. Not for the fainthearted! *Off the northbound George Washington Pkwy.* ☎ *703/289-2500.*

Seals at the National Zoo.

Historic Washington

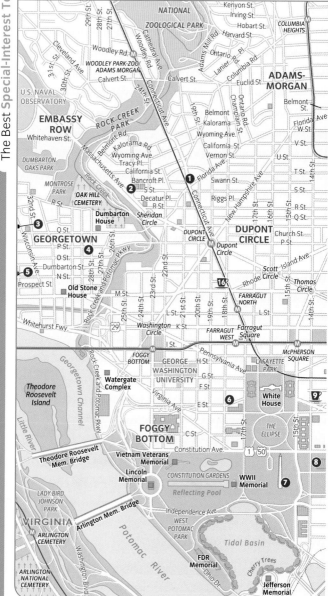

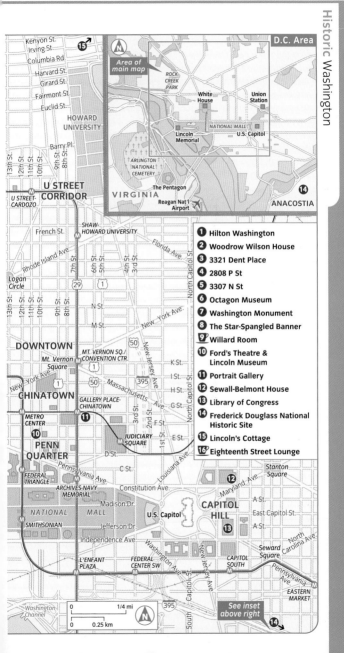

1 Hilton Washington
2 Woodrow Wilson House
3 3321 Dent Place
4 2808 P St
5 5307 N St
6 Octagon Museum
7 Washington Monument
8 The Star-Spangled Banner
9 Willard Room
10 Ford's Theatre & Lincoln Museum
11 Portrait Gallery
12 Sewall-Belmont House
13 Library of Congress
14 Frederick Douglass National Historic Site
15 Lincoln's Cottage
16 Eighteenth Street Lounge

In the 21st century, America's capital city bears little resemblance to the swampy Potomac River Valley lands that President George Washington staked out as the new site for Congress in 1790. Yet trying to separate historic Washington from the contemporary capital is like trying to take the red from blood. Because of its historic relevance, Washington exists on two planes in the collective consciousness: first, as a real city with magnificent structures and whimsical cherry trees juxtaposed against a backdrop of still-recovering pockets of poverty; and second, as a virtual city of suspenseful Hollywood lore, with its Deep Throat–esque covert operations, war games, and congressional plottings. The true Washington lies somewhere between fact and fiction, past and present, and that is why it never loses its intrigue or its allure. START: **Metro to Smithsonian**

1 ★★ **Hilton Washington (where President Reagan was shot).** In 1981, John Hinckley, Jr., an obsessed fan of actress Jodie Foster, ambushed Ronald Reagan here, just 69 days into the president's first term, in a misguided attempt to impress the star. Hinckley fired six shots, one of which struck Reagan's armpit. (Reagan's press secretary James Brady was also seriously injured; paralyzed from the waist down, he has been in a wheelchair ever since.) The Secret Service whisked Reagan away to a waiting hospital, where he underwent emergency surgery, making the now-legendary joke to his doctors: "I hope you're all Republicans." Despite being 70, the president recovered quickly—and went on to tackle other concerns, like the Cold War. The Hilton Washington is also known as the annual site for the National Press Foundation Awards Dinner. *1919 Connecticut Ave. NW.* ☎ *202/483-3000. www.hilton.com. Metro: Dupont Circle.*

2 **Woodrow Wilson House.** This historic, final residence of Nobel Peace Prize winner and 28th president of the United States Woodrow Wilson has been preserved to celebrate the great man's "Washington years," from 1913 to 1924. It is where he returned to civilian life after his 8-year term guiding Americans through World War I, giving women the right to vote, and launching the League of Nations (now known as the United Nations). He lived the last 3 years of his life at this grand brick house. Inside, tour his drawing room, kitchen, bedrooms, and garden. *See p 87, bullet 3.*

3 **3321 Dent Place.** If you are a JFK buff, you'll want to explore both the east and west villages of Georgetown—Wisconsin Avenue divides the historic neighborhood into two enclaves—to check out where the 35th president once lived, in some cases with his glamorous wife, Jackie, and their two children, Caroline and John, Jr. Between January and June 1954, 3321 Dent Place was the first home of Senator and Mrs. Kennedy after their marriage in September 1953.

4 **2808 P St.** After a stint in Virginia, the Kennedys moved back to Georgetown, to this tony address, where they lived from January to May 1957.

5 **3307 N St.** JFK purchased this home and presented it to Mrs. Kennedy after the birth of their

President Woodrow Wilson's original office desk.

daughter, Caroline. From here, they moved to the White House on January 20, 1961.

⑥ Octagon Museum. The Octagon is one of the oddest-looking buildings in downtown D.C., and its history is just as intriguing. Built in 1799 for the Tayloe family, James and Dolley Madison temporarily lived in the house after the White House was burned by the British in 1814. Ironically, the Treaty of Ghent, ending war with Great Britain, was signed on its second floor. In its storied history, the Octagon was also a girls' school, a tenement, and is presently home to the American Architectural Foundation. At press time, tours are temporarily suspended while it undergoes renovation, but a stroll past it is still a worthwhile detour. *1799 New York Ave. NW.* ☎ *202/638-3221. www.archfoundation.org/octagon. Metro: Farragut West*

⑦ ★★ Washington Monument. In 1838, architect Robert Mills designed the largest—and perhaps most famous—masonry structure in the world, the 550-foot (165m) Washington Monument, honoring George Washington. While it now resembles a solitary and unadorned Egyptian obelisk, Mills originally intended the marble shaft to rise from a circular building containing a huge statue of the first American president. After

President John F. and Jacqueline Kennedy in Georgetown.

Walk Through History

Cultural Tourism DC offers a series of guided and self-walking tours all around the District. Bus tours include tailored itineraries for individual groups, planned in advance with CTDC; "anecdotal" history tours conducted by author/historian guide Anthony Pitch (of whom the *Washington Post* says, "You'll follow him dreamily, mesmerized by his tales"); neighborhood tours of U Street and Capitol Hill; even a city scooter tour, where—you guessed it—travelers sightsee on scooters. Self-guided walking tours include the U Street Heritage Trail, where visitors follow numbered signs with information about this historic neighborhood; the Downtown Heritage Trail, which guides tourists though high and low points in D.C. history, from the Civil War through the civil rights era; and the Adams-Morgan Heritage Trail, a walk through this vibrant community of artists, immigrants, and start-up entrepreneurs. To plan a specialized tour, sign up for a bus tour, or learn how to take a self-guided walking tour, check out www.culturaltoursmdc.org.

much bickering over the design, years of construction, and halted progress during the Civil War (which led to its two-tone marble effect, still visible today), the monument was finally completed and opened to the public on October 9, 1888. Visitors may take an elevator to the top for spectacular views of The Mall; for those dying to walk up or down its 897 steps, you must first contact the National Park Service at least a month in advance for a special tour. *15th St. SW.* ☎ *202/426-6841, or 800/967-2283 (for reservations). Free timed tickets are available at the 15th Street kiosk on a first-come, first-served basis. Advanced tickets are available through the National Park Service. Tickets required for everyone 2 and up. Daily 9am–4:45pm. Closed July 4th and Dec 25. Metro: Smithsonian.*

❽ ★★★ The Star-Spangled Banner. O, say can you see the garrison flag that has come to represent our country and its democratic ideals? You'll find it and its companion

exhibit, The Flag That Inspired the National Anthem, at the newly reopened National Museum of American History. Backstory: In 1814, Francis Scott Key peered through the clearing smoke after a 25-hour British bombardment of Baltimore's Fort McHenry and saw this very flag flapping proudly in the wind. He immediately wrote a poem that was set to music and sung at the country's patriotic events ever after. In 1907, the worn and tattered but powerfully

The "star-spangled banner" that inspired the national anthem.

symbolic flag was donated to the museum; in 1931, the song became our national anthem. After undergoing several years of preservation, the flag is now resting in its new high-tech atrium in the museum, designed to keep it carefully protected but still allow throngs of visitors to see this American monument. *14th St. and Constitution Ave. NW.* ☎ *202/633-1000. www.americanhistory.si.edu. Daily 10am–5:30pm (until 7:30pm in summer). Metro: Smithsonian and Federal Triangle.*

Beaux-Arts architecture meets history at the formal, elegant Willard Inter-Continental, which has welcomed every president from Pierce to "W." It is the place where the Rev. Martin Luther King, Jr., wrote his legendary "I Have a Dream" speech. President Ulysses S. Grant held frequent meetings in the hotel lobby, and a host of celebrity visitors from Walt Whitman to P.T. Barnum have stayed. Contemporary heavyweights from Hollywood (like Tom Cruise) have reportedly overnighted here, too. Join in the weekday lunch rush at the 🍴 ★★ **Willard Room,** the in-hotel restaurant, which welcomes a virtual who's who of Washington. Romantics yearn for the hotel's Jenny Lind Room, named for a racy 19th-century opera singer; the suite's elevated Jacuzzi sits below a large window that perfectly frames the Washington Monument in all its vertical glory. *1401 Pennsylvania Ave. NW (at 14th St.)* ☎ *202/628-9100. www. washington.intercontinental.com. $$$$. Metro: Metro Center.*

John Wilkes Booth's assassination of Abraham Lincoln at Ford's Theatre.

14, 1865, when President Abraham Lincoln was killed as he watched a performance of *Our American Cousin.* The theatre was immediately closed, and remained so for another 103 years. In 1968, it reopened as a living, working tribute to our late leader, serving as a functioning playhouse and a Lincoln repository for historic materials such as assassin John Wilkes Booth's Derringer pistol, the gun that killed the president. In 2006, the theatre closed once again for renovations and reopened in early 2009, with an expanded museum on the president, plus a new lobby, box office, and seating. *511 10th St. NW.* ☎ *202/347-4833. www.fords theatre.org. Museum tours are free but do require a ticket. Daily 9am–5pm, except Dec. 25. Metro: Metro Center.*

🔟 ★★ **Ford's Theatre & Lincoln Museum.**
Another shot heard round the world was fired here on April

Booth's murder weapon.

The Frederick Douglass National Historic Site, in Anacostia.

⑪ ★★★ Portrait Gallery.

While the building itself has a rich history—it served as the National Patent Office for 92 years—the Gallery's contents might be considered even more important. Some of the most treasured

The Sewall-Belmont mansion.

paintings, sculptures, and artifacts from American history are housed in this ode to the presidents, first ladies, and stars. See the original Gilbert Stuart portrait of George Washington, saved by Dolley Madison in the War of 1812, along with modern depictions of Richard Nixon, John F. Kennedy, and even Barack Obama. *8th and F sts., NW.* ☎ *202/633-8300. www.npg.si.edu. Free admission. Daily, 11:30am–7pm except Dec. 25. Metro: Gallery Place/Chinatown.*

⑫ Sewall-Belmont House.

Including the works and words of "radicals" such as Susan B. Anthony and Gloria Steinem, this museum traces the evolution of a revolution: the women's movement, in all of its fits, starts, and back-and-forward progress. Check out authentic picketing banners, 5,000 prints and photographs, original cartoons, more than 50 scrapbooks from early suffragists, paintings, sculptures, publications, and more. ⏱ *1 hr. (by docent tour only). See p 100,* ➐.

Mount Vernon

Easily accessible from the District, **George Washington's Mount Vernon Estate and Gardens,** 3200 Mount Vernon Memorial Hwy. (☎ **703/780-2000;** www.mountvernon.org), is 16 miles (26km) south of the capital. This impressive, historic destination is entertaining, educational, and appealing to kids. Admission is $15 adults, $14 seniors, $7 kids 6 to 11, and free for kids under 6. The site is open to visitors daily April to August (8am–5pm), March and September to October daily (9am–5pm), and November to February daily (9am–4pm). The first president and his wife, Martha, lived here from their wedding in 1759 until Washington's death 40 years later. Tour the main house and see Washington's library, the dining room and parlors, and the bedrooms. The plantation's outbuildings include the kitchen, smokehouse, storeroom, overseer's house, and the cramped slaves' quarters, a somber testament to a dark period in U.S. history. A recently opened on-site museum and visitors center has more than 500 artifacts from the Washington family, including furnishings, china, silver, clothing, jewelry—even Revolutionary War artifacts and rare books. Activities, from musical events to garden parties, take place year-round. To reach Mount Vernon, take the Metro Rail Yellow Line (☎ **202/637-7000;** www.wmata.com) to Huntington Station, VA. Exit at the lower level to catch a Fairfax Connector (☎ **703/339-7200**) bus no. 101 (Fort Hunt Line) for the 20-min. trip to Mount Vernon.

⑬ ★ Library of Congress. Original presidential documents, plus photographs, multimedia, and more can be found at the Library of Congress, which houses the most comprehensive collection of archival material documenting this country's birth and growth as a nation. It occupies three adjacent buildings on Capitol Hill: the Thomas Jefferson Building (1897), the John C. Adams Building (1938), and the James Madison Building (1981). Docent-led, scheduled public tours depart Monday through Saturday, from the Great Hall of the Thomas Jefferson Building, at 10:30, 11:30am, 1:30, 2:30, and 3:30pm. 🕘 *1 hr. Arrive 30 min. before tour begins. 101 Independence Ave. SE. www.loc.gov. Mon–Fri 9am–4:30pm, except federal holidays. Metro: Capitol South or Union Station.*

⑭ Frederick Douglass National Historic Site. Born a slave, Frederick Douglass escaped his circumstances to become, as President Lincoln once said, "the most meritorious man" of the 19th century. An outspoken abolitionist, a feminist, a human-rights pioneer, an ambassador, a minister, a family man, and the father of the civil rights movement, Douglass settled here in southeast D.C. at a home he called Cedar Hill, where his personal belongings are now on display. National Park Service rangers lead tours of the house, sharing the stories and legacy of this important American icon. *1411 W St. SE.* ☎ *202/426-5961. Free*

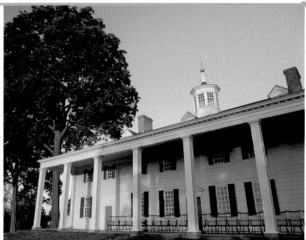

Mount Vernon, the former home of President George Washington.

admission. *Daily Apr 15–Oct 15 9am–5pm. Closed Jan 1, Thanksgiving, and Dec 25. Metro: Anacostia, then bus no. 2, which stops in front of the house.*

⑮ ★★ Lincoln's Cottage.
When the sweltering heat of D.C. got to be too much for President Lincoln and his family, they retreated to this cottage, originally known as the Soldier's Home. Each June through November during 1862 to 1864, the Lincolns would take in the cool breezes from this house, on the third highest area in Washington, 3 miles (5km) north of what was then downtown. After a restoration by the National Trust for Historic Preservation, this presidential landmark debuted to the public in 2008 and began offering 1-hour guided tours. The cottage is a straight shot up the Green Line on the Metro, and is well worth the detour if you can spare the time. ⏱ *2 hr., including commute. Rock Creek Church Rd. NW and Upshur St. NW. ☎ 202-829-0436. 3. Metro: Georgia Avenue/Petworth then taxi (to the Armed Forces Retirement Home campus, Eagle Gate entrance).*

The multi-level ⑯ **Eighteenth Street Lounge** is a happening spot for martinis and live music on the weekends, but at one point, Teddy Roosevelt called it home. Check it out—if you can find the unmarked door. *1212 18th St., NW; ☎ 202/466-3922. www.eighteenthstreet lounge.com. $–$$. Metro: Farragut North.* ●

National Gallery of Art

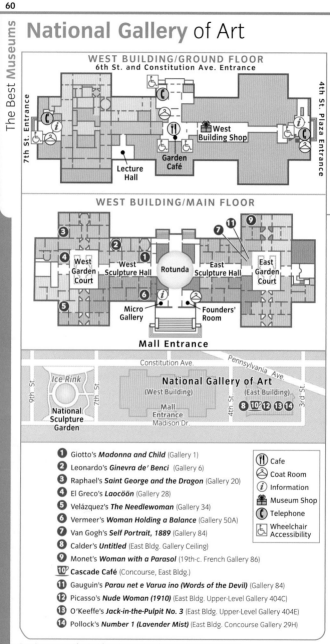

WEST BUILDING/GROUND FLOOR
6th St. and Constitution Ave. Entrance

7th St. Entrance

4th St. Plaza Entrance

West Building Shop

Garden Café

Lecture Hall

WEST BUILDING/MAIN FLOOR

❸

❷

❶

❹ West Garden Court

West Sculpture Hall

Rotunda

East Sculpture Hall

❼ ⓫ ❾ East Garden Court

❺

Micro Gallery

Founders' Room

Mall Entrance

Constitution Ave.

Pennsylvania Ave.

Ice Rink

9th St.

7th St.

National Gallery of Art
(West Building)

4th St.

(East Building)

3rd St.

❽ ❿ ⓬ ⓭ ⓮

National Sculpture Garden

Mall Entrance

Madison Dr.

❶ Giotto's *Madonna and Child* (Gallery 1)
❷ Leonardo's *Ginevra de' Benci* (Gallery 6)
❸ Raphael's *Saint George and the Dragon* (Gallery 20)
❹ El Greco's *Laocöön* (Gallery 28)
❺ Velázquez's *The Needlewoman* (Gallery 34)
❻ Vermeer's *Woman Holding a Balance* (Gallery 50A)
❼ Van Gogh's *Self Portrait, 1889* (Gallery 84)
❽ Calder's *Untitled* (East Bldg. Gallery Ceiling)
❾ Monet's *Woman with a Parasol* (19th-c. French Gallery 86)
❿ Cascade Café (Concourse, East Bldg.)
⓫ Gauguin's *Parau net e Varua ino (Words of the Devil)* (Gallery 84)
⓬ Picasso's *Nude Woman (1910)* (East Bldg. Upper-Level Gallery 404C)
⓭ O'Keeffe's *Jack-in-the-Pulpit No. 3* (East Bldg. Upper-Level Gallery 404E)
⓮ Pollock's *Number 1 (Lavender Mist)* (East Bldg. Concourse Gallery 29H)

🍴 Cafe
Coat Room
ⓘ Information
Museum Shop
Ⓒ Telephone
Wheelchair Accessibility

Previous page: The Smithsonian-National Air and Space Museum.

Founded in 1937 by philanthropist Andrew Mellon, with seed works from his personal collection, the National Gallery is one of the finest repositories of Western painting, sculpture, and graphic art on earth. And, unlike most its rivals, it's free to visitors. The collection ranges from revered early Renaissance paintings, including the only Leonardo da Vinci painting in the United States, to works by contemporary artists, such as Ellsworth Kelly. You will recognize many a masterpiece as you make your way through the galleries, organized by school, and arranged chronologically. The following itinerary features hallmark paintings of the collection. Plan to spend a couple of hours here; art lovers may want to linger an afternoon or a day. For more extensive coverage of modern and contemporary works, see "19th- & 20th-Century Art Museums" on p 72. START: **Metro to Archives, Judiciary Square, or Smithsonian**

❶ ★ Giotto's Madonna and Child (1320). A century before the Italian Renaissance, Giotto's explorations of three-dimensionality laid the groundwork for the breakthroughs to come 100 years later. This *Madonna and Child* exemplifies his emphasis on mass and volume, lending fleshy character and greater perspective to his subjects, rendered on otherwise conservative Byzantine backgrounds. *Gallery 1.*

❷ Leonardo's Ginevra de' Benci (1474). Leonardo da Vinci's portrait of a wealthy young Florentine woman, one of the most esteemed intellectuals of her day, was probably commissioned by Venetian ambassador to Florence Bernardo Bembo, with whom the sitter had a platonic affair, an accepted Renaissance convention. The juniper plant (*ginepro* in Italian, a pun on her name) symbolizes chastity, and the reverse side of the painting bears the motto "Beauty Adorns Virtue." *Gallery 6.*

❸ ★★ Raphael's Saint George and the Dragon (1506). Early Italian Renaissance painter Raphael created this work for the royal court of Urbino. In it, a Roman soldier of Christian faith subdues a dragon to save a pagan princess, whose

survival inspires a mass conversion to Christianity among her subjects. *Gallery 20.*

❹ El Greco's Laocöön (1610). Interpreting a story related to Troy's most famous debacle, the Spanish painter El Greco presents a doomsday scenario starring a Trojan priest named Laocöön, who tried to warn his countrymen about a certain wooden horse left outside the gates of the city. *Gallery 28.*

Ginevra de' Benci, the best-preserved example of Leonardo da Vinci's early work.

Sculptures in the National Gallery.

5 Velázquez's The Needle-woman (1640). Spain's golden age of painting is best represented by the works of Diego Velázquez, one of the greatest masters of 17th-century Europe. The muted tones in

The Needlewoman, by Diego Velázquez, at the National Gallery.

this unfinished work show a departure from his earlier, extreme contrasts in lights and darks. *Gallery 34.*

6 Vermeer's Woman Holding a Balance (1664). With his characteristically delicate treatment of light, Dutch master Johannes Vermeer depicts a woman quietly going about her everyday work, her facial expression serene. Seventeenth-century Dutch paintings often conveyed such messages: that God's work was evident in the smallest or most inconsequential of details. *Gallery 50A.*

7 Van Gogh's Self Portrait (1889). One of 36 self-portraits from this prolific artist, Van Gogh is thought to have executed this work in a single sitting without retouching. He portrays himself at work, dressed as an artist, and it is one of the last self-portraits he ever painted. *Gallery 84.*

8 ★★★ **Calder's Untitled (1976).** In 1972, Calder began constructing this 76-foot-long (23m) mobile, commissioned specifically for the National Gallery's East Building. Installed in 1977, 1 year after his death, it was the artist's last major work of art. *East Building, Gallery Ceiling.*

9 ★★★ **Monet's Woman with a Parasol (1875).** The Impressionists would certainly win a recognition contest if pitted against the proponents of other art movements, and Claude Monet just might take the prize for most popular artist. This well-known painting demonstrates his mastery of light, landscape, and vibrant color. *19th-century French Gallery 86.*

Enjoy views of a cascade waterfall while noshing on the likes of soups, salads, wood-fired pizzas, sandwiches, and fresh-baked desserts at the 10 **Cascade Café.** *No phone. Concourse, East Building. $.*

11 **Gauguin's Parau na te Varua ino (Words of the Devil) (1892).** Paul Gauguin escaped to Tahiti and fell in love with its innocent, unspoiled culture. His sense of paradise there—coupled with a biblical reference suggesting that Western civilization had lost it—is evident in this classic nude painting. *Gallery 84.*

12 ★★★ **Picasso's Nude Woman (1910).** One of the most radical movements in art history can be attributed in part to Spanish painter Pablo Picasso, whose Cubist explorations with Georges Braque created a window to a new, fractured sense of space and time. *East Building, Upper-Level Gallery 404C.*

Jan Vermeer's Girl with the Red Hat, at the National Gallery.

13 ★★★ **O'Keeffe's Jack-in-the-Pulpit No. 3 (1930).** Georgia O'Keeffe's sensuously abstracted flowers celebrate nature and make an overt nod to the female form. This painting, along with three others, was bequeathed to the Gallery by O'Keeffe herself. *East Building, Upper Level, Gallery 404E.*

14 ★★★ **Pollock's Number 1 (Lavender Mist) (1950).** Of his spontaneous, intuitive innovation—pouring paint directly onto unprimed canvas—Jackson Pollock once remarked, "There is no accident." *Lavender Mist* is one of the artist's most important drip paintings, in which his long, rhythmic movements are discernible. *East Building, Concourse Gallery, 29H.*

Tip:

The National Gallery is on the Mall, between 3rd and 7th sts (☎ **202/737-4215.** www.nga.gov. Free admission. Mon–Sat 10am–5pm; Sun 11am–6pm; closed Dec 25 and Jan 1).

Museum of **Natural History**

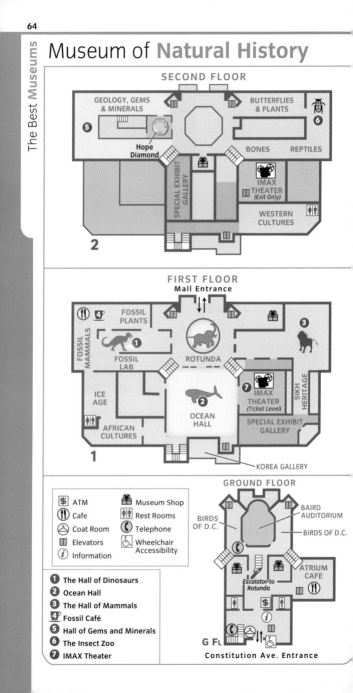

SECOND FLOOR

GEOLOGY, GEMS & MINERALS

5

Hope Diamond

BUTTERFLIES & PLANTS

6

BONES   REPTILES

SPECIAL EXHIBIT GALLERY

IMAX THEATER *(Exit Only)*

WESTERN CULTURES

2

FIRST FLOOR
Mall Entrance

FOSSIL PLANTS

4

FOSSIL MAMMALS

FOSSIL LAB

1

ROTUNDA

3

ICE AGE

OCEAN HALL

2

IMAX THEATER *(Ticket Level)*

7

SIKH HERITAGE

AFRICAN CULTURES

SPECIAL EXHIBIT GALLERY

1

KOREA GALLERY

$ ATM
Cafe
Coat Room
Elevators
i Information

Museum Shop
Rest Rooms
Telephone
Wheelchair Accessibility

1 The Hall of Dinosaurs
2 Ocean Hall
3 The Hall of Mammals
4 Fossil Café
5 Hall of Gems and Minerals
6 The Insect Zoo
7 IMAX Theater

GROUND FLOOR

BIRDS OF D.C.

BAIRD AUDITORIUM

BIRDS OF D.C.

ATRIUM CAFE

Escalator to Rotunda

$

i

G Fl
Constitution Ave. Entrance

Kids go ape over this museum, "dedicated to understanding the natural world and our place in it." This vast repository houses thousands of natural relics, some of which date back millions of years. If you care to learn about global warming, African cultures, the social constructs of insects, the Big Bang, fossilized bones, and other esoteric interests, you might end up wishing you'd devoted your entire trip to the largest of the Smithsonian Institution's 14 museums. Of the Smithsonian's 142 million objects, nearly 90%— that's 125 million artifacts—belong to this museum. Give yourself an hour at a minimum to explore this place. START: **Metro to Archives, Judiciary Square, or Smithsonian**

The Museum of Natural History's Hope Diamond—the world's largest deep blue diamond, a billion-plus years old.

❶ ★★ The Hall of Dinosaurs. If you have young children, you might want to make your first stop the first-floor Discovery Room, which is filled with creative hands-on exhibits "for children of all ages." On the first floor, beyond the rotunda with its giant woolly mammoth, you'll find the real Jurassic Park, with its towering exhibitions of those fascinating, larger-than-life creatures from the distant past—the dinosaurs. The collection includes a giant Diplodocus and the complete skeleton of an Allosaurus (think T. Rex, only smaller).

Mounted throughout the Dinosaur Hall are replicas of ancient birds, including a life-size model of the *Quetzalcoatlus northropi*, which lived 70 million years ago, had a 40-foot (12m) wingspan, and was the largest flying animal ever. Also residing above this hall is the jaw of an ancient shark, the *Carcharodon megalodon*, which lived in the oceans 5 million years ago. A

Stuffed giraffes quaff at the Smithsonian National Museum of Natural History.

A stuffed elephant at the Museum of Natural History.

monstrous 40-foot-long (12m) predator with teeth 5 to 6 inches (13–15cm) long, it could have consumed a Volkswagen Bug in one gulp.

2 The Ocean Hall. In late 2008, the museum debuted a brand-new, 22,000-square-foot (2,044-sq.-m) hall, the largest, most diverse exhibit of its kind in the world. Designed by the same firm that created the exhibits and spaces of the highly interactive International Spy Museum, the hall includes collections and state-of-the-art technology to demonstrate our oceans' essential role in life on earth. Also look for Ice Age animals and loads of fossilized plants, among other preserved treasures. Look for a model of a 45-foot-long (14m)

North American right whale and a 1,500-gallon (5,676L) coral reef aquarium with more than 70 live animals and 674 specimens.

3 The Kenneth E. Behring Hall of Mammals. This exhibit represents the "new" face of the museum: Set in the restored west wing, with up-to-date lighting and sound, it features interactive dioramas that explain how mammals evolved and adapted to changes in habitat and climate over millions of years. More than 270 stuffed mammals, from a polar bear to a tiger and a lion, are on display, along with a dozen mammal fossils. From time to time, the hall erupts

A stuffed leopard from the Hall of Mammals, at the Museum of Natural History.

with animal sounds, all part of the curatorial wizardry that helps make this a lifelike experience.

Before heading up to the second floor, make a pit stop for a quick sandwich, snack, or even a cold one at the **4** Fossil Café. *No phone. First Floor, in Dinosaur Hall. $.*

5 ★★★ **Hall of Gems and Minerals.** On the second floor, the Janet Annenberg Hooker Hall of Geology and Gems and Minerals features the famous, cursed Hope Diamond. Legend has it that the rare blue diamond was originally stolen in the late 17th century, in its native India, from a statue of the Hindu goddess Sita. The theft reputedly brought bad luck ever after to all who claimed it. From nasty French royals Louis XVI and Marie Antoinette to a consortium of wealthy playboys and socialites, all who "owned" it either met untimely deaths or watched their dearest loved ones die badly—very badly. Jeweler Harry Winston purchased the gem in 1947 and immediately gave it to the museum, probably with more than a little relief. Here you can also learn all you want about earth science, from volcanology to the importance of mining. Interactive computers, animated graphics, and a multimedia presentation of the "big picture" story of the earth are among the features that have advanced the exhibit and the museum a bit farther into the 21st century.

6 ★ **The O. Orkin Insect Zoo.** Also on the second floor, those with an interest in creepy-crawlies can view live spiders, ants, millipedes, and centipedes up close, and learn what made the arthropods the animal kingdom's biggest grouping. Kids enjoy looking at tarantulas, centipedes, and the like, and crawling through a model of an African termite mound.

7 **IMAX Theater.** You just might jump out of your seat as nature's untamed beasts come barreling at your theater seat. Whether you are exploring the aliens of the deep oceans, taking a wild safari, or visiting Harry Potter's Hogwarts School of Wizardry, here you'll find the wonders of the world (and supernatural world) up close and at their most thrilling. Films rotate regularly; check the website to see what's on during your visit.

Tip:

The **National Museum of Natural History** is on the north side of The Mall, on Constitution Avenue NW, between 9th and 10th streets (☎ **202/633-1000;** www.mnh. si.edu). It's open daily from 10am to 5:30pm (until 7:30pm in summer; call ahead to confirm), except December 25. Admission is free.

A T-Rex skeleton at the Museum of Natural History.

Museum of **American History**

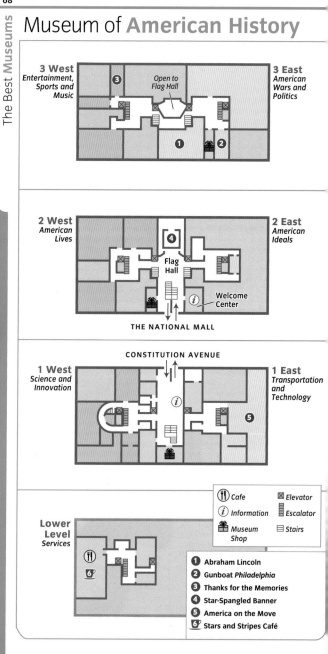

3 West
Entertainment, Sports and Music

Open to Flag Hall

3 East
American Wars and Politics

❸

❶ 🎁 ❷

2 West
American Lives

2 East
American Ideals

❹

Flag Hall

🎁

ⓘ Welcome Center

THE NATIONAL MALL

CONSTITUTION AVENUE

1 West
Science and Innovation

1 East
Transportation and Technology

ⓘ

❺

🎁

🍴 Cafe	⊠ Elevator
ⓘ Information	☰ Escalator
🏛 Museum Shop	☰ Stairs

Lower Level
Services

🍴

6️

❶ Abraham Lincoln
❷ Gunboat *Philadelphia*
❸ Thanks for the Memories
❹ Star-Spangled Banner
❺ America on the Move
6️ Stars and Stripes Café

Calling all pop culture fans and American history buffs: This seriously entertaining Smithsonian museum is home to more than 3 million national treasures. Check out Dizzy Gillespie's angled trumpet, Dorothy's ruby red slippers, Julia Childs' kitchen, and Muhammad Ali's boxing gloves. The original flag that inspired "The Star-Spangled Banner" is here too, housed in a new high-tech gallery dedicated to its preservation. Plan to spend a few hours soaking up your fill of good ole Americana. START: **Metro to Smithsonian**

❶ ★★ Abraham Lincoln: An Extraordinary Life.

Lincoln's top hat, Museum of American History.

On the third floor, you'll find tons of artifacts, documents, and photographs celebrating the life and legacy of the 16th President of the United States. The collection ranges from his everyday items, including an iron wedge he used to split wood in the 1830s, to more solemn treasures such as the top hat he wore on April 14, 1865, the night he was shot at Ford's Theatre. You'll also see photographs of the president at a young age and personal artifacts such as his gold watch, original plaster casts of his face and hands, campaign banners, and more. The ongoing exhibit debuted in January 2009 to coincide with the 200-year anniversary of the former president's birth.

❷ Gunboat *Philadelphia.*

The only surviving gunboat from the Revolutionary War, the *Philadelphia* is now on view on the museum's third floor. One of eight identical ships constructed, it measures 53 feet (16m) long and 15 feet (4.5m) wide and was mounted with two cannons and numerous swivel guns. The *Philadelphia* was sunk in battle

Gunboat Philadelphia, *at the American History Museum.*

The newly opened Star Spangled Banner gallery at the National Museum of American History.

with the British in New York's Lake Champlain, and remained at the bottom of Valcour Bay until 1935 when historians recovered it. The cold waters had kept its wood intact all those years, and it now rests here, along with the 24-pound (11kg) English cannonball that sent it to the bottom over 200 years ago.

Tip

The Museum of American History is located on the National Mall at 14th St (☎ **202/633-1000.** www.american history.si.edu. Free admission. Daily 10am–6:30pm, until 7:30pm in summer; closed Dec 25.)

❸ ★★★ Thanks for the Memories: Music, Sports, and Entertainment History. Pop culture icons and other mainstays get a front-row seat at this museum. Even non-Hollywood buffs will appreciate X-files memorabilia, Bruce Willis'

T-shirts from Die Hard (he donated them to the museum in 2007), Archie Bunker's armchair from the popular (and controversial) sitcom *All in the Family,* the original Kermit the Frog puppet, and a Dumbo the Flying Elephant Car Ride from 1955 Disneyland. An autographed Babe Ruth baseball, a 1989 Nintendo Gameboy, Julia Child's entire kitchen from her Cambridge, Massachusetts, home—donated part-and-parcel by the cook in 2001 when she moved residences—and the R2-D2 and C-3PO robots from the 1983 George Lucas blockbuster *Return of the Jedi,* are just some more of the favorites found in this museum's vast collection.

❹ ★★★ The Star-Spangled Banner: The Flag That Inspired the National Anthem. The British bombardment of Baltimore's Fort McHenry on September 14, 1814, lasted 25 hours, but at its conclusion, this "flag was still there." The poignant sight of its battle-weary stripes and stars inspired Francis Scott Key to write *The Defence of Fort McHenry,* a poem that would eventually become the nation's National Anthem, titled *The Star-Spangled Banner.* The Smithsonian acquired the flag in 1907, and it has been undergoing restoration at the museum ever since. The exhibit was an integral part to the museum's recent renovation and the nearly 200-year-old flag is now housed in a new, interactive gallery. A special environmentally-controlled chamber regulates the temperature and lighting conditions to protect the 30-by-34 foot (9 x 10m) flag from any more wear and tear, while giving visitors a fascinating glimpse of the storied symbol: The multistory gallery with floor-to-ceiling glass windows is designed to give visitors a sense of the same "dawn's early light" that Key

observed that morning in the harbor near Fort McHenry. The surrounding installation chronicles the story behind the flag's missing pieces, the Smithsonian's preservation efforts, and what this artifact represents to the country's history.

5 ★ America on the Move. Do you still reminiscence about your first muscle car? It's likely represented here, along with a Chicago Transit Authority car, a 1903 Winton—which was the first car driven across the U.S.—a 92-foot-long (28m) Southern Railway locomotive, and even 40 feet (18m) of the American Southwest's renowned Route 66 itself. Motor on down to the ground floor of the museum to see the nearly 20 life-size dioramas depicting America's transit history, from the first covered wagons that braved the Wild West to motor vehicles whose brethren still ply Route 66 and I-95 today. A range of some 300 artifacts—including railway markers, signs, and photographs—are displayed within period settings to illustrate the story of how America's railroad, canals, and roads changed the way its people traveled.

Vintage truck in the America on the Move exhibit at the National Museum of American History.

Tour the museum and then head to the aptly named **6 Stars and Stripes Café** on the lower level for a culinary slice of Americana: basic soups, salad, burgers, pizza, and desserts. *No phone. $–$$.*

Southern Railway's 1401 steam locomotive, in the America on the Move exhibit at the National Museum of American History.

19th- & 20th-Century Art
Museums

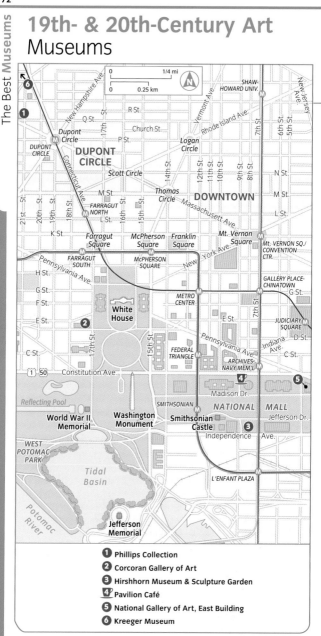

1 Phillips Collection
2 Corcoran Gallery of Art
3 Hirshhorn Museum & Sculpture Garden
4 Pavilion Café
5 National Gallery of Art, East Building
6 Kreeger Museum

In a world where what's considered current changes at an ever-faster pace—"That's so, like, 30 seconds ago!"—it's refreshing to view the art of the 1800s and 1900s, still thought of as modern, if not so subversive, well into the 21st century. It's also cool to put those art history classes to the test. START: **Metro to Dupont Circle (Q St. exit)**

❶ Phillips Collection. The building that houses the Phillips Collection, which is widely considered America's first museum of modern art, was once the home of Duncan Phillips, grandson of the cofounder of the Jones and Laughlin Steel Company. The modern-looking newer wing generally shows fresh exhibitions; the museum also plays host to special lectures and tours. Some of its 2,472 artworks include Pierre-Auguste Renoir's *Luncheon of the Boating Party* (1880–81), Vincent van Gogh's *The Road Menders in Saint Remy* (1889), Edgar Degas's *Dancers at the Barre* (1884–88), and Georges Rouault's *Christ & the High Priest* (1937). ⏱ *1 hr. 1600 21st St. NW.* ☎ *202/387-2151. www.phillips collection.org. Admission prices vary per exhibition. Tues–Sat 10am–5pm (Thurs to 5:30pm); Sun noon–7pm (June–Sept to 5pm).*

❷ ★★★ Corcoran Gallery of Art. Founded by William Wilson Corcoran, a "leading patron" of American art, the Corcoran contains a wildly varied selection of envelope-pushing contemporary art alongside 18th- and 19th-century masterworks. Under one roof, you can admire *The Departure,* one of the legendary landscapes by 19th-century artist Thomas Cole, and then walk a mere few steps away to analyze Andy Warhol's *Mao.*

Highlights include *Ground Swell* by Edward Hopper (1939); *Woman Sewing* by Winslow Homer (1878); *Repose* by **Jean-Baptiste-Camille**

Street Pavers, by Vincent van Gogh, at the Phillips Collection.

Louise Bourgeois' Crouching Spider, *at the Hirshhorn Museum.*

Corot (1860); *Mrs. Henry White* (1883) and *The Oyster Gatherers of Cancale* (1878), both by John Singer Sargent; *Singing a Pathetic Song* by Thomas Eakins (1881); and *Young Girl at a Window* by Mary Cassatt (1883). ⏱ *1 hr. 500 17th St. NW.* ☎ *202/639-1700. www.corcoran. org. Admission $10; $8 for students with ID; free for children; Thurs 5–9pm is pay what you wish. Wed–Sun 10am–5pm (Thurs until 9pm); closed Mon except holidays, Tues, Thanksgiving, Dec 25, and Jan 1.*

❸ ★ Hirshhorn Museum & Sculpture Garden. First opened in 1974, the Hirshhorn Museum—built 14 feet (4.2m) above ground on sculptured supports—is a unique vessel for a singular collection of modern and contemporary art. Amassed around Latvian émigré Joseph Hirshhorn's original donation of more than 9,500 works to the United States, the collection now includes works by Christo, Joseph Cornell, Arshile Gorky, and others. In the outdoor Plaza, visitors can gawk at the giant fountain and sur-real sculptures such as Juan Muñoz's *Last Conversation Piece*

(1994–95), which features a cluster of characters right out of an old-school fairy tale. The Hirshhorn also has a sculpture garden across the street, with some 60 works of art. Other highlights of touring this eclectic outdoor exhibition are Emile-Antonine Bourdelle's *Great Warrior of Montauban* (1898–1900, cast 1956); Alexander Calder's *Sta-bile-Mobile* (1947) and *Deux Discs* (1965); Edward Hopper's *City Sun-light* (1954); Rodin's *The Burghers of Calais* (1884–89); and Alberto Gia-cometti's *Walking Man II* (1948). ⏱ *1 hr. Independence Ave. at 7th St. NW.* ☎ *202/633-4674. www. hirshhorn.org. Free admission. Daily 10am–5:30pm; plaza 7:30am–5:30pm, except Dec 25; sculpture garden 7:30am–dusk.*

The **❹ Pavilion Café** is a cafeteria-style lunch spot that serves salads, veggie wraps, grilled meats, sandwiches, pizza, espresso drinks, and yummy baked goods, near the National Gallery of Art Sculpture Garden. Dine outdoors on warm days, or admire the ice-skating rink on cold ones, from inside the cafe's family-friendly environs. *9th St. and Constitution Ave. NW (near Sculpture Garden).* ☎ *202/289-3360. $.*

5 ★★★ National Gallery of Art, East Building. The trademarks of this 1978 I. M. Pei–designed building are its adjoining triangles, in pink Tennessee marble (from the same quarry as the neoclassical West Wing), that form sharp, acute angles at the corners. Inside, the centerpiece is the 76-foot-long (23m), 920-pound (417kg) mobile by Alexander Calder, which hangs from the ceiling of the main atrium. Returned for display after restoration work, the mobile's construction includes aluminum tubing and aluminum honeycomb panels, which allow its arms to slowly and gracefully rotate. On the concourse hang nine color field paintings by Mark Rothko; with 295 paintings and more than 650 sketches, the National Gallery has one of the largest collections of Rothko artwork in the world. In the tower of the East Building are large "cutouts" by Henri Matisse, featuring beautiful color shapes on large white backgrounds; it's one of the world's biggest collections of these works as well. ⏱ *1 hr. The National Mall, between 3rd and 7th sts.* ☎ *202/737-4215. www.nga.gov. Free admission. Mon–Sat 10am–5pm; Sun 11am–6pm; closed Dec 25 and Jan 1.*

6 Kreeger Museum. This private museum is housed in the former residence of David and Carmen Kreeger, well-known collectors who amassed a sizable holding of 19th- and 20th-century paintings and sculptures. Highlights include works by Monet, van Gogh, Pisarro, Miro, Kandinksy, and Renoir. As you tour the museum, take note of its own modern architecture. Designed by architect Philip Johnson, it features a steel and concrete frame with glass walls and a free-form design. *2401 Foxhall Rd., NW;* ☎ *202/337-3050. Reservations:* ☎ *202/338-3552. Adults, $10; students (with ID) and seniors over 65, $7. Tour reservations are required. www.kreeger museum.org. No Metro access.*

Whistler at the Freer Gallery of Art

Founded by businessman Charles Lang Freer, and opened to the public in 1923, the **Freer Gallery of Art** is the very first Smithsonian museum for fine arts. It houses a world-renowned collection of artworks from China, Japan, Korea, and Southeast Asia—as well as the largest collection of paintings by American artist James McNeill Whistler, who so famously produced a study of his mama in her rocking chair (*Whistler's Mother,* 1871). While this may strike some as a bit of a disconnect, art lovers recognize how strongly influenced Whistler was by Japanese prints and Chinese ceramics. In fact, it was Whistler himself who, after befriending Freer in 1890, convinced the collector of primarily American works to begin buying art from the East, which Freer bequeathed to the museum. Whistler fans will be thrilled to learn the Freer houses more than 1,300 paintings and drawings by this principal American artist. *Jefferson Dr. at 12th St.* ☎ *202/633-1000. www.asia.si.edu. Free admission. Daily 10am–5:30pm, except Dec 25.*

Special-Interest Museums

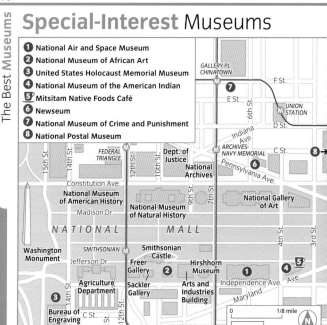

1. National Air and Space Museum
2. National Museum of African Art
3. United States Holocaust Memorial Museum
4. National Museum of the American Indian
5. Mitsitam Native Foods Café
6. Newseum
7. National Museum of Crime and Punishment
8. National Postal Museum

Maybe you fantasize about galaxies far, far away, and the spaceships that transport starry explorers. Perhaps you want to learn more about another ethnic group's art, culture, and storied history. Whatever your inclination may be, Washington can satisfy it, as home to many renowned special-interest museums. Here are a few of distinction. START: **Metro to L'Enfant Plaza or Smithsonian**

1 ★★★ **National Air and Space Museum.** The most visited museum on the National Mall, this monument to avionics holds some 30,000 aviation artifacts and 9,000 space artifacts. The Wright Brothers' 1903 Flyer, the first successful powered airplane, is here, along with a reproduction of the original sketches for the machine. A complete collection of planes from World War II includes the famed Supermarine Spitfire Mk VII and a Mitsubishi A6M5 Zero, and Amelia Earhart's red Lockheed Vega (the one she flew

solo across the Atlantic Ocean in 1932). For those more interested in the stars, the National Air and Space Museum holds an original Apollo Lunar Module, 1 of 12 built for the program; astronaut and cosmonaut space suits; and, in one of the newest additions, SpaceShipOne, the first privately designed and built vehicle to reach space, and a harbinger of space tourism. It also houses the Lockheed Martin IMAX Theater, where you can explore the galaxies from the safety of your movie seat. ⏱ *1 hr. Independence Ave. at 4th St.*

NW. ☎ 202/633-1000. www.nasmi.
si.edu. Free admission. Daily 10am–
5:30pm (til 7:30pm in summer),
except Dec 25.

2 National Museum of African Art. The only national
museum solely dedicated to the
acquisition, study, and exhibition of
African art, this collection features
both traditional and contemporary
pieces, including everything from
the spiritual (a Koranic writing board
from Mali, an ivory pendant from
the Congo) to the beautiful and
practical (a carved wood fly whisk
handle from Cote d'Ivoire). Ongoing
exhibits include "The Art of the Personal Object," which focuses primarily on utilitarian objects from
eastern and southern Africa (chairs,
bowls, baskets, and so on) with particularly notable decorations and
designs. Another exhibit features
more than 140 contemporary and
traditional ceramics from the continent. The museum also features
regular music programs and tours.
🕐 1 hr. 950 Independence Ave. NW.
☎ 202/633-4600. www.nmafa.
si.edu. Free admission. Daily 10am–
5:30pm, except Dec 25.

3 ★★ United States Holocaust Memorial Museum.
Be prepared to take an emotional journey when you
enter this space, a living
memorial to "never forgetting" the genocide of
Europe's Jews, and the
murder of all who opposed
the rise of Germany's Nazi
party, before and during
World War II. Upon entering, you will be given (to
keep) a faux passport of an
actual man, woman, or
child who went through
the Holocaust; some
survived, but the great
majority did not. The
museum's centerpiece

*Wooden fertility figures from
Guinea, at the National Museum
of African Art.*

is its three-floor exhibit, entitled
"The Holocaust." It's broken up into
three subsections: "Nazi Assault,"
"Final Solution," and "Last Chapter."
Through hundreds of artifacts and
film footage, the story of one of
humankind's biggest tragedies is laid
out in exhaustive detail. The
museum recommends that visitors
be 11 years of age or older, due to
the intensity of the material. There is
also a museum shop, a cafe, and the
Wexner Learning Center on the second floor, where visitors can explore
the survivors' registry and view
materials about topics such as the
Nuremberg Trials and the contemporary genocide emergency in Darfur. 🕐 1hr. 100 Raoul Wallenberg
Place SW. ☎ 202/488-044. www.
ushmm.org. Free admission, but
timed passes are necessary for visiting the permanent exhibition, and
can be obtained at the museum on
the day of your visit or in advance by
calling Tickets.com (☎ 800/400–
9373). Each day, the museum distributes a large but limited number of
timed-entry passes, on a first-come,
first-served basis, for use that same
day. Daily 10am–5:30pm, except
Yom Kippur and Dec 25.

**4 ★★ National Museum of
the American Indian.**
The newest big
museum on The Mall is
also one of the most
distinctive, its exterior
walls organically
curved to suggest rock
worn down by water.
Dedicated to preserving
the culture and history
of Native Americans, the
museum is also one of the
most technologically
advanced: Exhibits routinely incorporate
video and other
multimedia, including "Our Lives,"

which shows how Native American tribes live, striving to keep their ethnic identity, in contemporary times. ⏱ *1hr. 4th St. and Independence Ave. NW.* ☎ *202/633-1000. www. nmai.si.edu. Free admission. Daily 10am–5:30pm, except Dec 25.*

On the American Indian museum's first floor, **5** **Mitsitam Native Foods Café** serves meals based on traditional Native American cuisines. *No phone. $–$$.*

6 ★★★ Newseum. All the news that's fit to print and more can be found in this seven-level high-tech monument to journalism. The history of news is told through interactive games and close-up views of hundreds of publications. Hear first-person accounts from reporters in the field, see a comprehensive collection of Pulitzer-Prize winning photojournalists' images, and discover the secrets to electronic news reporting. The "Be a Reporter" exhibit puts visitors in the hot seat: With a deadline looming and a breaking news story to report, grab a microphone and test your skills in front of the camera. How would you fare as the next Walter Cronkite? *555 Pennsylvania Ave. NW.* ☎ *888/ 639-7386. www.newseum.org Daily 9am–5pm, except Thanksgiving, Dec. 25, and Jan. 1. Adults, $20, seniors and students, $18, kids 7–18, $13, children under 6, free. Metro: Archives/Navy Memorial.*

7 National Museum of Crime and Punishment. CSI it's not, but this museum devoted to the history of crime is as close to a real-life experience as you can get (without all the danger). The hands-on exhibits outline the pillaging of pirates and medieval knights to the Wild West and the infamous robbers Bonnie and Clyde. Exhibits include a full-scale model police station, a simulated FBI shooting range, and the actual television set of *America's Most Wanted.* Try your hand at cracking a safe or hacking into a computer and see if you could make it as a crook. *575 7th St. NW.* ☎ *202/393-1099. www.crime museum.org. Mar 20–Aug 31 9am– 9pm, Sept 1–Mar 19, 10am–8pm. Adults $18; child, senior, and military $15. Metro: Gallery Place/Chinatown.*

A chief's headdress from the Tsimshian Culture, at the National Museum of the American Indian.

8 National Postal Museum. Calling all stamp collectors: Nirvana awaits you right next door to Union Station. One of the world's largest stamp collections resides at this ode to the U.S. Mail Service, established in 1886. Listen to tales of the early Pony Express and browse a vast assortment of historic postage dating back to the nation's infancy, plus international stamps, the first piece of correspondence to be flown across the Atlantic, and some original 24-cent inverted stamps. *2 Massachusetts Ave. NE.* ☎ *202/ 633-5555. www.postalmuseum.si. edu. Free admission. Daily 10am– 5:30pm, except Dec 25. Metro: Union Station.* ●

4 The Best Neighborhood Walks

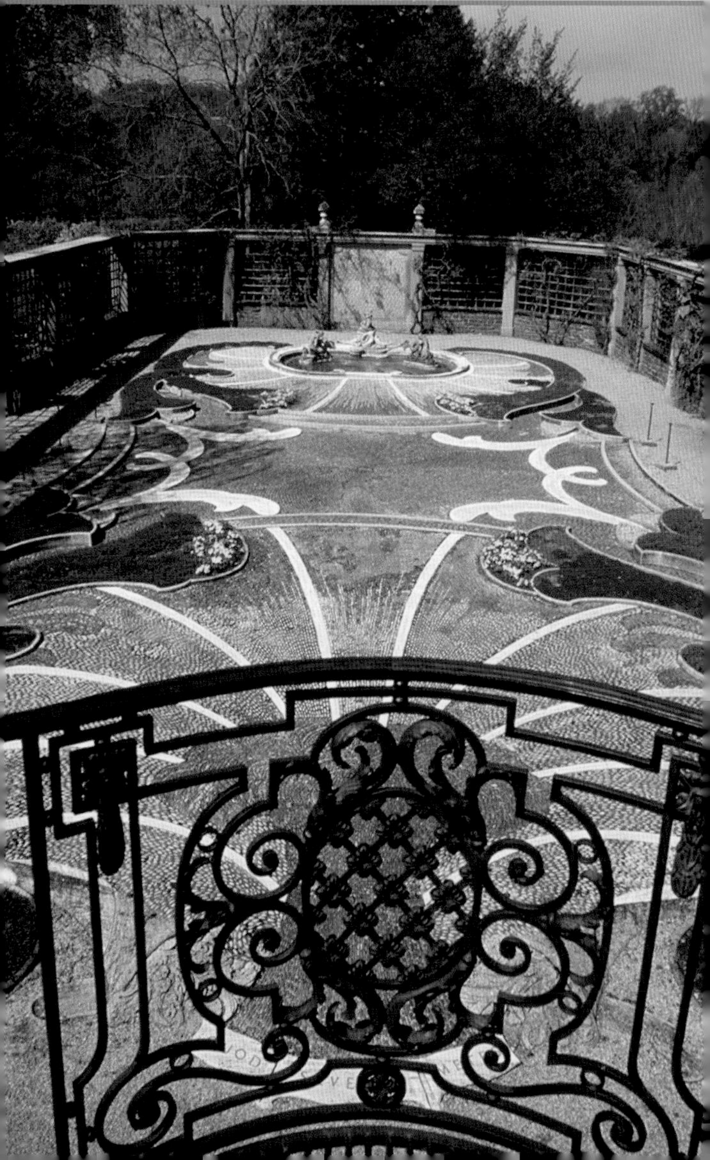

Adams Morgan

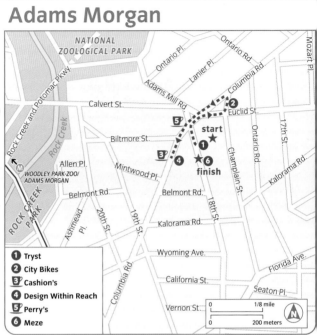

1 Tryst
2 City Bikes
3 Cashion's
4 Design Within Reach
5 Perry's
6 Meze

If you love New York's East Village, you'll feel right at home in this neighborhood, which is all about youthful verve, bohemian values, diversity, and a thriving street scene. Concentrate your explorations on 18th Street and the intersecting Columbia Avenue where you'll discover authentic ethnic restaurants, world-bazaar shops, girlie boutiques, funky lounges, coffeehouses with sidewalk seating, and young people on display in their various rebellious uniforms. START: **Metro to Woodley Park–Zoo/Adams Morgan**

1 ★★ **Tryst** is one of those coffeehouses whose regulars seem to live in the place—you almost expect to find Ross, Rachel, Joey, and the gang camped out in the corner. A bar, a lounge, a diner, and a cafe, it shelters students doing homework; writers on their laptops; artists hanging their work; and mohawked 8-year-olds running around, pastries

Previous page: Dumbarton Oaks' formal garden, in Georgetown.

in hand. Opens very early, closes very late. *See p 150 for service details.*

2 **City Bikes.** With their motto, "There are no stupid questions," this free-wheeling retailer specializes in diagnosing the best brand for each bicyclist's particular needs. Choose from hundreds of bikes, which you can test-ride, plus safety

The newly revitalized Adams Morgan.

One of the buzziest rooftop scenes in the city is **5 ★ Perry's,** where GW students and 40-somethings collide for well-prepared Asian-fusion fare including sushi, tuna steaks, and even unusual pizzas. Cocktails and conversation are also on the menu, best ordered on a warm spring evening with the scent of cherry blossoms in the air. *1811 Columbia Rd. NW.* ☎ *202/234-6218. Sun–Thurs 5:30–10:15pm; Fri 5:30–11:15pm. $12–$20. Metro: Woodley Park–Zoo/Adams Morgan.*

gear, kids' tricycles, and accessories. *2501 Champlain St. NW.* ☎ *202/265-1564. www.citybikes.com. Mon–Wed and Fri–Sat 10am–7pm; Thurs 10am–9pm, Sun 11am–5pm. MC, V. Metro: Woodley Park–Zoo/Adams Morgan.*

Carnivores roar with delight at **3 ★★ Cashion's Eat Place;** this neighborhood mainstay is a darkly sophisticated if somewhat cramped restaurant with a mahogany bar that virtually beckons you to order a strong martini with your buffalo hanger steak. *See p 137 for service details.*

4 Design Within Reach. The San-Francisco–based retailer opened this 3,300-square-foot (3,066 sq. m) space in perennially hip Adams Morgan to cater to modern furniture fans seeking to outfit their home or office. Think sleek tables, minimalist chairs, and stylized accessories from top designers at slightly more modest prices. *1838 Columbia Rd. NW.* ☎ *202/265-5460. www.dwr.com.*

6 Meze. Since Adams Morgan is one of the most diverse areas in the city, it's easy to stumble across restaurants that offer alternatives to your average American burger. More exotic fare such as stuffed grape leaves, creamy hummus, and savory kebabs are all options when you book a table at this popular Mediterranean restaurant that is also a lively bar and dance floor late at night. *2437 18th St. NW.* ☎ *202/797-0017. Daily 5:30pm–1:30am or later. Metro: Woodley Park–Zoo/Adams Morgan*

Diners at Tryst.

U Street Corridor/14th Street

1 **ACKC Cocoa Bar**
2 **The Galleries on 14th Street**
3 **The Studio Theatre**
4 **Black Cat**
5 **Home Rule**
6 **Café Saint-Ex**
7 **Greater U Street Heritage Trail**
8 **Marvin**
9 **The Lincoln Theatre**
10 **Ben's Chili Bowl**
11 **African American Civil War Memorial and Museum**
12 **Howard University**

The riots of 1968—ignited by the assassination of Martin Luther King—subjected the Corridor to 3 days of looting and devastation. Once known as the grand and glorious "Black Broadway," the strip was a shadow of its former self for decades afterward, known better for its crack houses than for its theater companies. Fourteenth Street, which intersects historic U Street and runs north to south, was also decimated during the riots. But new signs of life appeared late in the last century to both of these areas: A frenzied real-estate boom brought homesteaders to the neighborhood and the requisite art galleries, one-off boutiques, scene-making cafes, and happening restaurants followed. It's best to start this walk after noon: No early opening hours here. **START: Metro to U Street/Cardozo**

1 **ACKC Cocoa Bar.** Chocolate lovers, rejoice. This quaint shop and cafe will get your body and mind moving any time of day with delectable coffee drinks or cocoa treats. Walk off with some exotic chocolates, such as the spicy smoked jalapeño and cinnamon

truffle. *1529C 14th St. NW.* ☎ *202/387-2626. www.thecocoagallery.com. $. Metro: See Start, above.*

2 **The Galleries on 14th Street.** Explore D.C.'s emerging contemporary art scene at this consortium of

Café St.-Ex is popular among those on the microbrewed beer circuit.

independent galleries: Begin your crawl at 1515 14th St. NW, which houses several talk-of-the-town galleries: G Fine Art (☎ 202/462-1601), Hemphill Fine Arts (☎ 202/234-5601), Adamson Gallery (☎ 202/232-0707), and Curator's Office (☎ 202/387-1008). Then check out Transformer (1404 P St. NW; ☎ 202/483-1102) and Gallery plan b (1530 14th St. NW; ☎ 202/234-2711) down the block. *Metro: Cardozo/U St.*

❸ ★★ The Studio Theatre. The best venue in town for contemporary playwrights and their sometimes-scathing works (Neil LaBute's provocative *Fat Pig* was a huge hit here), the Studio Theatre also houses an Acting Conservatory, with workshops and classes for young thespians. *1501 14th St. NW (at P St.).* ☎ *202/332-3300. www.studiotheatre.org. Tickets $32–$62. Metro: Cardozo/U St., Dupont Circle, or McPherson Sq.*

If you hang out at **❹ ★★ Black Cat,** are you (a) a live music fan; (b) an alternative type; (c) sporting vibrantly hued hair; (d) a possessor of original vinyl recordings from X, the Meat Puppets, and Siouxsie and the Banshees; or (e) all of the above? The answer, of course, is "e." *1811 14th St. NW.* ☎ *202/ 667-7960. www.blackcatdc.com. $. Metro: Cardozo/U St.*

❺ Home Rule. Need a milk frother? Stainless steel martini shaker? How about a pair of "potholder dogs," oven mitts that look like your mutt? Of course you do! Look no further than this culinary outpost for creative, colorful kitchen and bar accessories. *1807 14t St. NW (at S St.).* ☎ *202/797-5544. www.homerule.com. Mon–Sat 11am–7pm; Sun noon–5:30pm. Closed holidays. AE, DISC, MC, V. Metro: Cardozo/U St.*

❻ ★★★ Café Saint-Ex. A New American café with a Francophile vibe, this eatery has a warm red-and-gold interior and bistro-style entrees. A DJ spins in the sometimes overcrowded downstairs lounge. *1847 14th St. NW.* ☎ *202/265-7839. www.saint-ex.com. $$–$$$. Metro: Cardozo/U St.*

Home Rule, which helped revitalize the 14th Street/Logan Circle area.

❼ ★★ Greater U Street Heritage Trail. As you explore this section of town—the former home of Duke Ellington and the vital heart of African-American culture in the capital—you might notice 14 poster-size signs, with historic images and compelling stories. By following these visual cues, you can take a 90-minute, self-guided tour of historic U Street. The first sign is at 13th and U streets NW, near the Cardozo/U Street/African-American Civil War Memorial Metro stop; each sign will direct you to the next. Highlights include the Thurgood Marshall Center for Service and Heritage (home to the first African-American YMCA), the Whitelaw Hotel (the segregated capital's first luxury hotel for African Americans), the revived Bohemian Caverns (where the Ramsey Lewis Trio recorded the album "In Crowd"), and the restored Lincoln Theatre. (These last two stops are included in the Lincoln Theatre tour, below, as well.) Walkers are encouraged to follow the trail at their own pace, sampling neighborhood character, businesses, and restaurants along the way. ☎ 202/661-7581. www. culturaltourismdc.org (click on "Tours & Trails").

The restaurant and bar is always packed at **❽ Marvin,** the new hipster joint in the Corridor. In summer, you can find most of the crowd sipping beer and wine on the outdoor back deck. *2007 14th St. NW. ☎ 202/797-7171. www.marvindc. com. $$. Metro: U Street/Cordozo.*

❾ ★ The Lincoln Theatre. The jewel of what was once called "Black Broadway," the Lincoln hosted the likes of Ella Fitzgerald and Cab Calloway before desegregation. The theater went dark in 1979 but reopened 15 years later and was eventually restored to its original

Historic Ben's Chili Bowl.

1920s splendor. Today, it books jazz, R & B, gospel, and comedy acts—even events such as the D.C. Film Festival. The Lincoln Theater is also hosting Arena Stage productions throughout 2009 while Arena's new theater is under construction (see p 157). *1215 U St. NW. ☎ 202/ 397-SEAT [397-7328]. www.thelincoln theatre.org. Tickets $20–$200. Metro: Cardozo/U St.*

Open since 1958, **❿ ★★ Ben's Chili Bowl** is a Washington institution. If this old-time diner's walls could talk, they would speak volumes about historic figures such as Martin Luther King, Jr.; Redd Foxx; Bill Cosby; and others who've sat at the Formica tables here. President Barack Obama has also visited: You just might catch him here inhaling a Chili Half-Smoke—a quarter-pound half pork/half beef smoked sausage smothered in chili, of course—with a side of chili fries and an iced tea. *Tip:* Ben's is cash-only, but they have an ATM in back in case you get caught short. *1213 U St. NW. ☎ 202/667-0909. www.benschili bowl.com. $. Metro: Cardozo/U St.*

⓫ ★ **African American Civil War Memorial and Museum.** This relatively new museum, opened in 1999, uses photography, audiovisual presentations, and historical documents and artifacts to commemorate the estimated 228,000-plus African-American soldiers and sailors who fought, largely unheralded, in the U.S. Civil War. Unveiled in 1998, the "Spirit of Freedom" sculpture, 2 blocks away, honors the sacrifices made by black soldiers and their families during the war. Designed by Ed Hamilton, of Louisville, Kentucky, it is also the first major artwork created by an African-American sculptor to reside on federal land in the capital. *1000 and 1200 U St. NW (between 10th and 12th sts).* ☎ *202/667-2667. www. afroamcivilwar.org. Free admission. Mon–Fri 10am–5pm; Sat 10am–2pm. Metro: Cardozo/U St.*

The African American Civil War Museum.

Howard University.

⓬ **Howard University.** Established in 1867 by a charter of the U.S. Congress, this educational institution was named after General Oliver Howard, a Civil War hero and commissioner of the Freedman's Bureau, which was instrumental in providing funds for the upstart university. Howard U. has come to be a bastion for the liberal and scientific arts, attracting the nation's best and brightest African-American students, and other students of color, who are proud to continue the legacy of a school so involved in the civil rights movement of the 1960s. Current enrollment hovers near 11,000, with more than 7,000 undergraduates. Famous alumni include Thurgood Marshall, Debbie Allen, Sean "P. Diddy" Combs, Marlon Wayans, and Roberta Flack. *2400 6th St. NW.* ☎ *202/806-6100. www.howard. edu. Metro: Cardozo/U St.*

Dupont Circle

1 **Kramerbooks & Afterwords Café**

2 **Phillips Collection**

3 **Woodrow Wilson House**

4 **Brickskeller**

5 **Dupont Memorial Fountain**

6 **Blue Mercury**

7 **Betsy Fisher**

8 **National Geographic Explorer's Hall**

9 **Hank's Oyster Bar**

10 **Komi**

11 **Eighteenth Street Lounge**

Capitol Hill and The Mall may represent Washington to the world, but for locals, Dupont Circle is the heart of the District—a central point for meeting, lunching, strolling, shopping, and people-watching. Famed for being gay-friendly, it's just plain old friendly to newcomers. Be sure to sit on a bench, rest your feet, and watch the world go by within the Circle itself, and ogle the master artworks at Duncan Phillips' private home turned museum, The Phillips Collection (see below). For a nice mix of retailers, restaurants, bars, and clubs, check out Connecticut Avenue and nearby 17th Street.

START: Metro to Dupont Circle

1 **★★ Kramerbooks & Afterwords Café.** Is it a restaurant? A bookstore? A coffeehouse? Open early and late (all night on weekends), it's the perfect spot to chat over lattes, browse bestsellers, grab a quick sandwich, and people-watch the Washingtonians who flock here in droves. The outdoor tables are at a premium in good weather, and weekend brunch is a popular time to rendezvous with friends. *1517 Connecticut Ave. NW.* 📞 *202/387-1400. www.kramers.com. $$. Metro: See Start, above.*

2 **★★ Phillips Collection.** Before leaving Dupont Circle for points north, make a stop at the original home of renowned art

collector Duncan Phillips. On opening his personal collection to the public in 1921, he established America's first modern art museum. His collection is still on view, and the museum remains one of the most popular in the District. Rooms in this historic brownstone feature works by Picasso, Degas, van Gogh, and O'Keeffe, along with several contemporary artists. Auguste Renoir's *Luncheon of the Boating Party* occupies an entire wall on the museum's second floor, and is the Phillips' most celebrated piece. *2 hr. 1600 21st St. NW. ☎ 202/387-2151. www.phillipscollection.org. Admission varies. Metro: Dupont Circle*

③ ★ Woodrow Wilson House.

Tour the former home of the 28th president, preserved as it was when he lived here during his final years in the 1920s. Docents guide visitors on hour-long tours of the Georgian Revival–style building, pointing out objects d'art, such as the French Gobelin tapestry given to Wilson by the French ambassador, and telling stories about our 28th president (such as the fact that he liked to whistle the tune "Oh You Beautiful Doll" to his beloved wife, Edith). You'll see Wilson's movie projector in the library (he was a film buff); the typical 1920s kitchen, with one of the nation's first electric refrigerators; and Wilson's office, which his family called "the dugout." Office treasures include a baseball given to him at an Army-Navy game he

President Woodrow Wilson's radio microphone.

attended with England's George VI. Upstairs, on his bedside table, lies *Imitation of Christ*, by Thomas à Kempis. See also "Historic Washington" on p 52. *2340 S St. NW. ☎ 202/387-4062. www.woodrowwilsonhouse.org. Free admission, but groups of 10 or more must book in advance, with at least 3 days' notice, for a $7.50 fee. Tues–Sun 10am–4pm; closed major holidays. Metro: Dupont Circle.*

If you love beer, have we got a place for you. At ④ **Brickskeller,** you'll find an awesome selection of 1,000-plus international ales, stouts, and lagers here—plus the requisite college kids who make this pub and restaurant their second home. The no-frills beer bar was voted *Washington City Paper*'s Best of DC winner for "Best Beer Menu"

The iconic fountain at Dupont Circle was designed by Daniel Chester French and Henry Bacon and installed in 1921.

Hank's Oyster Bar.

in 2009. *1523 22nd St. NW.* ☎ *202/ 293-1885. www.lovethebeer.com/ brickskeller.html. $. Metro: Dupont Circle.*

⑤ Dupont Memorial Fountain.

A trip to Dupont Circle will undoubtedly include a stroll through this urban park, from which the neighborhood radiates in all directions. A giant marble statue of three classical figures representing sea, wind, and sky anchors the circular area that attracts dog walkers, musicians,

bookworms, and lunchbreakers. Designed by Daniel Chester French—sculptor of the seated Abraham Lincoln at the Lincoln Memorial—and erected in 1921, it was placed on the National Register of Historic Places in 1978. *Connecticut Ave. and New Hampshire Ave., NW. Metro: Dupont Circle.*

⑥ Blue Mercury.

This regional skin care, cosmetics, and bath shop has a beautiful clientele—women and men who can't buy enough of the store's Shu Uemera, Fresh, Decleor, and Paula Dorp product lines. Limited spa and beauty treatments are also available. *1619 Connecticut Ave. NW.* ☎ *202/462-1300. www.bluemercury. com. Mon–Sat 10am–8pm; Sun noon–6pm. AE, DISC, MC, V. Metro: Dupont Circle or Farragut North.*

⑦ ★★ Betsy Fisher.

In a world where so many of us can spot our own outfits on others, it's nice to find a boutique with unique, fashion-forward apparel, shoes, and accessories for women—not girls—that are modern without

Bathysphere and brass sculpture at the National Geographic Society's Explorer's Hall.

being trendy. A good place to grab some basic accessories, too—think belts, boots, shoes, and bags. *See p 108 for service details.*

8 ★★ kids **National Geographic Explorer's Hall.** If you, or your little ones, are a fan of world travel, space exploration, or both—or if you've been a reader of *National Geographic* all your life and simply want to see where the magazine is put together—this museum is a must visit. Check out the society's rotating exhibits related to exploration, adventure, world cultures, and earth sciences, which incorporate interactive programs and artifacts. Conclude your expedition with a stop by the gift shop whose ample collection of toys, gadgets, and gear will amuse your whole scouting party. *17th and M sts. NW.* ☎ *202/857-7588. www. nationalgeographic.com/museum. Free admission (to most exhibits; call ahead to check). Mon–Sat 9am– 5pm; Sun 10am–5pm. Closed Dec 25. Metro: Farragut North (Connecticut Ave. and L St. exit).*

If your ideal evening (or afternoon) involves beer and oysters, you will find no better place than 🍵 ★★ **Hank's Oyster Bar.** This casually sophisticated, modern restaurant caters to low-key diners with a taste for fresh seafood. *1624 Q St. NW.* ☎ *202/462-4265. www. hanksdc.com. $$. Metro: Dupont Circle.*

Fresh catch at Hank's Oyster Bar.

🔟 ★★ **Komi.** Komi and its young chef/owner Johnny Monis have swapped the formally minimalist decor here for something more romantic. But the fantastic Mediterranean fare remains as consistently delicious as always. *See p 140 for service information.*

⓫ **Eighteenth Street Lounge.** Whether you arrive early in the evening to rest your feet as you sip a cocktail and sit, salon-style, on a sofa, or you show up later at night to listen to a live band with all the beautiful people, this legendary destination is all about mingling, chilling to music, and posing pretty. *See p 150 for service details.*

Georgetown

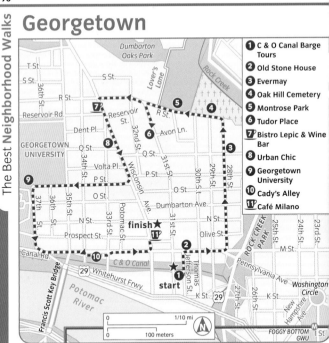

1. C & O Canal Barge Tours
2. Old Stone House
3. Evermay
4. Oak Hill Cemetery
5. Montrose Park
6. Tudor Place
7. Bistro Lepic & Wine Bar
8. Urban Chic
9. Georgetown University
10. Cady's Alley
11. Café Milano

No visit to Washington is complete without a trip to historic and hip Georgetown—which somehow manages to balance frenzied consumerism with cultural relevance. For a detailed tour, check out "The Best of D.C. in Two Days" on p 14. Here are a few additional points of interest, high-end restaurants, and outstanding retailers. START: **Bus no. 30, 32, 34, 35, 36, or 38B to Thomas Jefferson and M streets**

① C & O Canal Barge Tours.
Perfect for families and history buffs, these scenic, 1-hour barge tours employ guides who don period clothes to share stories of the region's history while floating down the Georgetown section of the Chesapeake and Ohio Canal. The 185-mile (298km) waterway would take you to Cumberland, Maryland, if you were to follow its course. *1057 Thomas Jefferson St.*

NW. ☎ 202/653-5190. www.nps. gov/choh. Admission $8 adults, $6 seniors, $5 children 4–14, free for children 3 and under. Mid-Apr to late Oct Wed–Sun 9am–4:30pm. No direct Metro access (Metro to Foggy Bottom is a 15-min. walk). Bus: See Start, above.

② ★ Old Stone House.
On M Street—between modern attractions like Sephora and Hu's Shoes—is the Old Stone House, one of the

Georgetown University.

capital's oldest buildings, built in 1765. Give your credit card a rest; explore its interior, and learn how Washingtonians lived nearly 250 years ago. *3051 M St. NW.* ☎ *202/895-6070. www.nps.gov/rocr/olst. Free tours of 10 or more by reservation only. No Metro access. See "Traveling to Georgetown" on p 93.*

③ ★★ **Evermay.** Built between 1792 and 1794, one of Georgetown's greatest mansions had an original owner who was both eccentric and obsessed with privacy. He went so far as to advertise dire predictions (bordering on threats) in the daily papers, warning the curious of trespassing on his property. Today it's privately owned, so you still can't tour the grounds, but you can steal a look through the iron gates. *1623 28th St. NW. No Metro access (see box, p 93).*

④ **Oak Hill Cemetery.** This historic cemetery is just a short walk uphill from the shops of Georgetown's M Street. One of the oldest cemeteries in the city, it was established in 1849 and now holds the

remains of many famous Washingtonians: Senators, Civil War generals, artists, designers, and Philip Graham, longtime publisher of the *Washington Post*, are all buried here. Among the grounds' great buildings and monuments are Renwick Chapel, designed by James Renwick, Jr., architect of the Smithsonian Building; and the Van Ness Mausoleum. *30th and R Sts. NW.* ☎ *202/337-2835. www.oakhill cemeterydc.org. Mon–Fri, 10am–4pm; closed to the public during funerals. Metro: Foggy Bottom.*

⑤ ★ **Montrose Park.** Right next door to Oak Hill, Montrose was founded as a place "for the recreation and pleasure of the people." Rope-making tycoon Robert Parrott claimed the land in the early 1800s, and by the early 1900s, it had become the premier spot in town for picnics and leisurely strolls. Street noises are so muffled, you might even feel you've left the city. *On the block of 3000 R St. NW, next to Dumbarton Oaks. Open daily April–Oct, 2–6pm; Nov–Mar, 2–5pm. No Metro access (see box, p 93).*

The pre-Revolutionary Old Stone House.

Tudor Place, a massive Georgetown mansion.

6 ★ **Tudor Place.** One of the longest blocks in Georgetown is the stretch between Q and R streets on 31st Street NW. In a neighborhood where even the rich and famous get dog-eat-dog over square footage, it doesn't get more impressive than this estate that sprawls nearly a full square block. This 1816 mansion was home to Martha Washington's granddaughter and her descendants until 1984. *1644 31st St. NW.* ☎ *202/ 965-0400. www.tudorplace.org. Admission $6 adults, $5 seniors, and $3 students. No reservations necessary for groups of 10 or less. Tues–Fri 10am–4pm; Sat 10am–3pm; Sun noon– 4pm. No Metro access (see box, p 93).*

French-born chef Bruno Fortin brings authentic Gallic flavors to Georgetown at **7** ★ **Bistro Lepic & Wine Bar,** whose intimate decor feels both upscale and casual. The wine bar upstairs is ideal for a romantic tête a tête, and for Sideways-loving pinot noir snobs. Bon Appétit named it one of the nation's top 10 restaurants. *1736 Wisconsin Ave. NW.* ☎ *202/333-0111. www.bistrolepic. com. $$. No Metro access (see box, p 93).*

8 ★ **Urban Chic.** Not so long ago, D.C. was all about pearls and twin-sets but, thank goodness, times have changed. This boutique is where the district's trendsetters select high-end denims; cool looks from Chloe, Marc Jacobs, and other designers; and saliva-inducing accessories, from wide belts to embellished earrings. *See p 109 for service details.*

9 ★★★ **Georgetown University.** Like Harvard, Princeton, and Brown, Georgetown University evokes images of ivy-covered buildings, historic colleges, polo-wearing students, and academic types with furrowed brows appearing from their ivory towers. The campus grounds do not disappoint, from the architecture to the soccer pitch, and make for a lovely stroll on a nice day. Because the university is in the heart of Georgetown just a hop, skip, and a jump from M Street's main drag (west of Wisconsin), the curious should not hesitate to tour it. (Look for the nearby *Exorcist* stairs, too, which were featured in a climactic scene in the 1973 horror film, and connect the campus to M St. from Prospect St.) Founded by Father John Carroll (an appointed

Traveling to Georgetown

Georgetown is not exactly convenient to reach. There are no Metro stops here—or even close to here; you will need to rely on bus or taxi transport for access. If you don't mind a walk, however, get off the Metro at either Foggy Bottom in D.C. or at the first stop in northern Virginia, at Roslyn (both are on the blue and orange lines), and hike 15 to 20 minutes. Foggy Bottom is a simple stroll west on Pennsylvania, which merges into M Street, Georgetown's main drag. Roslyn is just across Key Bridge; traverse it and you're at the other end of Georgetown—perfect for a stop at Dean & Deluca for a snack. For bus schedules, check out **www.wmata.com**.

superior of the American Mission by the pope in 1784), the school officially opened its doors for study in 1789. More than 2 centuries later, the school is a top draw for continuing education and boasts

Shoppers on M St.

formidable alums such as President William Jefferson Clinton, and yes, the guy who wrote *The Exorcist,* William Peter Blatty. *37th and O sts. NW.* ☎ *202/687-0100. www. georgetown.edu. No Metro access (see box above).*

🔟 ★★ **Cady's Alley.** Looking for that perfect armchair to go with your new lamp? You'll likely find it here in D.C.'s design district. Sidled next to the C&O Canal in George-town, this cluster of shops features international and local contempo-rary furnishings and accessories. Artefacto, Contemporaria, and Ligne Roset are just a few of the purveyors you'll find in this lofty design center. *3318 M St. NW (between 33rd and 34th sts.). www. cadysalley.com. Store hours vary. Metro: Foggy Bottom or Roslyn.*

Busy 11️⃣ ★ **Café Milano** is a ven-erable who's who of D.C. socialites, senators, and playboys. Although somewhat pretentious, it dishes out middling-to-good Italian fare. *3251 Prospect St. NW (at Potomac).* ☎ *202/333-6183. Entrees $–$$$. Metro: Foggy Bottom or Roslyn.*

Penn Quarter

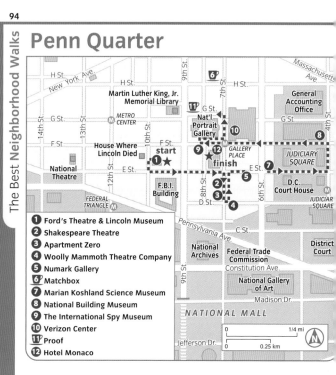

1. Ford's Theatre & Lincoln Museum
2. Shakespeare Theatre
3. Apartment Zero
4. Woolly Mammoth Theatre Company
5. Numark Gallery
6. Matchbox
7. Marian Koshland Science Museum
8. National Building Museum
9. The International Spy Museum
10. Verizon Center
11. Proof
12. Hotel Monaco

Just 10 years ago, this section of town induced more fear than fanfare. Now Penn Quarter has certifiably transformed, drawing beautiful young things in droves to explore it. The former redlight district has been replaced with scene-making lounges and high-end hotels. And art galleries, edgy theater companies, and groovy retailers have taken over aging buildings and given them new life. Throw in the Verizon Center for major sporting events and stadium concerts, and you've got one happening neighborhood.
START: **Metro to Archives/Navy Memorial**

1 ★★ **Ford's Theatre & Lincoln Museum.** On April 14, 1865, gun-wielding assassin John Wilkes Booth killed President Abraham Lincoln here, as the president watched a performance of *Our American Cousin*. Everyone was laughing at a funny line from Tom Taylor's celebrated comedy, when Booth crept into the president's box; shot him; and leapt to the stage, shouting, "Sic semper tyrannis!" ("Thus ever

to tyrants!"). With his left leg broken from the vault, Booth mounted his horse in the alley and galloped off. Doctors carried Lincoln across the street to the house of William Petersen, where the president died the next morning. The theater closed immediately, and the War Department used the building as an office until 1893, when three floors collapsed, killing 22 clerks. Subsequently, the structure fell into disuse until 1968, when it reopened—restored to its appearance on the night of Lincoln's murder—as a functioning playhouse and a repository for historical artifacts surrounding the assassination and the trial of Booth's conspirators. The museum just underwent another 2-year renovation and reopened in 2008, with expanded exhibits on the president, a new lobby and box office (the latter was previously located outside), and 21st-century lighting, seats, and concessions. The collection of museum artifacts includes Booth's derringer pistol, Lincoln's overcoat from the night he was shot, and the theatre binoculars that were found on the floor of the president's box. *511 10th St. NW. ☎ 202/347-4833. www.fordstheatre.org. Free museum admission. Daily 9am–5pm, except Dec. 25. Metro: See Start, above. Also see "Historic Washington" on p 55.*

② ★★ **Shakespeare Theatre.** From *Love's Labor Lost* to *Pericles,* this renowned outfit stages the best of the Bard in one of the District's hottest new neighborhoods. So you can fill up on highbrow culture and then hit the town for some low-down gallivanting after the show. *See p 157 for service details.*

The newly renovated Ford's Theatre.

③ ★ **Apartment Zero.** Form meets function at this temple for modern interiors and accessories. Think stainless steel, simple lines, bright- and solid-colored fabrics, and very expensive price tags. *406 7th St. NW. ☎ 202/628-4067. www.apartmentzero.com. Metro: Gallery Place/Chinatown.*

④ ★★ **Woolly Mammoth Theatre Company.** Provocative and experimental, this theater company is committed to defying boundaries, with the aim of igniting discussion after every performance. *641 D St. NW. ☎ 202/289-2443. www.woolly mammoth.net. Tickets $22–$52. Metro: Gallery Place/Chinatown.*

⑤ **Numark Gallery.** One of the few dynamic, contemporary galleries outside the explosive new 14th Street art zone, this space spotlights the works of emerging national and local artists. *625–27 E St. NW. ☎ 202/628-3810. www.numark gallery. Metro: Gallery Place/Chinatown.*

Built into a 15-foot (4.5m) wide, three-story tall building, **⑥** **Matchbox** is quite simply the place for pizza. You'll happily nosh on fire-cooked pizza pies, mini-burgers,

The International Spy Museum.

and salads—if you can get a table. **Note:** Your entire party must be present before they'll seat you. *713 H St. NW.* ☎ *202/289-4441. www. matchboxdc.com. $$. Metro: Gallery Place/Chinatown.*

7 Marian Koshland Science Museum. Want to know how DNA works, or how global warming will affect us? You don't have to be a science geek to immerse yourself for

Home furnishings at Apartment Zero.

hours in this museum. *6th and E sts. NW.* ☎ *202/334-1201. www. koshland-science-museum.org. Admission $5 adults, $3 children 5–18. Wed–Sun 10am–6pm (last admission 5pm), except Thanksgiving, Dec 25, and Jan 1–13. Metro: Gallery Place/Chinatown.*

8 ★★ National Building Museum. Architects of the world, rejoice! Finally, a museum is dedicated to American achievements in the building arts. *401 F St. NW.* ☎ *202/272-2448. www.nbm.org. Suggested $5 donation. Mon–Sat 10am–5pm; Sun 11am–5pm. Metro: Gallery Place/Chinatown.*

9 ★★ International Spy Museum. Spies used to conjure up romantic images of James Bond and trench-coated secret agents. Now, in the wake of 9/11 and terrorist cells, it's a whole new world. To learn about the history of espionage and the uncharted territory we now must learn to navigate, tour this museum, which features the largest collection of international espionage artifacts ever put on public display. Exhibits include a re-creation of a tunnel beneath the divided city of Berlin during the Cold War; the intelligence-gathering stories of those behind enemy lines and of those involved in planning D-Day in World War II; an exhibit on escape and evasion techniques in wartime; the tales of more recent spies, told by the CIA and FBI agents involved in identifying them; and a mockup of an intelligence agency's 21st-century operations center. The Spy Museum's executive director was with the CIA for 36 years and his advisory board includes two former CIA directors, two former CIA disguise chiefs, and a retired KGB general. Also see p 31. *800 F St. NW.* ☎ *202/393-7798.* www.spymuseum. org. *Metro: Gallery Place/Chinatown.*

🔟 **Verizon Center.** Time it right and you could catch Gilbert Arenas in his famous "zero" shirt playing hoops for the Wizards, or the puckish Alex Ovechkin making goals for the Caps. You might even see Madonna or another touring legend in concert when you come here for stadium-size entertainment. *601 F St. NW.* ☎ *202/628-3200.* www. verizoncenter.com. *Call for admission prices. Metro: Gallery Place/ Chinatown.*

Wine bars exploded onto the D.C. scene in recent years, and 🔟 **★★★ Proof** continues to be at the top of the heap. A tax attorney–turned-restaurateur, Mark Kuller, opened this wine-centric restaurant in 2007 and devoted much of his own wine collection to its list, which boasts 1,000 different bottles. A dinner of glazed Alaskan sablefish or grilled beef hanger steak isn't bad either. *775 G St. NW.* ☎ *202/ 737-7663.* www.proofdc.com. *$$–$$$. Metro: Gallery Place/Chinatown.*

🔟 **Hotel Monaco.** In a former historic post office, this luxury hotel has 15-foot (4.5m) ceilings and marble, 19th-century neoclassical architecture, but the interior is utterly contemporary and cool. Hotel guests, NBA stars, and neighborhood hipsters flock to the in-house lounge, Poste. It's dog-friendly too. *See p 164 for service details.*

The National Building Museum.

Capitol Hill

1. Washington Navy Yard
2. Eastern Market
3. Barracks Row
4. Trover Shop
5. Bartholdi Park
6. Folger Shakespeare Library
7. Sewall-Belmont House & Museum
8. Johnny's Half Shell
9. Union Station
10. Hawk 'n' Dove

Although it's the seat of U.S. government, crowned by the Capitol's graceful dome, and encompassing the Supreme Court and the Library of Congress, "the Hill" is also a quiet residential district bounded by the Capitol in the West, the Armory in the East, H Street to the North, and the Southwest Freeway to the South. Capitol Hill has plenty for travelers, beyond the government buildings: tree-lined streets with Victorian homes, restaurants, the U.S. Botanic Garden, and the Folger Shakespeare Library. For a more extensive tour of this historical neighborhood and its essential landmarks, see "The Best of D.C. in Two Days" on p 14. Here are a few additional highlights, for a more relaxed day of exploration rather than sightseeing. START: **Metro to Eastern Market**

1 Washington Navy Yard. If you're already in the Capitol Hill area, it's a relatively short walk to the Washington Navy Yard and Museum. Off the beaten track and often overlooked—and therefore, blessedly uncrowded—this museum celebrates the Navy's heroes, ships,

diplomacy, and battles. Among its many exhibits are submarines, swords, and firearms from Revolutionary ship captains, artifacts from salvaged Naval vessels dating back to 1800, and a range of Naval uniforms that span the years. *805 Kidder Breese SE.* ☎ *202/433-6897.*

The Folger Shakespeare Library.

www.history.navy.gov. *Mon–Fri, 9am–5pm, weekend and holidays, 10am–5pm. Call in advance for tour reservations. Free admission. Metro: Eastern Market or Navy Yard.*

2 ★★ Eastern Market. You'll have many "have-to-have-it" moments during your stroll through the shops of this D.C. landmark that has been in continuous operation since 1873. A 2007 fire nearly decimated the 135-year-old East Hall building, but the city government—and devoted fans of the market—vowed to rebuild it. The farmer's market operated from temporary quarters in South Hall across the street until Eastern Market's reopening in June 2009. Snack on treats from various vendors to stay fueled as you browse the wares of more than 175 exhibitors who showcase their handmade pottery, jewelry, crafts, furniture, and—on the weekends—fresh produce from the surrounding states. Saturday morning is once again the best time to go experience a D.C. tradition: blueberry pancakes at the Market Lunch counter (Sat 7am–6pm, Sun 9am–4pm, Tues–Fri from 7am). *7th St. & North Carolina Ave., SE.* ☎ *202/543-7293 or 703/534-7612. Tues–Fri*

7am–7pm, Sat 7am–6pm, Sun 9am–5pm. Metro: Eastern Market.

3 ★★ Barracks Row. The strip along 8th St., SE, became the first commercial center in D.C. after Thomas Jefferson centered the Marine Corps there in 1801. The neighborhood has ridden out some downturns since then, but in more recent years, Washingtonians have

The Sewall-Belmont House.

flocked to the lively district for housing, dining, and shopping. Restaurants, outdoor cafes, and taverns such as the Ugly Mug and Belga Café are always packed, and stores such as Groovy DC and Homebody cater to artsy types seeking those one-of-a-kind finds. *8th and Eye Sts. SE.* ☎ *202/544-3188. www.barracks row.org. Metro: Eastern Market.*

4 ★ **Trover Shop.** If you're looking for international newspapers, periodicals, congressional directories, and lobbyist guides, make a beeline to this family-run shop. A local fixture for 40 years, it still attracts the biggest names in government to peruse its well-stocked racks. *221 Pennsylvania Ave. SE (between 2nd and 3rd sts.).* ☎ *202/543-8006. www.trover.com. Metro: Capitol South.*

5 ★★ **Bartholdi Park.** Part of the U.S. Botanic Garden, this flower-filled park is about the size of a city block and is named for the French sculptor who created its 30-foot-high (9m) cast-iron "fountain of light and water." Frederic Auguste Bartholdi (1834–1904), who is most famous for that other large sculpture he did—the Statue of Liberty in New York Harbor—constructed this work for the 1876 International Exposition in Philadelphia. When the exposition closed, the U.S. government purchased the sculpture for the National Mall; it was moved to its current location in 1932. Come to view it, and to enjoy the surrounding sunflowers, petunias, morning glories, tall ornamental grasses, and creeping vines. *1st St. and Independence Ave. SW. Free admission. Daily 10am–5pm. Metro: Union Station.*

6 ★★ **Folger Shakespeare Library.** Founded in 1932 by ardent Shakespeare fan (and wealthy Standard Oil executive)

Henry Clay Folger and his wife, Emily, this repository houses the world's largest collection of the Bard's printed works. In addition to its 250,000 books—100,000 of which are classified as rare—the library also provides an important research center for students of the master playwright and Renaissance literature. The permanent exhibits in the Great Hall include period costumes, musical instruments, historic playbills, and more. Also see p 39. *201 E. Capitol St. SE.* ☎ *202/544-7077. www.folger.edu. Mon–Sat 10am–4pm, with docent tours at 11am; closed on federal holidays. Metro: Capitol South or Union Station.*

7 **Sewall-Belmont House & Museum.** You might find yourself humming "Sister Suffragette" from *Mary Poppins*—"We're clearly soldiers in petticoats, and dauntless crusaders for women's votes"—as you tour this museum. This Federal/Queen Anne–style house was once the home of Alice Paul (1885–1977), who founded the National Women's Party in 1913 and wrote the original Equal Rights Amendment to the Constitution (ERA). Paul, who held three law degrees and a Ph.D. in sociology, was jailed seven times in the U.S. and Great Britain for the cause of women's suffrage. Paul lived here from 1929 to 1972, but now the National Women's Party owns and maintains the house. Exhibitions trace the path of the women's movement, from the better-known activist, Susan B. Anthony, to 59¢ buttons and the ERA. Check out picketing banners, 5,000 prints and photographs, original cartoons, more than 50 scrapbooks from early suffragists, paintings, sculptures, publications, and more. Also see "Historic Washington" on p 56. *144 Constitution Ave. NE.* ☎ *202/546-1210. www.sewallbelmont.org.*

Daniel Burnham's Beaux-Arts masterwork, Union Station.

Suggested donation $5. Wed–Sun noon–4pm by docent tour only. Metro: Union Station.

Capitol Hill is known for its stuffy, only-in-D.C. restaurants, but **8 ★ Johnny's Half Shell**—a lively seafood eatery, with close tables and a neighborly feel—is anything but. Prices are steep, but the variety of fresh seafood is usually worth dishing out the extra dough. *400 N. Capitol St. NW. ☎ 202/737-0400. www.johnnyshalfshell.net. Breakfast, lunch, dinner. $$–$$$$. Metro: Union Station.*

9 ★ Union Station. Take one step inside and you'll know that this is no typical train station. As ornate as it is functional, this 1907 Beaux Arts–style building was designed by noted architect Daniel Burnham. As a member of the illustrious McMillan Commission (assembled in 1900 to beautify the city in a manner befitting an important world capital), Burnham counseled, "Make no little plans. They have no magic to stir men's blood." Union Station, one of the commission's "big plans" (at its

opening, it was the largest train station in the world), was modeled after the Baths of Diocletian and the Arch of Constantine in Rome. The Main Hall features a nine-story, 96-foot (29m) barrel-vaulted ceiling inlaid with 70 pounds (32 kilograms) of 22-carat gold-leaf, acres of white marble floors punctuated by red Champlain dots, bronze grilles, and rich Honduran mahogany paneling.

The Hawk 'n' Dove.

Diners at Hawk 'n' Dove.

The adjacent East Hall has scagliola marble walls and columns; a gorgeous, hand-stenciled skylight ceiling; and stunning murals inspired by the frescoes of Pompeii. In the heyday of rail travel, many important events took place in Union Station: Visiting royalty and heads of state were honored here, as were World War I General Pershing, upon his return from France; South Pole explorer Rear Admiral Byrd; and President Franklin Delano Roosevelt, whose funeral train was met here by thousands of mourners in 1945. Today Union Station is a crossroads for D.C. locals, commuters from Baltimore and the suburbs, and visitors from farther afield. It also houses loads of shops such as Nine West, Swatch, and Victoria's Secret, plus a solid section of fast-food and fine-fare dining options. *50 Massachusetts Ave. NE.* ☎ *202/371-9441. www.unionsationdc.com. Free admission. Daily 24 hr. Metro: Union Station.*

The venerable ⑩ **Hawk 'n' Dove** is where everyone—Democrats, Republicans, staffers, and Hill members—goes for strong drinks when the working day is done. Eavesdrop on conversations as you snack on appetizers and you might just hear some of those famous D.C. secrets. *329 Pennsylvania Ave. SE.* ☎ *202/ 543-3300. www.hawkanddove online.com. $$. Metro: Eastern Market or Capitol South.* ●

Shopping Best Bets

Best **Interior Design District**
Cady's Alley, *3318 M St. NW,
Georgetown (p 112)*

Best **Antiques (to $10K)**
Carling Nichols, *1675 Wisconsin
Ave. NW (see "Antique Row," p 112)*

Best **Antiques (to $100)**
Eastern Market, *7th St. and North
Carolina Ave. SE (p 114)*

Best **"Bling"**
Tiny Jewel Box, *1147 Connecticut
Ave. NW (p 112)*

Best **Shoes for $500**
Hu's Shoes, *3005 M St. NW. (p 114)*

Best **Shoes for $50**
Shake Your Booty Shoes, *2206
18th St. NW (p 114)*

Best **Apparel for Serious
Fashionistas**
Urban Chic, *1626 Wisconsin Ave.
NW (p 109)*

Best **Commercial Shopping
Drag**
M Street and Wisconsin Avenue

Best **Hidden Gem**
Simply Home, *1412 U St. NW
(p 113)*

Best **Hood for Contemporary
Art**
The Galleries on 14th Street, *14th
St. NW (p 109)*

Best **Place for a Power Tie**
Thomas Pink, *1127 Connecticut
Ave. NW (p 109)*

Best **Gourmet Snack**
Dean & Deluca, *3276 M St. NW
(p 111)*

Best **Flowers**
Ultra Violet Flowers, *1218 31st St.
NW (p 111)*

Best Bookstore to **Catch a Senator Reading about Himself**
Trover Shop, *221 Pennsylvania Ave.
SE (p 111)*

Best for Cool **Mid-20th-Century
Finds**
Miss Pixie's, *1626 14th St. NW
(p 113)*

Best **Baby Stuff**
★★ Piccolo Piggies, *1533 Wisconsin Ave. NW (p 110)*

Best **Contemporary Home**
Design Within Reach, *1838 Columbia Rd. NW. (p 81)*

Best **Denim**
★★ Denim Bar, *4939 Cordell Ave,
Bethesda, MD (p 108)*

Best **Cards & Gifts**
★ Pulp, *1803 14th St. NW (p 111)*

Where **Musicians Jam**
★ The Guitar Shop, *1216 Connecticut Ave. NW (p 113)*

Best **Bones to Pick**
★★ Pet Essentials, *1722 14th St.
NW (p 113)*

Best **If You Forgot to Pack
Elmo**
★ Sullivan's Toy Store, *3412 Wisconsin Ave. NW (p 110)*

*Previous page: Home Rule (p 83), in
14th Street/Logan Circle.*

Capitol Hill & Penn Quarter

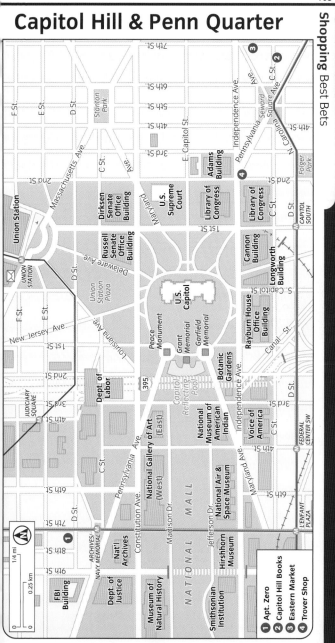

1 Apt. Zero
2 Capitol Hill Books
3 Eastern Market
4 Trover Shop

Georgetown & Dupont Circle

Vice-President's House

US NAVAL OBSERVATORY

Observatory Ln.

Normanstone Dr.

Woodland Dr.

McGill Terrace

28th St.

30th St.

30th St.

Normanstone Park

Edgevale Terrace

EMBASSY ROW

ROCK CREEK PARK

Benton Pl.

Rock Creek Dr.

Rock Creek and Potomac Pkwy.

Belmont Rd.

Connecticut Ave.

Observatory Circle

Whitehaven St.

Kalorama Circle

Whitehaven Pkwy.

2

Whitehaven St.

Wisconsin Ave.

35th Pl.

Dumbarton Oaks Park

Wyoming Ave.

Tracy Pl.

Massachusetts Ave.

Waterside Dr.

23rd St.

Bancroft Pl.

24th St.

T St.

S St.

35th St.

36th St.

S St.

R St.

S St.

Montrose Park

R St.

Decatur Pl.

Reservoir Rd.

Winfield Ln.

Reservoir St.

31st St.

Avon Pl.

Avon Ln.

R St.

Dumbarton Oaks & Gardens

Sheridan Circle

Dent Pl.

3 **4**

32nd St.

Cambridge Pl.

Q St.

30th St.

29th St.

28th St.

26th St.

27th St.

GEORGETOWN UNIVERSITY

5

Q St.

Tudor Place

34th St.

Q St.

Volta Pl.

6

33rd St.

P St.

O St.

P St.

Rock Creek and Potomac Pkwy.

Rock Creek

36th St.

35th St.

O St.

Wisconsin Ave.

Dumbarton Ave.

GEORGETOWN

N St.

N St.

Prospect St.

Potomac St.

Olive St.

13

Congress Ct.

14

Canal Rd.

7

9 **10** **11** **12**

Th. Jefferson St.

Old Stone House

M St.

Pennsylvania Ave.

Washington Circle

Francis Scott Key Bridge

K St.

Whitehurst Frwy.

C & O Canal

27th St.

26th St.

25th St.

K St.

Queen Annes Ln.

I St.

New Hampshire Ave.

Potomac River

Potomac Pkwy.

Virginia Ave.

Watergate Complex

Theodore Roosevelt Island

George Washington Memorial Pkwy.

Theodore Roosevelt Memorial

19th St N.

Kent St.

N Lynn St.

Arlington Ridge Rd.

JFK Center for Performing Arts

8

0   1/10 mi

0   0.10 km

N

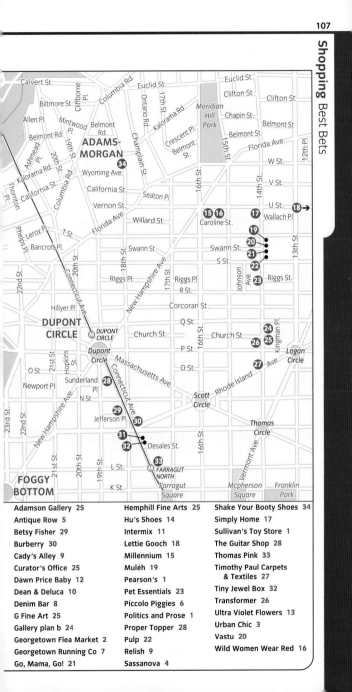

Shopping A to Z

Go, Mama, Go! in 14th Street/Logan Circle.

Apparel

★ Betsy Fisher DUPONT

CIRCLE You follow *Vogue*, so peruse the racks of this boutique—buzz to gain entry, please—designed to suit the caviar tastes of well-dressed women who must look smashing at D.C. dinner parties and occasional dates with high-ranking officials. *1224 Connecticut Ave. NW (at 18th St.).* ☎ *202/785-1975. www. betsyfisher.com. AE, DISC, MC, V. Metro: Dupont Circle. Map p 106.*

★★ Burberry DOWNTOWN Yes,

it's a chain store. But despite its English roots, there is something about that famous signature plaid—found in the linings of its cloth umbrellas, tony and tailored clothing, and camel-hair coats for men and women—that is quintessentially Washington, too. *1155 Connecticut Ave. NW (at M St.).* ☎ *202/463-3000.*

www.burberry.com. AE, DISC, MC, V. Metro: Farragut North. Map p 106.

★★ Denim Bar BETHESDA We

wouldn't send a D.C. newcomer to shop outside the District for anything but the ultimate pair of jeans. Men and women devoted to upscale designer denim should take the easy Metro ride here, where an expert staff will guide you (sometimes cruelly, to be kindly) to the perfect fit. *4939 Cordell Ave, Bethesda, MD.* ☎ *301/986-5260. AE, DISC, MC, V. Metro: Bethesda. Map p 106.*

Georgetown Running Co.

GEORGETOWN If you're light on your feet—meaning the prospect of running 5 miles (8km) fills you with joy, not dread—jog this way for state-of-the-art track shoes and gear. *3401 M St. NW (at 34th St.).* ☎ *202/ 337-8626. www.runningcompany.net. AE, DISC, MC, V. No Metro access. See "Traveling to Georgetown" on p 93. Map p 106.*

★★ Intermix GEORGETOWN What

started in NYC has landed in D.C.: a satellite store for Marc Jacobs jackets, Diane von Furstenberg wrap dresses, rhinestone cowboy boots, Norma Kamali jumpsuits, and over-size shades—priced to make you feel as though the paparazzi are waiting at the front door. *3222 M St. NW (at Wisconsin Ave.).* ☎ *202/298-8080. www.intermixonline.com. AE, DC, DISC, MC, V. No Metro access. See "Traveling to Georgetown" on p 93. Map p 106.*

Lettie Gooch SHAW A little bit of

NYC's Soho is found in this unique boutique that stocks one-of-a-kind feminine fashions from Tricia Fix, SaltWorks, Hype, Jak & Rae, and local designers. *1911 9th St. NW.* ☎ *202/ 332-4242. www.lettiegooch.com. Metro: U Street/Cardozo. Map p 106.*

Drinking glasses from Home Rule, p 83.

Proper Topper DUPONT CIRCLE From the name alone, you can probably guess what this tiny shop specializes in. Every type of hat, cap, and beret in stylish designs are represented, along with picture frames, gift books, and funky clothes. *1350 Connecticut Ave. NW. ☎ 202/ 842-3055. www.propertopper.com. Metro: Dupont Circle. Map p 106.*

★★★ **Thomas Pink** DOWNTOWN Dapper gentlemen from the nation's capital descend upon this London outpost for well-cut business suits, power ties, cufflinks, crisp and color-ful shirts, and tailored service. Inside the Mayflower Hotel. *1127 Connecti-cut Ave. NW (between L and M sts.). ☎ 202/223-5390. www.thomas pink.com. AE, MC, V. Metro: Farragut North. Map p 106.*

★ **Urban Chic** GEORGETOWN If you dress like a casual-but-chic Hol-lywood starlet, and you're intent on finding chandelier earrings, a slouched hobo bag, flirty blouse, or

pricey designer denim, then off you go: Urban Chic awaits. *1626 Wiscon-sin Ave. NW (between Q St. and Res-ervoir Rd.). ☎ 202/338-5398. www. urbanchic-dc.com. AE, DISC, MC, V. No Metro access. See "Traveling to Georgetown" on p 93. Map p 106.*

Art
★★★ **The Galleries on 14th Street** 14TH STREET/LOGAN CIRCLE Fusebox, the most famous of these galleries, just got an offer they couldn't refuse and moved to San Francisco. But the creative mark made by its owners inspired other curators to open galleries on this emerging main street for modern and contemporary works. Don't miss these highlights: **G Fine Art** *(1515 14th St. NW, at Church St.; ☎ 202/462-1601; www.gfineartdc. com; no credit cards);* **Hemphill Fine Arts** *(☎ 202/234-5601; www. hemphillfinearts.com; AE, DC, DISC, MC, V);* **Adamson Gallery** *(☎ 202/ 232-0707; www.adamsoneditions. com; MC, V);* **Curator's Office** *(☎ 202/387-1008; www.curators office.com; MC, V);* **Transformer** *(1404 P St. NW, at 14th St.; ☎ 202/ 483-1102; www.transformergallery. com);* and **Gallery plan b** *(1530 14th St., NW, at Q St.; ☎ 202/234-2711; www.galleryplanb.com; AE, MC, V).* Metro: Cardozo/U St. Map p 106.

Muléh, in 14th Street/Logan Circle.

Timothy Paul Carpets & Textiles, in 14th Street/Logan Circle.

Babies & Kids

★★ Dawn Price Baby GEORGE-
TOWN If you're a member of the stroller set whose bundle of joy must have the latest Bugaboo model, head to this small but stocked shop. Clothing, shoes, and toys are also for sale. *3112 M St. NW (at 31st St.).* ☎ *202/333-3939. www. kbaby.com. AE, DC, DISC, MC, V. No Metro access. See "Traveling to Georgetown" on p 93. Map p 106.*

★★ Piccolo Piggies GEORGE-
TOWN Is your baby or preschooler a tiny fashionista? Don't miss this charming, utterly French boutique stocked with beautifully made knits, adorable jumpers, handcrafted sweaters, and cool shoes for kids. It's pricey, but everything here is well made and worth it. *1533 Wisconsin Ave. NW (at Q St.).* ☎ *202/333-0123. www.piccolo-piggies.com. AE, MC, V. No Metro access. See*

"Traveling to Georgetown" on p 93. Map p 106.

★ Sullivan's Toy Store CLEVE-
LAND PARK Forgot to pack Elmo? This tantrum-quashing shop is jam-packed with every conceivable plaything, puzzle, costume, wheeled wonder, art supply, and entertaining distraction imaginable. *3412 Wisconsin Ave. (at Newark St.).* ☎ *202/362-1343. AE, DISC, MC, V. Metro: Cleveland Park, then walk west to Wisconsin. Map p 106.*

Books

★ Capitol Hill Books CAPITOL
HILL Feel like losing yourself on a rainy afternoon in dusty stacks bursting with amazing old books? This used bookstore, steps from Eastern Market, has more than a century's worth of history and is a mine for modern first editions, lit-crit, and unusual subjects. *657 C St. SE (between 6th and 7th sts.).* ☎ *202/544-1621. www.capitolhill books-dc.com. AE, DC, MC, V. Metro: Eastern Market. Map p 105.*

★★ Politics and Prose CLEVE-
LAND PARK If on principle you'd rather give your hard-earned cash to Mom and Pop than a big chain, head north of downtown to this two-story shop. It's famed in D.C. for its warm vibe, nearly nightly author readings, excellent selection, and cozy coffeehouse. *5015 Connecticut Ave. NW (at Fessenden St.).*

Mid-20th-century modern furniture from Muléh.

Friendship Heights, D.C.

Known and loved for its off-the-beaten-path boutiques and shops, this bustling strip is billed as D.C.'s Fifth Avenue. If it's the extremely high-end you're looking for, take a 15-minute Metro ride—or better yet, hail a cab—to this busy Wisconsin Avenue corridor that caters to luxury buyers with outposts of Sak's Fifth Avenue, Tiffany's, Louis Vuitton, Jimmy Choo, Neiman Marcus, Bloomingdales, and more. Be prepared to drop some serious Benjamins on designer dresses, impeccable suits, handbags, and jewelry in this pricey neighborhood along the Maryland border. *Wisconsin and Western aves. Metro: Friendship Heights.*

☎ 202/364-1919. www.politics-prose. com. AE, DISC, MC, V. Metro: Van Ness–UDC, then walk or transfer to an "L" bus for 1 mile (1.6km). Map p 106.

★ **Trover Shop** CAPITOL HILL
For more than 40 years, this family-owned bookstore has attracted Washington's movers and shakers (yes, that was a senator you spotted near the periodicals) for its international newspapers, congressional directories, and lobbyist guides. *221 Pennsylvania Ave. SE (at Independence Ave.).* ☎ 202/543-8006. www. trover.com. AE, DISC, MC, V. Metro: Capitol South. Map p 105.

Flowers & Gifts
★ **Pulp** 14TH STREET A former San Francisco AIDS activist opened this community-welcoming gift shop in 2001. People can sit at the "card bar" to journal; write notes on unusual, handcrafted cards; or chat with neighbors. *1803 14th St. NW (at S St.).* ☎ 202/462-7857. www.pulp dc.com. AE, DISC, MC, V. Metro: Cardozo/U St. Map p 106.

★ **Ultra Violet Flowers** GEORGE-TOWN In the doghouse? Wooing your beloved? Mother's Day? No matter. Call Ultra Violet for a floral concoction exploding with color and

sweet, intoxicating scents. *1218 31st St. NW (near M St.).* ☎ 202/ 333-3002. www.ultravioletflowersdc. com. AE, MC, V. No Metro access. See "Traveling to Georgetown" on p 93. Map p 106.

Gourmet Tastes
★ **Dean & Deluca** GEORGE-TOWN Crave a dark chocolate bar from Switzerland? How about a custard fruit tart? Gourmands with a nose for fragrant cheeses, fresh fish, out-of-season fruit, choice-cut meats, aged wines, Kona coffee beans, and European crackers nosh and shop here. In fine weather try lunch at the outdoor cafe. *3276 M St. NW (at Potomac St.).* ☎ 202/342-2500. www.deandeluca.com. AE,

Housewares from Vastu, in 14th Street/ Logan Circle.

Cady's Alley interior design district, in Georgetown.

DISC, MC, V. No Metro access. See "Traveling to Georgetown" on p 93. Map p 106.

★ **Pearson's** GLOVER PARK This neighborhood standby sells more than 2,000 fine wines, liqueurs, and spirits. A knowledgeable staff of 15 experts hosts regular wine tastings. *2436 Wisconsin Ave. NW (37th St.).* ☎ *202/333-6666. www.pearsons wine.com. MC, V. Bus line: D1 or D2. Map p 106.*

Jewelry

★★★ **Tiny Jewel Box** DOWN-TOWN Thinking of popping the question or surprising your sweetie with a fabulous bauble, expensive watch, or eye-popping ring from an estate sale? Look no further than this D.C. mainstay, a peddler of romantic, unique adornments. *1147 Connecticut Ave. NW (at M St.).* ☎ *202/393-2747. www.tinyjewelbox.com. AE, MC, V. Metro: Farragut North. Map p 106.*

Interiors

Antique Row GEORGETOWN Depending on which way you're walking, Antique Row is either a cool cruise downhill or a steep trek up it. In any event, antiques lovers

won't care—they'll be too busy gaping at the storefronts with mint-condition, 18th-century divans; beautifully painted Persian consoles; weathered ceramic water jugs; and other singular finds. The best of the lot: Carling Nichols; Gore-Dean; and, for early-20th-century fans, Random Harvest. Bring your Black AmEx card for this shopping stroll—prices are that steep. *Wisconsin Ave., from S St. to N St. No Metro access. See "Traveling to Georgetown" on p 93. Map p 106.*

★ **Apartment Zero** PENN QUARTER If you never met a sleek line or hard edge you didn't love, head to this mecca for modern chic. The store stocks unfettered, functional tables and chairs, stainless steel candlesticks, fine linens, and more. *406 7th St. NW.* ☎ *202/628-4067. www.apartmentzero.com. AE, DISC, MC, V. Metro: Gallery Place/China-town. Map p 105.*

★★ **Cady's Alley** GEORGE-TOWN Make tracks to Washington's newest district devoted to furnishings and accessories. Not long ago, Cady's Alley was all industrial space and abandoned lofts. Now, if you walk through a bricked archway off M Street and descend a flight of stairs into a hidden alcove,

Housewares from Go, Mama, Go!

you'll discover shops such as Contemporaria for Italian furniture, Bulthaup for ultraluxe culinary gadgets, Illuminations for European lighting, and Poggenpohl Studio for German kitchen fixtures. *3300 block of M St. NW. www.cadysalley.com. No Metro access. See "Traveling to Georgetown" on p 93. Map p 106.*

Go, Mama, Go! 14TH STREET In this colorful, offbeat store (named by the owner to inspire her success), you'll score unique Asian ceramics and Japanese *furoshiki* (rayon crepe wall hangings). *1809 14th St. NW (at Swann St.).* ☎ *202/299-0850. www. gomamago.com. AE, MC, V. Metro: Cardozo/U St. Map p 106.*

Miss Pixie's U STREET Scavenger hunters will love Miss Pixie's giant new space that's filled with second-hand furnishings, funky chandeliers, table settings, figurines and other crazy knick-knacks (plastic flamingos, anyone?). *1626 14th St. NW.* ☎ *202/ 232-8171. www.misspixies.com. Metro: U Street/Cardozo. Map p 106.*

★★ **Muléh** 14TH STREET Owner Christopher Reiter mixes it up at Muléh (pronounced "moo-lay") with his Asian-inspired collection of wooden benches and tables, minimalist bed frames, sophisticated bric-a-brac, and racks of city-slick clothing by young designers. *1831 14th St. NW (at Swann St.).* ☎ *202/ 667-3440. www.muleh.com. AE, MC, V. Metro: Cardozo/U St. Map p 106.*

★ **Simply Home** 14TH STREET If you can't make it to Thailand, let brother-and-sister team Somsak and Nannapat Pollert bring Bangkok to you. Simply Home carries one-of-a-kind ceramics, handmade papers, silk pillows, embroidered blouses, woven baskets, and traditional Thai dinnerware—75% of which is designed by the siblings themselves. *1412 U St. NW (at 14th St.).* ☎ *202/ 986 8607. www.simplyhomedc.com.*

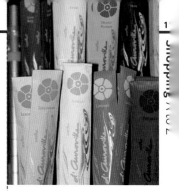

Specialty papers from Pulp, in 14th Street/Logan Circle.

AE, DISC, MC, V. Metro: Dupont Circle. Map p 106.

Timothy Paul Carpets & Textiles LOGAN CIRCLE Interior design enthusiasts, make a mental note to visit this husband-and-wife-owned boutique/gallery, specializing in custom-colored textiles, upscale carpet lines, antique rugs, and unusual lighting fixtures. *1404 14th St. NW (at Rhode Island Ave.).* ☎ *202/319-1100. www.timothypaulcarpets.com. AE, MC, V. Metro: McPherson Sq. or Dupont Circle. Map p 106.*

Music
★ **The Guitar Shop** DUPONT CIRCLE Aspiring Cobains, Springs-teens, and Youngs converge here to pluck strings, caress Fenders and Rickenbackers, and brag about their next (or last) gigs to the authentic (if occasionally bitter) musicians behind the cash registers. *1216 Connecticut Ave. NW (at Jefferson St.).* ☎ *202/331-7333. www.theguitar shop.com. DISC, MC, V. Metro: Dupont Circle. Map p 106.*

Pets
★★ **Pet Essentials** 14TH STREET Spoiled felines and diva dogs know where to send their masters for all-organic kibble; irresistible catnip; pigs' ears; and designer bones,

collars, harnesses, and other supplies. *1722 14th St. NW.* ☎ *202/986-7907. www.greenpets.com. AE, DISC, MC, V. Metro: Cardozo/U St. Map p 106.*

Shoes

★★ Hu's Shoes GEORGETOWN

A rather daunting showroom—you might be the only customer fending off several hungry salespeople—displays the latest and greatest in women's "rebellious" designer shoes, including Sonia Rykiel, Chloé, Proenza Schouler, and more. *3005 M St. NW (at 30th St.).* ☎ *202/342-0202. www.hushoes.com. AE, DC, DISC, MC, V. See "Traveling to Georgetown" on p 93. Map p 106.*

★★ Sassanova GEORGETOWN

"Stylish women in Washington" is no longer an oxymoron since Sassanova opened up in 2004, carrying designers such as Bettye Muller, Lambertson Truex, Hollywould, and Lulu Guinness, in sweet slingbacks, saucy stilettos, wicked wedges, and funky flats. *Warning:* Expect to blow at least $200. *1641 Wisconsin Ave. NW (at 33rd St.).* ☎ *202/471-4400. www. sassanova.com. AE, MC, V. No Metro access. See "Traveling to Georgetown" on p 93. Map p 106.*

★ Shake Your Booty Shoes

ADAMS MORGAN Trend-loving hipster chicks without a lot of cash to burn should walk this way for cool sandals, sneakers, and, yes, boots in sensational, seasonal styles, priced to move. *2206 18th St. NW (between Columbia and Belmont).* ☎ *202/518-8205. www.shakeyourbootyshoes. com. AE, DISC, MC, V. Metro: Woodley Park–Zoo/Adams Morgan. Map p 106.*

Thrift & Flea Markets

★★ Eastern Market CAPITOL

HILL If Washingtonians could name only one institution endemic to the city that had nothing to do with politics, 9 out of 10 would say Eastern Market. Locals gather here on weekends for the flea market, outdoor vendors, artisans, and brunch spots. Its permanent buildings are open year-round, Tuesday through Sunday; the outdoor lot fills on weekends (Mar–Dec) with farmers and fresh produce, plus bargain-hunters looking to score great deals. *306 7th St. SE (between North Carolina Ave. and C St. SE).* ☎ *202/544-0083. www.easternmarketdc.com. Metro: Eastern Market. Map p 105.*

Georgetown Flea Market

GEORGETOWN Every Sunday (unless it's pouring rain or freezing cold outside), bargain hunters troll the lot at the Corcoran School for cheap treasures. Score handmade and antique jewelry, velvet Elvis paintings, secondhand leather jackets, and used furniture from weathered vendors smoking cigarettes, ready to haggle. *Wisconsin Ave. NW (at Whitehaven St. NW). No Metro access. See "Traveling to Georgetown" on p 93. Map p 106.*

★★ Millennium U STREET/

CARDOZO Do you groove on pleather chairs, mid-20th-century coffee tables, stainless steel bookcases, even white vinyl microminis? Millennium is a must for fans of design from the '50s, '60s, and '70s. *1528 U St. NW (at 15th St.).* ☎ *202/483-1218. Metro: Cardozo/U St. Map p 106.* ●

6 The Best Outdoor Activities

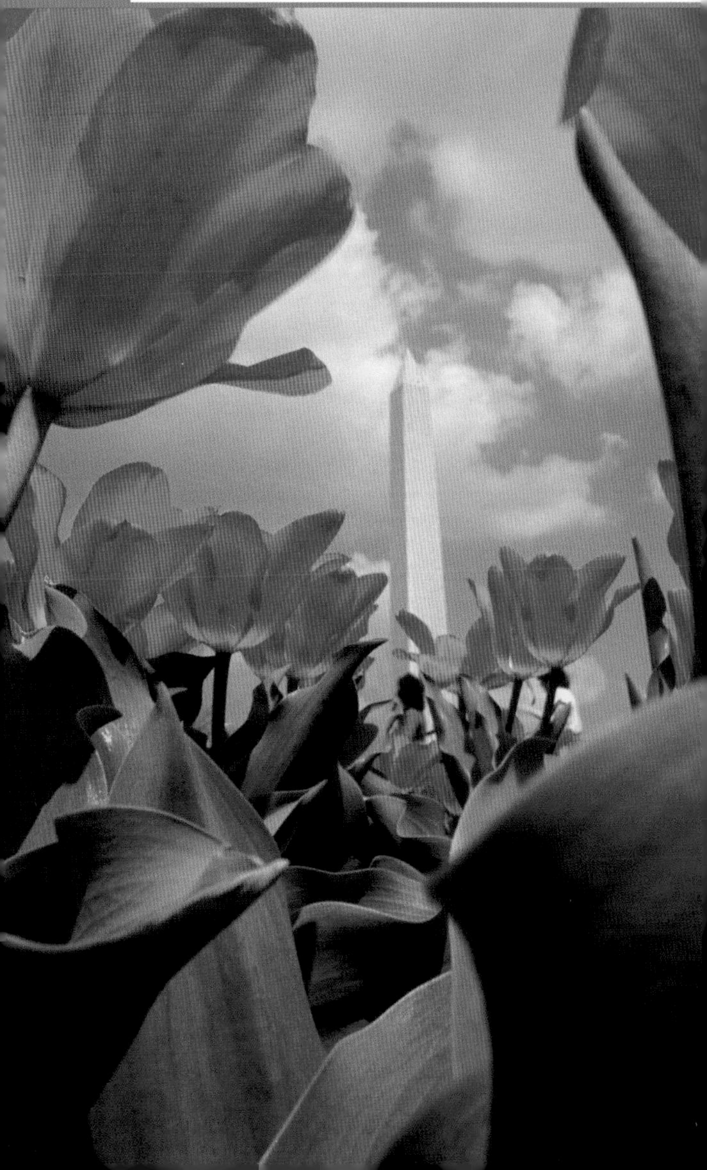

Rock Creek Park

1 Rock Creek Park Planetarium
2 Rock Creek Horse Center
3 Carter Barron Amphitheater
4 Rock Creek Park Tennis Center
5 Picnic in the park

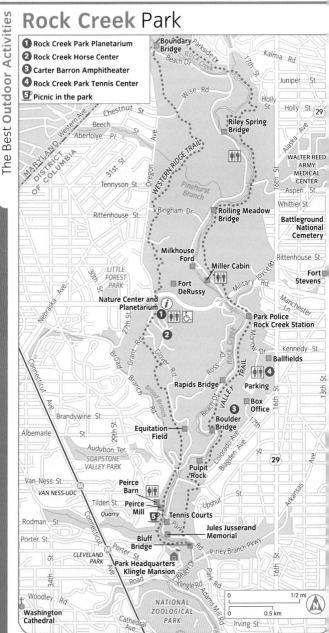

How many other major American urban areas have 3,000 acres (1,214 hectares) of natural woodlands smack dab in the middle of the city? Established in 1890 by the Rock Creek Park Historic District and protected by the U.S. Congress, this green resource is to Washingtonians what Central Park is to New Yorkers—except New Yorkers can't camp, canoe, or lose themselves for miles on trails that wind beneath canopies of lush-leaved trees, so thick in spots that civilization seems a distant memory. Accessible through numerous entrance points throughout northwest Washington, this urban oasis offers shade and cooler temperatures on hot days, historic parks, great golf, horseback riding, bird watching, a refuge for deer and raccoons, even a 1-mile (1.6km) stretch of rapids. It also borders the National Zoo. It does have isolated areas, however, so avoid visiting early in the morning or past dusk. Remain alert, and bring a friend if you can. START: **Metro to Friendship Heights or Fort Trotten, then the E2 bus to Glover (also called Oregon) and Military roads; walk 300 feet (30m) south on the trail to the planetarium**

Tip

Take a **virtual tour** of Rock Creek Park and explore its activities and offerings at www.nps.gov/rocr/home. The park runs along Rock Creek and its tributaries from the National Zoo to the D.C. boundary. *Accessible to the public 24 hr. Metro: Woodley Park–Zoo.*

Rock Creek Park.

1 ★ kids **The Rock Creek Park Planetarium and Nature Center.** Stargazers come to the Planetarium to stare at the heavens. Track the night skies here with the whole family, and take your little ones (ages 4 and up, please) to special astronomical programs on the weekends. The Nature Center is also the scene of numerous activities, including nature films, crafts demonstrations, live animal demonstrations, guided nature walks, and a daily mix of lectures and other events. Self-guided nature trails begin here. All activities are free, but for planetarium shows you need to pick up tickets a half-hour in advance. There are also nature exhibits on the premises. For a schedule, check out www.nps.gov/rocr/planetarium.

Not far from the Nature Center is **Fort DeRussey,** one of 68 fortifications erected to defend the city of Washington during the U.S. Civil War. From the intersection of Military Road and Oregon Avenue, walk a short trail through the woods to reach the fort, the remains of which include high earth mounds with openings where guns were

Cyclists in Rock Creek Park.

mounted, surrounded by a deep ditch/moat. *Metro: See Start, above.*

2 ★★ **kids The Rock Creek Horse Center.** Next door to the planetarium, beginners can take private lessons in the ring, and more experienced riders can sign up for trail rides on weekdays with a professional trail guide. Supervised pony rides for very young children are also quite popular; there is no age limit, but your tyke must be at least 30 inches (.76m) tall to join in

the fun. *5100 Glover Rd.* ☎ *202/362-0117. www.rockcreekhorsecenter. com. Tues–Fri noon–6pm; Sat–Sun 9am–5pm.*

3 ★★★ **Carter Barron Amphitheater.** Want to see Shakespeare under the stars, or catch a symphony concert or dance performance? This amphitheater, in Rock Creek Park on Colorado Avenue off 17th Street, seats 1,500 patrons. It opened in 1950 to commemorate the 150th anniversary of Washington as the nation's capital city. Nearly 60 years later, it's a local favorite among nature lovers and theater fans.

Some shows are free but require tickets, distributed on the day of performance at the Carter Barron Box Office (noon–8pm), and at the Washington Post building, 1150 15th St. NW (8:30am on weekdays). Shows with admission fees are $23 at the Carter Barron Box Office, or through Ticketmaster outlets (www. ticketmaster.com). All sales are final, even if the show is canceled. *Bus: S1, 2, or 3. Take 16th St. N, and get off at Colorado Ave. The tennis*

Rock Creek Park offers visitors 3,000 acres (1,214 hectares) of unsullied grounds to wander.

The Rock Creek Horse Center.

center is a few blocks north, visible from 16th St., at Kennedy St.

④ Rock Creek Park Tennis Center. The home of the annual Legg Mason Tennis Classic offers excellent hard and soft court facilities, a pro shop, and a stadium (16th and Kennedy sts. NW; reservations: ☎ 202/722-5949; www.rockcreek tennis.com). Free tennis courts can be found throughout the District. If you love a good match and aren't too particular about the state of the facilities—expect faded hard courts, piles of leaves in the corners, and somewhat sagging nets—hurry to public parks such as Montrose (R St., between 30th and 31st sts.), Rose (P and 28th sts.), and Volta

(34th and Volta sts.) in Georgetown, and wait your turn. Courtesy allows for players to use the courts for 1 hour before relinquishing them to those waiting on the sidelines.

Once you enter wooded Rock Creek Park, you won't stumble upon too many fast-food joints in the underbrush. Bring along a lunch for a **⑤ picnic in the park** and stop at any of the 30 picnic areas throughout the grounds; some have rain shelters. Many can be reserved for groups up to 100. *Reservations must be made in person at the D.C. Department of Parks and Recreation, 3149 16th St. NW.* ☎ 202/673-7647.

Theodore Roosevelt Island Park

A serene, 91-acre wilderness preserve, ★★ **Roosevelt Island Park** (☎ **703/289-2500.** www.nps.gov/this. Free admission. Daily dawn–dusk. Metro: Rosslyn, then walk 2 blocks to Rosslyn Circle and cross the bridge) is a memorial to the nation's 26th president and his contributions to conservation. The swamp, marsh, and upland forest is a haven for rabbits, chipmunks, great owls, foxes, muskrats, turtles, and groundhogs. You can observe these flora and fauna in their natural environs on 2.5 miles of foot trails. By car, take the George Washington Memorial Parkway exit north from the Theodore Roosevelt Bridge. Parking is accessible only from the northbound lane; a pedestrian bridge connects the lot to the island.

C&O **Canal**

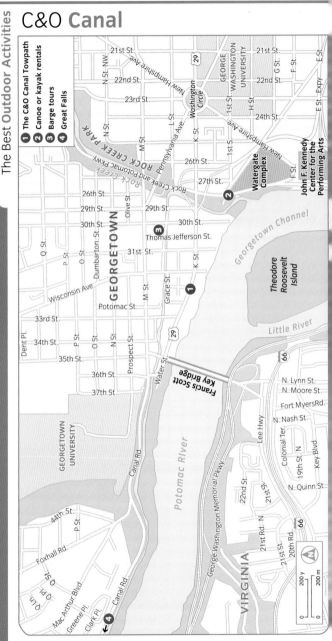

21st St. NW
22nd St.
23rd St.
N St. N.W
N. St. NW
N. St.
M St.

29

GEORGE
WASHINGTON
UNIVERSITY

21st St.
G St.
F St.
E St.
E St.–Expy.

Washington
Circle

22nd St.

New Hampshire Ave.
21st St.
21st St.

24th St.
H St.

New Hampshire Ave.

Pennsylvania Ave.
L St.
K St.

ROCK CREEK PARK

Rock Creek and Potomac Pkwy.
Rock Creek and Potomac Pkwy.

26th St.
27th St.

Watergate
Complex

John F. Kennedy
Center for the
Performing Arts

F St.

26th St.
29th St.
30th St.
Olive St.

29th St.
30th St.
Thomas Jefferson St.
31st St.

Georgetown Channel

GEORGETOWN

Q St.
P St.
O St.
N St.
Dumbarton St.

K St.

Theodore
Roosevelt
Island

Wisconsin Ave.
Potomac St.
M St.
Grace St.

Little River

33rd St.
34th St.
35th St.

Dent Pl.

P St.
O St.
N St.
Prospect St.

29

66

Water St.

Francis Scott
Key Bridge

36th St.
37th St.

N. Lynn St.
N. Moore St.
Fort Myers Rd.
N. Nash St.

Lee Hwy
Colonial Ter.
19th St. N
Key Blvd
N. Quinn St.

GEORGETOWN
UNIVERSITY

Canal Rd.

Potomac River

George Washington Memorial Pkwy.

44th St.
P St.

Foxhall Rd.

VIRGINIA

22nd St. N
21st Ct.

21st St. N
21st Rd. N
20th Rd.

66

O Pl.
O St.

Mac Arthur Blvd.
Greene Pl.
Clark Pl.

Canal Rd.

200 y
200 m
0
0

This towpath, along the Chesapeake and Ohio Canal, is another stunning natural escape in Washington. A stretch of tree-lined land curves along the Potomac River at the canal's start in Georgetown, then winds north along the border of West Virginia before ending in Cumberland, Maryland. First opened in 1828, for the purpose of hauling coal between these two ports, the 185-mile (298km) canal and its path are now peopled with leisure boaters, joggers, bikers, power walkers, lovers out for afternoon strolls, campers, and kids. The stunning Potomac River Valley serves as an ever-changing backdrop to all this outdoor activity; summers are gorgeously green, autumn is ablaze in color, and the river itself can be placid or turbulent, but it always makes for prime viewing. START: **The Potomac River, at M or K streets in Georgetown; no Metro access**

❶ ★ The C & O (Columbia & Ohio) Canal Towpath. During milder months, when tourists take over The Mall, you'll find Washingtonians biking, jogging, or walking here en masse, unwinding after a hard week of policy wonking. Start in Georgetown at the western end of K Street (beneath the Whitehurst Fwy.), and then make your way west, following the river. The first few miles are inundated with walkers, so bikers might want to take the parallel Capital Crescent Trail, which is paved and closer to the river. The Capital Crescent trail eventually intersects with the Rock Creek Trail. Take the latter for a convenient circular trip of about 22 miles (35k). This trail and the C&O towpath meet near the 3-mile (5k) marker; track

your progress with regular mile markers along the route. To rent a bike nearby, visit either of these pro shops on M Street: **Revolution Cycles** (3411 M St. NW; ☎ 202/965-3601) or **Bicycle Pro Shop** (3403 M St. NW; ☎ 202/337-0311). Or stop by **Thompson's Boat Center** (at the start of the trail in Georgetown at 2900 Virginia Ave. NW; ☎ 202/333-9543; www.thompsonboatcenter. com), which rents bicycles in addition to canoes and other river craft.

❷ Rent a canoe or kayak. There are two convenient boat rental centers near the start of the towpath: The aforementioned Thompson's Boat Center (2900 Virginia Ave. NW; ☎ 202/333-9543), and Fletcher's Boathouse (4940

A barge on the C&O Canal.

Snacks & Facts

C&O Canal Visitors' Centers are scattered along the route, but only two will likely interest travelers to Washington. The first is in Georgetown (1057 Thomas Jefferson St. NW; ☎ 202/653-5190), near the start of the towpath. It offers historical information and a quick place for a bathroom break. Hungry explorers will find no shortage of food options nearby, on K Street, the Washington Harbor, and nearby M Street. The second center is **Great Falls Tavern** (11710 MacArthur Blvd., Potomac, Md.; ☎ 301/767-3714), which provides information, restrooms, and a small snack bar. If you make it to Great Falls, consider stopping at **Old Anglers Inn** (10801 MacArthur Blvd., Potomac, MD; ☎ 301/299-9097; entrees $29–$39; AE, DC, MC, V; Tues–Sun noon–11pm), for great New American fare and a fireplace.

Canal Rd. NW; ☎ 202/244-0461) at the 3-mile (5k) marker, which is easiest to reach on foot or by bicycle. Both outfits rent kayaks and canoes (Thompson's even offers instructional programs), and Fletcher's has a snack bar and nearby picnic grounds, too.

Rental boats along the canal.

❸ ★ kids Take a barge tour. Take your family for a ride on a mule-drawn canal boat. Park rangers don period costumes as they operate replica canal boats and share the history of the canal during these 60-minute round-trips from Georgetown. *Georgetown*

Rental boats along the canal.

Information Center, 1057 Thomas Jefferson St. NW ☎ 202/653-5190. 1-hr. round-trips are also available at Great Falls, Potomac, Maryland. Georgetown and Great Falls barge rides: $5 per visitor. Children age 3 and under ride free. Call Great Falls to confirm boats are running.

❹ ★★★ Explore Great Falls. A day trip worth taking, this 800-acre (320-hectare) park is known for its scenic beauty, steep gorges, and dramatic waterfalls and rapids, with several overlooks along the river that may take your breath away. It's along the C&O Canal, 14 miles (23km) upriver from Washington in McLean, Virginia, but ambitious bikers can reach it via the towpath. *From D.C. by car: Take Constitution Ave. NW/US-50 to I-66 W/US-50 W. out of the city across Roosevelt Bridge. Continue until you reach the US-50 W/Arlington Blvd./GW Pkwy. exit. Turn north onto George Washington Memorial Pkwy (GWMP or GW Pkwy). Follow the GWMP to the* exit for I-495 S. When you are on the ramp, stay in the right-hand lane, which will turn into the exit ramp for Rte. 193, Georgetown Pike. Take a left at the traffic light onto Rte 193 West. In 3 miles, make a right at Old Dominion Dr. to access the park.*

The towpath in Georgetown.

Georgetown

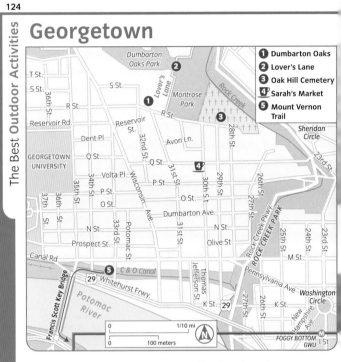

1. Dumbarton Oaks
2. Lover's Lane
3. Oak Hill Cemetery
4. Sarah's Market
5. Mount Vernon Trail

The capital's most exclusive neighborhood—with its prize-winning gardens, gargantuan homes, and boldface names out walking their dogs—offers visitors an ideal balance of eye candy and history, best enjoyed under a canopy of trees and blue skies. Tour the parks, stop to smell the flowers, study the statuary, and picnic on the grass with a great bottle of wine. START: **Dumbarton Oaks garden entrance at 31st and R streets in Georgetown; no Metro access**

For an outdoor walking tour of Georgetown, see p 90.

1 ★★ **Dumbarton Oaks.** Enjoy the traditional French, Italian, and English gardens at this once-private home, now open to the public for tours. Discover bubbling fountains, stone archways, romantic hideaways, tiled pools, and even a Roman-style amphitheater. Flora includes an orangery, a rose garden, wisteria-covered arbors, groves of cherry trees, and magnolias. When everything is in bloom,

you could spend as long as an hour here. *1703 32nd St. NW.* ☎ *202/339-6410. www.doaks.org. Gardens: Tues–Sun year-round; Mar 15–Oct 21 2–6pm, Nov 1–Mar 14 2–5pm (except national holidays and Dec 24). $8 adults, $5 seniors and children.*

2 ★ **Lover's Lane.** Follow the downhill, paved road that hugs Dumbarton Oaks's bricked wall next to Montrose Park. At the bottom, hang to the left and discover a gently cultivated enclave of gurgling brooks, weeping willow trees,

Getting some fresh air in Georgetown.

Just off the corner of 30th and Q streets is **4** **Sarah's Market,** a sweet, family-owned deli stocked with upscale treats. Choose from a small selection of prepared sandwiches in the cooler, or grab some British shortcakes, a snack bar, fresh fruit, a bag of nuts, and/or a decent bottle of wine to take with you into the great outdoors. *3008 Q St. NW (at 30th St.). $*

wildflowers, and carefully placed benches for maximum romance and relaxation.

3 ★ **Oak Hill Cemetery.** Reminiscent of Europe's historic cemeteries, the iron-gated, hilly grounds here are both beautifully kept and visually breathtaking. Spot a wild fox or a deer among the hundreds of 19th- and 20th-century headstones and the wealth of ornate statuary; stroll down toward the creek on winding paths as you tour yesterday's VIPs—and tell them to RIP.

5 ★★ **Mount Vernon Trail.** Just across the river from downtown Georgetown, on Theodore Roosevelt Island, bikers, hikers, and joggers enter this scenic 18-mile (30k) trail. The path hugs the Virginia side of the Potomac River and offers breathtaking views of the classic monuments, memorials, and the river itself. Follow its course over bridges and through parks, and you'll eventually arrive at George Washington's historic Mount Vernon home (p 57). ☎ *703/289-2500. www.nps.gov/gwmp/mtvernontrail. htm. Metro: Roslyn.*

The formal gardens of Dumbarton Oaks.

The **Mall & Tidal Basin**

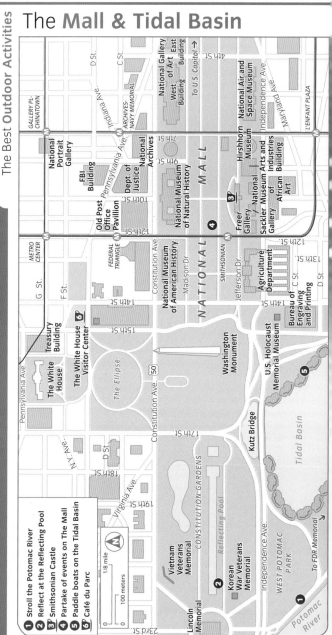

1 Stroll the Potomac River
2 Reflect at the Reflecting Pool
3 Smithsonian Castle
4 Partake of events on The Mall
5 Paddle boats on the Tidal Basin
6 Café du Parc

Before it was the nation's capital, Washington, D.C. was a swamp. And if you wander The Mall and Tidal Basin in July or August, you'll have no trouble imagining what it was like way back when. But few American urban environments can beat The Mall and Tidal Basin's outdoor appeal in spring, when Japanese cherry blossoms transform the cityscape, or in fall, with its perfect sweater weather. Throw in miles of bike and jogging paths in the heart of the city; botanical gardens; a galloping river; and plenty of green spaces, and you've got a rationale for avoiding the indoors. (Shhh, don't tell the museum curators I said that!) START: **Metro to Smithsonian**

1 ★ kids **Stroll the Potomac River.** Whether you begin your walk in Georgetown, at Washington Harbor, or head toward the river near the Watergate Hotel or the Lincoln Memorial, spend some time promenading. You'll pass a legion of resident joggers (have you ever seen so many in your life?); admire university crew teams sliding through the waves; capture grand glimpses of the memorials, monuments, and bridges from a new perspective; see historic Georgetown from afar; duck as Dick Cheney's helicopter buzzes loudly overhead; pass 10 or more volleyball games in progress; observe a few college-age touch-footballers; picnic on the grass with kindred spirits inclined to stop and smell the roses; and root for fishermen who cast their rods in hopes of catching "the big one." On a beautiful day, nothing beats it.

2 **Reflect at the Reflecting Pool.** Pedestrian paths surround this ½-mile-long (.5km) body of water that visually connects the Lincoln Memorial and Washington Monument. It's also the site where thousands gathered to hear Rev. Martin Luther King, Jr., recite his legendary "I Have a Dream" speech in 1963. His followers stood around the pool— and in it—as they listened to the words that would change a nation.

The **3** ★★ **Smithsonian Castle,** just off The Mall on Independence Avenue, is an ideal spot to rest (if your dogs are barking) and to snack (if you're hungry like the wolf). It's

The Tidal Basin is a popular course for strollers, joggers, and cyclists.

Cherry Blossoms in Washington

It's been nearly 100 years since Tokyo gave Washington 3,000 delicately flowering, fragrant cherry trees in recognition of the growing friendship between the two cities. In 1965, Tokyo gave an additional 3,800 trees. Today, an estimated 700,000 travelers from all around the world arrive en masse every April, the peak of the cherry blossom season, to wander amid their riotous color and heady fragrance during the 2-week Cherry Blossom Festival. For a complete schedule of events, visit the official website, www.nationalcherry blossomfestival.org.

also information central for the Smithsonian museums, so grab a sandwich or muffin and pick up a brochure to plan your next adventure. *1000 Jefferson Dr. NW. Daily 8:30am–5:30pm. Metro: Smithsonian. $–$$.*

4 ★★★ **kids Partake of events on The Mall.** Depending on the time of year when you arrive in Washington, you may stumble upon ethnic festivals, fireworks, kite-flying celebrations, dance performances, dedication ceremonies, children's workshops, orchestra concerts, holiday happenings, and much more on the National Mall. *Check out www. nps.gov/nama to find out what's happening during your visit.*

5 ★ **kids Paddle Boats on the Tidal Basin.** Whether you're a kid or just a kid at heart, head to the Tidal Basin, weather permitting, and get ready to exercise your right to see the Jefferson Memorial while working up a sweat. *2-passenger boat $8 per hr.; 4-passenger boat $16 per hr. Mar 15 to Labor Day daily 10am–6pm. Metro: Smithsonian Station (Blue/Orange lines; use the 12th St. and Independence Ave. exit). Walk west on Independence*

toward 15th St. Turn left on Raoul Wallenberg Place/15th St. and continue toward the Jefferson Memorial; look for the Tidal Basin Paddle Boat dock.

Order some frites and a bottle of Bordeaux at **6 Café du Parc,** the bustling French bistro and sidewalk cafe adjacent to the Willard Hotel. *1401 Pennsylvania Ave., NW. ☎ 202/942-7000. www.cafeduparc. com. AE, DC, DISC, MC, V. Metro: Federal Triangle. $$–$$$$.* ●

The Smithsonian Kite Festival on the National Mall.

Capitol Hill & Penn Quarter

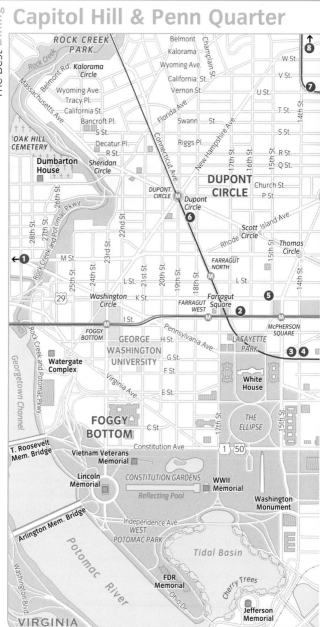

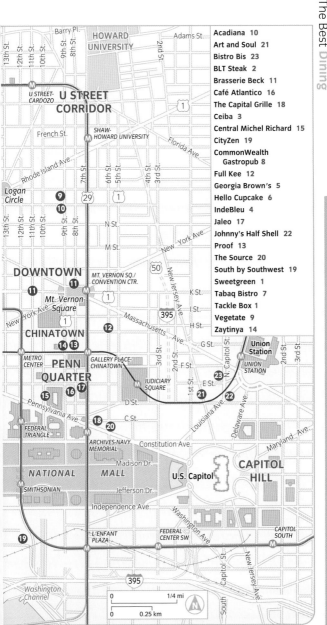

Acadiana 10
Art and Soul 21
Bistro Bis 23
BLT Steak 2
Brasserie Beck 11
Café Atlantico 16
The Capital Grille 18
Ceiba 3
Central Michel Richard 15
CityZen 19
CommonWealth
  Gastropub 8
Full Kee 12
Georgia Brown's 5
Hello Cupcake 6
IndeBleu 4
Jaleo 17
Johnny's Half Shell 22
Proof 13
The Source 20
South by Southwest 19
Sweetgreen 1
Tabaq Bistro 7
Tackle Box 1
Vegetate 9
Zaytinya 14

Georgetown & Dupont Circle

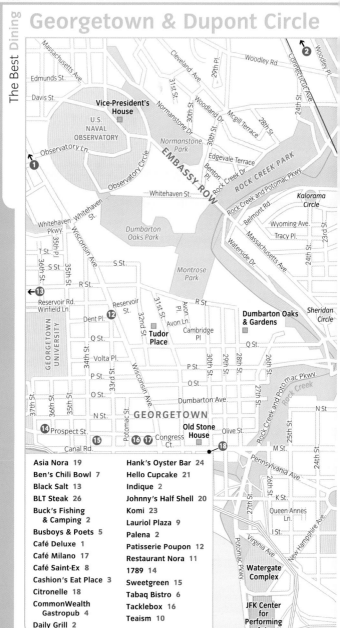

Asia Nora **19**

Ben's Chili Bowl **7**

Black Salt **13**

BLT Steak **26**

Buck's Fishing
& Camping **2**

Busboys & Poets **5**

Café Deluxe **1**

Café Milano **17**

Café Saint-Ex **8**

Cashion's Eat Place **3**

Citronelle **18**

CommonWealth
Gastropub **4**

Daily Grill **2**

Hank's Oyster Bar **24**

Hello Cupcake **21**

Indique **2**

Johnny's Half Shell **20**

Komi **23**

Lauriol Plaza **9**

Palena **4**

Patisserie Poupon **12**

Restaurant Nora **11**

1789 **14**

Sweetgreen **15**

Tabaq Bistro **6**

Tacklebox **16**

Teaism **10**

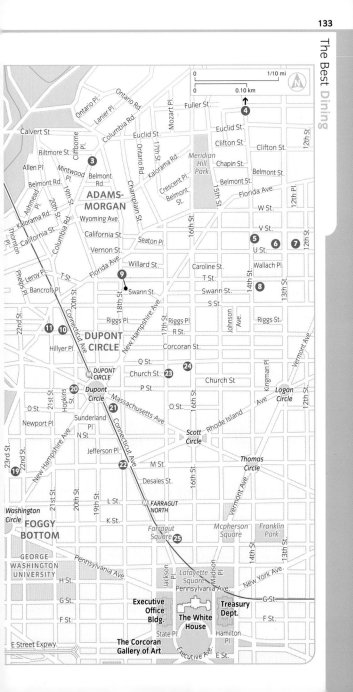

Dining Best Bets

Best Newcomer
★★★ The Source $$$ *555 Pennsylvania Ave. NW* (p 141)

Best Manhattan Rival
★★★ CityZen $$$$ *1330 Maryland Ave. SW* (p 137)

Best for Avoiding Carnivores
★ Vegetate $$ *1414 9th St. NW* (p 142)

Best Hotel Eats
★★ Art and Soul $$$ *415 New Jersey Ave. NW* (p 135)

Best Fussy French
★★★ Citronelle $$$$ *3000 M St. NW* (p 137)

Best Mussels and Beer
★★ Brasserie Beck $$ *1101 K St. NW* (p 136)

Best All-Organic
★★ Restaurant Nora $$$ *2132 Florida Ave. NW* (p 140)

Best for Under 10 Bucks
★★ Full Kee $ *509 H St. NW* (p 138)

Best Casual Mediterranean
★ Meze $$ *2437 18th St. NW* (p 81)

Best Sexy Tapas Place
★★ Zaytinya $$ *701 9th St. NW.* (p 142)

Best for Flirting with Elected Officials
The Capital Grille $$$$ *601 Pennsylvania Ave. NW* (p 137)

Best for Winos
★★ Proof $$$ *775 G St. NW.* (p 140)

Best for Blue Bloods
★ Café Milano $$$ *3252 Prospect St. NW* (p 136)

Best Fireside Dining
1789 $$$$ *1226 36th St. NW* (p 135)

Best Fresh Fish
★★★ Black Salt $$$ *4883 MacArthur Blvd. NW* (p 135)

Best for Moody Political Debates
★ Busboys and Poets *2021 14th St. NW* (p 136)

Best Hipster Joint
★ Café Saint-Ex $$ *1847 14th St. NW* (p 137)

Best for Rowdy Rugrats
★★ Café Deluxe $$ *3228 Wisconsin Ave. NW* (p 136)

Best South of the Border
★ Lauriol Plaza $$ *1835 18th St. NW* (p 140)

Best Crab Cakes
★ Johnny's Half Shell $$$ *2002 P St. NW* (p 139)

Best Historic Diner
★ Ben's Chili Bowl $ *1213 U St. NW* (p 135)

Best Sweet Confections
ACKC Cocoa Bar $ *1529C 14th St. NW* (p 82)

Best for Expat Parisians
★★ Patisserie Poupon $ *1645 Wisconsin Ave. NW* (p 140)

Restaurants A to Z

★★★ 1789 GEORGETOWN *AMERICAN* Go for the feel of old money, antiques, and old-fashioned service—plus romantic lighting and a fireplace on cold nights. The quintessential Georgetown experience, serving new American fare and fabulous wines. *1226 36th St. NW (at Prospect St.).* ☎ *202/965-1789. www.1789restaurant.com. Entrees $18–$38. AE, DC, DISC, MC, V. Dinner daily. No Metro access. Bus: DC Circulator. Map p 132.*

★★★ Acadiana DOWNTOWN *CAJUN* New Orleans is still rebounding, but its legacy is strong here, in Cajun fare by Jeff Tunks, who cooked in the Big Easy for years. Try gumbo with andouille, crawfish pies, or fried okra in this upscale, ornate, but unfussy setting. *901 New York Ave. NW (K and 9th sts.).* ☎ *202/408-8848. www.acadianarestaurant.com. Entrees $21–$26. AE, DISC, MC, V. Lunch Mon–Fri; dinner Mon–Sat. Metro: Gallery Place/Chinatown. Map p 130.*

★★ Art and Soul CAPITOL HILL *AMERICAN* Not every hotel restaurant can give off this kind of stylish demeanor. In the new Liaison Hotel, politicos dine on American fare with flair. *415 New Jersey Ave. NW.* ☎ *202/393-7777. www.artandsoul dc.com. Entrees $18–$34. AE, DISC, MC, V. Lunch & dinner Mon–Sat. Metro: Union Station. Map p 130.*

★★ Ben's Chili Bowl U STREET CORRIDOR *AMERICAN* Known for its Formica tables, sloppy chili dogs, and late-night banter, this old-time diner has drawn a who's who of African-American history since 1958—from Martin Luther King, Jr. to Redd Foxx and President Barack Obama. *1213 U St. NW (at 12th St.).* ☎ *202/667-0909. www.benschilibowl.com.*

Entrees $10. No credit cards. Mon–Sat breakfast, lunch & dinner; Sun lunch, dinner. Metro: Cardozo/U St. Map p 132.

★★ Bistro Bis CAPITOL HILL *FRENCH* This bistro in the St. George Hotel is always buzzing with the power-tie and pumps-and-pearls set on Capitol Hill. Breakfast is served for early birds. *15 E St. NW (N. Capitol St.).* ☎ *202/661-2700. www.bistrobis.com. Entrees $20–$32. AE, DC, DISC, MC, V. Breakfast, lunch & dinner daily. Metro: Capitol South or Union Station. Map p 130.*

★★★ Black Salt PALISADES *SEAFOOD* Local seafood fans rave for chef Jeff Black's newest D.C. catch—this restaurant/fish market, with perfectly cooked black sea bass, fried Ipswich clams, fish stews, and more. *4883 MacArthur Blvd. NW (at V St.).* ☎ *202/342-9101. www.blacksalt restaurant.com. Entrees $25–$35. DC, DISC, MC, V. Lunch Tues–Sat; dinner Tues–Sun. No Metro access. Bus: B6. Map p 132.*

★ BLT Steak DOWNTOWN *AMERICAN* Despite its background as an upscale chain, the comfortable eatery serves quality steak with different sauces, and fish from the raw bar. The chef's warm popovers are just right. *1625 Eye St. NW.* ☎ *202/689-8999. www.bltsteak.com. Entrees $29–$45.*

Hank's Oyster Bar.

Cafe Atlantico, downtown.

AE, DISC, MC, V. Lunch Mon–Fri, dinner Mon–Sat. Metro: Farragut West. Map p 130.

★★ **Brasserie Beck** DOWNTOWN *BELGIAN* Travel to Europe or head to this Belgian bistro for authentic brews and dishes such as steamed mussels, lamb sausage, roasted rabbit, and more than 50 beers. *1101 K St. NW.* ☎ *202/408-1717. www.beck dc.com. Entrees $23–$32. AE, DISC, MC, V. Lunch Mon–Fri, dinner daily. Metro: Metro Center. Map p 130.*

★★ **Buck's Fishing & Camping** CLEVELAND PARK *AMERICAN* The rough-hewn communal table, perfect for large groups, plus a revolving menu of comfort food cooked with loving care makes Buck's a mainstay among tourists and townies. *5031 Connecticut Ave. NW (Nebraska Ave.).* ☎ *202/364-0777. Entrees $15–$35. Dinner Tues–Sun. Metro: Tenleytown/AU. Map p 132.*

★ **kids Busboys & Poets** 14TH STREET/LOGAN CIRCLE *AMERICAN* Local lit majors, groovy families, and budget fashionistas flock here for pizzas, burgers, and sandwiches, artfully prepared and affordable. *2021 14th St. NW (V St.).* ☎ *202/387-POET [7638]. www.busboysand poets.com. Entrees $9–$17. AE, DC, DISC, MC, V. Dinner daily. Metro: Cardozo/U St. Map p 132.*

★★ **Café Atlantico** DOWNTOWN *LATIN AMERICAN* The three-floor dining room is a carnival, and the South American–fused fare is a zesty

reminder that policy wonks in Washington don't always play it safe. Tropical cocktails, sexy crowd. *405 8th St. NW (D and E sts.).* ☎ *202/393-0812. www.cafeatlantico.com. Entrees $18–$24. AE, DC, DISC, MC, V. Lunch Mon–Fri; dinner daily. Metro: Archives/Navy Memorial. Map p 130.*

★★ **kids Café Deluxe** CATHEDRAL *AMERICAN* Can one bistro really serve all? Seems this one does: Guys hang out at the bar and watch sports. Families come early for the kids menu and buckets of crayons. Foodies swear by the tuna steak sandwich. Young lovers sip cocktails and gaze at each other. Everyone else simply enjoys the solid New American fare. *3228 Wisconsin Ave. NW (at Macomb St.).* ☎ *202/628-2233. www.cafedeluxe. com. Entrees $12–$20. AE, MC, V. Lunch Mon–Thurs & Sun; dinner Mon–Sun. No Metro access. Map p 132.*

★ **Café Milano** GEORGETOWN *ITALIAN* Pushy lobbyists, the society set, smug playboys, and ambitious young women in skimpy dresses don't flock here for the decent, but unremarkable, Italian food. They do come here to make

Café Saint-Ex, in 14th Street/U Street Corridor.

the scene, close a deal, drink too much, touch the hems of power, and let loose, Washington-style, at this supercharged, always-packed restaurant and lounge. *3252 Prospect St. NW (at M St.).* ☎ *202/333-6183. www.cafemilano.net. Entrees $14–$42. AE, DC, DISC, MC, V. Lunch & dinner daily. Metro: Foggy Bottom or Roslyn. Map p 132.*

★★★ **Café Saint-Ex** 14TH STREET/U STREET CORRIDOR *AMERICAN* This Eurochic bar and bistro attracts goateed hipsters and their supercilious dates for New American fare. A DJ spins in the lounge. *1847 14th St. NW (T St.).* ☎ *202/265-7839. www. saint-ex.com. Entrees $15–$25. AE, DISC, MC, V. Lunch Tues–Sun; dinner daily. Metro: Cardozo/U St. Map p 132.*

★★★ **The Capital Grille** PENN QUARTER *AMERICAN* Cut through the cigar smoke and throng of short-skirted interns and married officials at the bar—for juicy steak and gossip from power players talking too loudly at nearby tables. *601 Pennsylvania Ave. NW (6th St.).* ☎ *202/737-6200. www.capitalgrille.com. Entrees $20–$45. AE, DC, DISC, MC, V. Lunch Mon–Sat; dinner Sun–Sat. Metro: Archives/Navy Memorial. Map p 130.*

★★ **Cashion's Eat Place** ADAMS MORGAN *AMERICAN* Carnivores roar with delight at this darkly sophisticated, cramped restaurant. The mahogany bar will likely possess you to order a martini with your buffalo hanger steak. *1819 Columbia Rd. NW (at Biltmore).* ☎ *202/797-1819. www.cashionseatplace.com. Entrees $19–$35. MC, V. Dinner Tues–Sat; brunch Sun. Metro: Adams-Morgan/Woodley Park. Map p 132.*

★★ **Ceiba** DOWNTOWN *LATIN AMERICAN* If you love Latin American ceviches (think fresh tuna marinated in lime and mango juice), zingy mojitos, and fashion, book a table at this outpost popular with young

Comfort food at Bucks Fishing & Camping, in Cleveland Park.

scenesters after work. *701 14th St. NW (at G St.).* ☎ *202/393-3983. www.ceibarestaurant.com. Entrees $16–$29. AE, DC, DISC, MC, V. Lunch Mon–Fri; dinner Mon–Sat. Metro: Metro Center. Map p 130.*

★★ **Central Michel Richard** DOWNTOWN *AMERICAN/FRENCH* Citronelle's casual, less expensive brother, Central Michel Richard dishes out unstuffy fare such as French onion soup, mussels, Lobster burgers, and soft shell crab. *1001 Pennsylvania Ave. NW.* ☎ *202/626-0015. www.centralmichelrichard. com. Entrees $16–$35. Lunch Mon–Fri; dinner daily. Metro: Federal Triangle. Map p 130.*

★★★ **Citronelle** GEORGETOWN *FRENCH* Fanatic foodies with cash to burn: Make reservations now. Citronelle's white-jacketed waiters, linen-dressed tables, and delicate foie gras carpaccio, caviar penguins, and squab (served three ways) won't disappoint. See "The Best of D.C. in One Day" (p 137). *3000 M St. NW (at 30th St.).* ☎ *202/625-2150. www.citronelledc.com. Dinner entrees $85–$150. AE, DC, MC, V. Breakfast & dinner daily. Metro: Foggy Bottom. Map p 132.*

★★★ **CityZen** WASHINGTON HARBOR *AMERICAN* In the posh Mandarin Oriental Hotel, Chef Eric Zeibold—formerly of French

Bistro Bis, on Capitol Hill.

Laundry, and voted "Best Mid-Atlantic Chef" by James Beard in 2008—makes gourmands swoon with his adventurous cuisine (think black bass, rabbit loin). *1330 Maryland Ave. SW (at 12th St.).* ☎ *202/787-6006. www.mandarinoriental.com. Entrees $75–$125. AE, DC, DISC, MC, V. Dinner Tues–Sat. Metro: Smithsonian. Map p 130.*

★★ **CommonWealth Gastropub** COLUMBIA HEIGHTS *BRITISH* Owner Jamie Leeds and her business partner traveled to England and back before opening this bar/restaurant featuring pot pies, fish 'n' chips, and roasts. *1400 Irving St. NW.* ☎ *202/265-1400. www.commonwealthgastropub.com. Lunch & dinner daily. Entrees $11–$19. AE, DISC, MC, V. Metro: Columbia Heights. Map 130.*

★★ kids **Daily Grill** DUPONT CIRCLE *AMERICAN* With several locations, this Washington staple is perfect for a quick lunch or dinner with kids, whether you're craving a burger and fries or seared salmon and baked potato. Roomy booths, after-work bar scene. *1200 18th St. NW (Connecticut Ave.).* ☎ *202/822-5282. www.dailygrill.com. Entrees $16–$30. AE, DC, DISC, MC, V. Lunch & dinner daily. Metro: Dupont Circle. Map p 132.*

★★ **Full Kee** CHINATOWN *ASIAN* The city's best chefs eat here on their days off (Eric Zeibold is a fan). Try the Hong Kong–style shrimp dumpling soup, oyster casserole, or any stir-fry. Open late. *509 H St. NW (at 6th St.).* ☎ *202/371-2233. www.fullkeedc.com. Entrees $10. No credit cards. Lunch & dinner daily. Metro: Gallery Place/Chinatown. Map p 130.*

Georgia Brown's DOWNTOWN *SOUTHERN* The dining room may seem formal, but the food is fit for a down-home, Southern jubilee: golden-fried chicken; cornmeal-crusted catfish fingers; shrimp and grits; and sweet, crunchy fried okra. *950 15th St. NW (at K St.).* ☎ *202/393-4499. www.gbrowns.com. Entrees $17–$26. AE, DC, DISC, MC, V. Lunch Mon–Fri; dinner daily; brunch Sun. Metro: Farragut North. Map p 130.*

★★ **Hank's Oyster Bar** DUPONT CIRCLE *SEAFOOD* Chef-owner Jamie Leeds mismatched the furnishings in this homey space so it wouldn't be "too perfect" a setting for beer, oysters, lobster rolls, and the like. *1624 Q St. NW (at 17th St.).* ☎ *202/462-4265. www.hanksdc. com. Entrees $12–$19. AE, MC, V. Dinner daily; brunch Sat–Sun. Metro: Dupont Circle. Map p 132.*

Hello Cupcake DUPONT CIRCLE *DESSERTS* Owner Penny Karas bakes her gourmet cupcakes from scratch, every day, and includes more than 20 flavors such as tiramisu, triple coconut, and "24 carrot." Vegan

Proof, in Penn Quarter.

and gluten-free flavors available. *1351 Connecticut Ave. NW. ☎ 202/861-2253. www.hellocupcakeonline. com. Mon–Sat. Cupcakes $3–$3.50. AE, DISC, MC, V. Metro: Dupont Circle. Map p 130.*

★ **IndeBleu** PENN QUARTER *FRENCH* Spot celebrities, in town to film political thrillers, at this swank spot for French fusion cuisine. Well-heeled hipsters sip Manhattans and sway in the lounge to DJ grooves. *707 G St. NW (next to Verizon Center). ☎ 202/551-0042. Entrees $22–$55. AE, DC, DISC, MC, V. Lunch & dinner Mon–Sat. Metro: Gallery Place/Chinatown. Map p 130.*

★ **Indique** CLEVELAND PARK *INDIAN* Curry, naan, biriyani. All of the flavors of India are here at this chic two-floor restaurant known for its consistently good fare. *3512 Connecticut Ave. NW. ☎ 202/244-6600. www.indique.com. Lunch and dinner daily. $14–$19. AE, DC, DISC, MC, V. Metro: Cleveland Park. Map p 132.*

★ **Jaleo** PENN QUARTER *SPANISH* Chef José Andrés started the "small plates" revolution in Washington with this sexy, casual tapas bar and restaurant in the heart of

Pastry chef at Komi, in Dupont Circle.

Penn Quarter. *480 7th St. NW (at E St.). ☎ 202/628-7949. www.jaleo. com. Entrees $16–$18, tapa $3.25–$9.95. AE, DC, DISC, MC, V. Lunch & dinner daily. Metro: Gallery Place/Chinatown. Map p 130.*

★ kids **Johnny's Half Shell** CAPITOL HILL *SEAFOOD* Maryland is famous for its crab cakes, and this small, no-frills neighborhood restaurant cooks them to perfection, with loads of meat and very little filler.

D.C. Dining Tips

Washington, D.C.: not just a center of political power, but of sensational dining. This chapter presents you with choices from as many different tastes, budgets, and styles. If a place beckons, call ahead for **reservations,** especially for Saturday night. At **www. opentable.com**, you can often reserve your table online. If you wait until the last minute to make a reservation, expect to dine really early, say 5:30 or 6pm, or after 9:30pm. Or you can sit at the bar and eat; see "A Seat at the Bar," p 141. Better yet, consider a restaurant that doesn't take reservations. At a place like Lauriol Plaza, where the atmosphere is casual, the wait can become part of the experience. If you're driving, call ahead to inquire about valet parking, complimentary or otherwise.

– Elise Hartman Ford

Ceiba, downtown.

Casual and kid-friendly. *400 N. Capitol St., NW (at Louisiana Ave).* ☎ *202/737-0400. www.johnnyshalfshell.net. Entrees $7.50–$24. AE, MC, V. Breakfast & lunch Mon–Thurs; dinner Mon–Sat. Metro: Dupont Circle. Map p 130.*

★★ **Komi** DUPONT CIRCLE *AMERICAN* Wow: Chef Johnny Monis's savory Mediterranean cooking, homemade breads, and light, lively desserts. The tiny dining room is casual, the service perfect. Worth the wait. *1509 17th St. NW (near P St.).* ☎ *202/332-9200. www.komirestaurant.com. Tasting menu $90–$125; wine pairing $42–$68. AE, MC, V. Dinner Tues–Sat. Metro: Dupont Circle. Map p 132.*

★ **Lauriol Plaza** DUPONT CIRCLE *MEXICAN* Is this multilevel place ever not packed to the roof, where singles flirt and drink? The Mexican fare is worth its salt—as are the strong margaritas. *1835 18th St. NW (at S St.).* ☎ *202/387-0035. www.lauriolplaza.com. Entrees $6.50–$16. AE, DC, DISC, MC, V. Lunch & dinner daily. Metro: Dupont Circle. Map p 132.*

★★★ **Palena** CLEVELAND PARK *ITALIAN/FRENCH* Former White House chef Frank Ruta and pastry queen Ann Amernick offer some of Washington's finest dining (upscale contemporary with Italian and French influences, with a special bar menu). *3529 Connecticut Ave. NW (at Porter St.).* ☎ *202/537-9250. www.palenarestaurant.com. Prix-fixe dinner $55–$69; entrees $28 (tasting menu), $10–$15 (cafe). AE, DISC, MC, V. Dinner Tues–Sat. Metro: Cleveland Park. Map p 132.*

★★ **kids Patisserie Poupon** CLEVELAND PARK *FRENCH* A sliver of a cafe, with lovely, brisk coffees, sandwiches, and confections, amid Georgetown's Antique Row. Expat Parisians camp out here. *1645 Wisconsin Ave. NW (Q St. and Reservoir Rd.).* ☎ *202/342-3248. Entrees $5–$10. AE, DISC, MC, V. Breakfast & lunch Tues–Sun. No Metro access. Bus: D2 or D6. Map p 132.*

★★★ **Proof** PENN QUARTER *AMERICAN* Choose from some 1,000 bottles of wine, or off a rolling champagne cart, then dine on freshly prepared contemporary dishes that make a nod toward eco-friendly cuisine. *775 G St. NW.* ☎ *202/737-7663. www.proofdc.com. Entrees $24–$29. Lunch Mon–Fri, dinner daily. Metro: Gallery Place/Chinatown. Map p 130.*

★★ **Restaurant Nora** DUPONT CIRCLE *ORGANIC* As an early advocate of fresh, seasonal ingredients,

Sesame-crusted tofu at Vegetate.

chef-owner Nora Pouillon's free-range chicken and tender roasted pork are testament to how good a simple, organic meal can be. Great wine list. *2132 Florida Ave. NW (at R St.).* ☎ *202/462-5143. www.noras. com. Entrees $24–$32. AE, MC, V. Dinner Mon–Sat. Metro: Dupont Circle. Map p 132.*

★★★ The Source DOWNTOWN
ASIAN-AMERICAN Wolfgang Puck made his D.C. debut with this Asian-Fusion restaurant in the new Newseum. *575 Pennsylvania Ave. NW.* ☎ *202/637-6100. www.wolfgang puck.com. Entrees $26–$45. Lunch Mon–Fri, dinner Mon–Sat. Metro: Archives/Penn Quarter. Map p 130.*

★★ South by Southwest
WASHINGTON HARBOR *AMERICAN* By day, the Mandarin Oriental Hotel's white-on-blond decor is the calm setting for afternoon tea. Later, come for Southern "Chesapeake" fare such as blue crab soup, hush puppies—and chicken and dumplings—and views of the memorials and Washington Harbor. *1330 Maryland Ave. SW (at 12th St.).* ☎ *202/787-6868. www.mandarin*

Brasserie Beck, downtown.

oriental.com. Entrees $20–$25. AE, DC, DISC, MC, V. Breakfast, lunch & dinner daily. Metro: Smithsonian. Map p 130.

A Seat at the Bar

Dining out in Washington can be many things: a culinary adventure, a happy pastime, a chance to transact business, a romantic interlude . . . and a competitive sport. Most restaurants require reservations, and in this cutthroat town, all the best seem always to be booked. Oh pooh! What's a hungry, reservation-less, good-food lover to do? Head to the bar, of course. In an effort to please those who haven't managed to reserve a table in their main dining rooms, but who nevertheless hope to sample some of their food, glorious food, a number of the city's top restaurants have started serving modified versions of their regular menus at the bar. The experience often proves more intimate and convivial than that in the main dining room, and here's the kicker: it's always less expensive.

– Elise Hartman Ford

★ **Sweetgreen** GEORGETOWN *SALADS* Healthy salads made-to-order with bold ingredients like Wasabi peas, gaucamole, and shrimp are featured at this casual joint owned by recent Georgetown grads. *3333 M St. NW.* ☎ *202/337-9338. www.sweetgreen.com. Salads from $6. AE, DC, DISC, MC, V. Lunch daily. Metro: Roslyn. Map p 130.*

★ **Tabaq Bistro** U STREET *MEDITERRANEAN* The glass-ceilinged third floor of this trendy restaurant offers unparalleled views of D.C.'s Washington Monument, not to mention tasty Moroccan fare served on small plates. *1336 U St. NW.* ☎ *202/265-0965. www.tabaqdc.com. Entrees $14–$22. AE, DC, DISC, MC, V. Dinner daily. Metro: U Street/Cardozo. Map p 130.*

★ **Tackle Box** GEORGETOWN *AMERICAN* New Englanders, this one's for you. Evoking a classic beach shack with communal tables and chalkboard menus, Tackle Box offers the best seafood without the fuss. *3245 M St. NW.* ☎ *202/337-TBOX (337-8269). Entrees $9–$13. AE, DC, MC, V. Lunch & dinner daily. No Metro access (See "Traveling to Georgetown" on p 93). Map p 130.*

kids **Teaism** DUPONT CIRCLE *ASIAN* Spot *Vanity Fair* scribe

Christopher Hitchens outside on warm days, or eavesdrop on moody political debates inside as you sup on healthy noodle dishes and baked goods. *2009 R St. NW (Connecticut Ave. and 21st St.).* ☎ *202/667-3827. www.teaism.com. Entrees $1.50–$10. AE, MC, V. Breakfast, lunch & dinner daily. Metro: Dupont Circle. Map p 132.*

★ **Vegetate** 14TH STREET *VEGETARIAN* This place serves a garden variety of tastefully prepared vegetarian dishes in a sleekly designed setting, with green walls and all. Occasionally a DJ spins tracks. *1414 9th St. NW.* ☎ *202/232-4585. www.vegetatedc.com. Entrees $12–$25. AE, DISC, MC, V. Dinner Thurs–Sun; brunch Sun. Metro: Cardozo/U St., Vernon Sq., or Shaw/Howard University. Map p 130.*

★★★ **Zaytinya** PENN QUARTER *MIDDLE EASTERN* Zaytinya is a must for fans of tapas-style dining—with its soaring ceilings, white-washed walls, communal tables shared by beautiful people, and modern Middle Eastern mezze. *701 9th St. NW (at G St.).* ☎ *202/638-0800. www.zaytinya.com. Entrees $18–$23. AE, DC, DISC, MC, V. Lunch & dinner daily. Metro: Gallery Place/Chinatown. Map p 130.* ●

Dinner at Proof, in Penn Quarter.

D.C. **Nightlife**

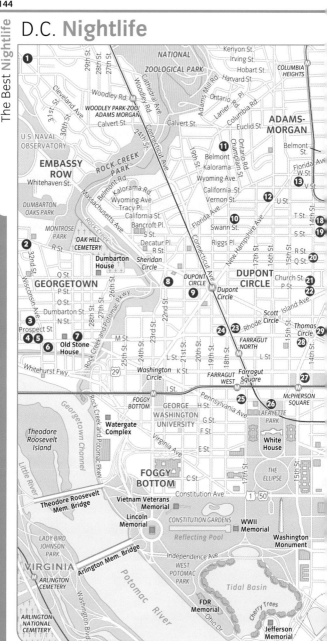

❶

NATIONAL
ZOOLOGICAL PARK

Kenyon St.
Irving St.
Hobart St.
Harvard St.

COLUMBIA
HEIGHTS

26th St.
24th St.
27th St.

Cleveland Ave.

Woodley Rd.
Woodley Rd.
Cathedral Ave.

WOODLEY PARK-ZOO/
ADAMS MORGAN

Calvert St.

Calvert St.

Adams Mill Rd.
Ontario Rd.
Lanier Pl.
Columbia Rd.

Euclid St.

ADAMS-
MORGAN

31st St.
30th St.

U.S. NAVAL
OBSERVATORY

24th St.

Connecticut Ave.

19th St.

Ontario Rd.
Champlain St.

Belmont
St.

⓫

Belmont

Florida Ave.

EMBASSY
ROW

Whitehaven St.

ROCK CREEK
PARK

Kalorama
Wyoming Ave.
California St.
Vernon St.

U St.

W St.
V St.

⓭

⓬

DUMBARTON
OAKS PARK

MONTROSE
PARK

32nd St.

Wisconsin Ave.

Massachusetts Ave.

Belmont Rd.

Kalorama Rd.
Wyoming Ave.
Tracy Pl.
California St.
Bancroft Pl.
S St.

Florida Ave.

New Hampshire Ave.

Florida Ave.

Swann St.

U St.

❿

T St.
S St.

14th St.

⓲
⓳

OAK HILL
CEMETERY

Rock Creek

Dumbarton
House

Decatur Pl.
R St.

Riggs Pl.

17th St.
16th St.
15th St.

R St.
Q St.

⓴

❷

Sheridan
Circle

DUPONT
CIRCLE

DUPONT
CIRCLE

GEORGETOWN

Dumbarton St.

Rock Creek and Potomac Pkwy.

26th St.
28th St.
27th St.

Q St.
P St.
O St.
N St.

❽

❾

Dupont
Circle

Church St.
P St.

㉑
㉒

Wisconsin Ave.

Prospect St.

❸

❹❺

❻

Old Stone
House

❼

25th St.
24th St.
23rd St.

22nd St.

M St.

L St.

21st St.
20th St.
19th St.

Scott
Circle

Rhode Island Ave.

FARRAGUT
NORTH

L St.

Island Ave.

Thomas
Circle

15th St.
14th St.

㉘

㉙

㉔

㉓

Whitehurst Fwy.

(29)

Washington
Circle

K St.

FARRAGUT
WEST

Farragut
Square

Farragut
Square

㉗

McPHERSON
SQUARE

Theodore Roosevelt
Island

Georgetown Channel

Rock Creek and Potomac Pkwy.

I St.

FOGGY
BOTTOM

Watergate
Complex

GEORGE
WASHINGTON
UNIVERSITY

Virginia Ave.

Pennsylvania Ave.
H St.
G St.
F St.
E St.

㉕

17th St.

LAFAYETTE
PARK

White
House

㉖

THE
ELLIPSE

15th St.

Little River

Theodore Roosevelt
Mem. Bridge

FOGGY
BOTTOM

C St.

Vietnam Veterans
Memorial
Lincoln
Memorial

Constitution Ave.

CONSTITUTION GARDENS

Reflecting Pool

1 50

WWII
Memorial

Washington
Monument

LADY BIRD
JOHNSON
PARK

VIRGINIA

ARLINGTON
CEMETERY

Washington Blvd.

Arlington Mem. Bridge

Arlington Mem. Bridge

Potomac

Independence Ave.

WEST
POTOMAC
PARK

Tidal Basin

Cherry Trees

ARLINGTON
NATIONAL
CEMETERY

River

FDR
Memorial

Ohio Dr.

Jefferson
Memorial

Previous page: Nighttime at the Capitol.

1789 4
2 Amys 1
9:30 Club 16
Black Cat 19
Blues Alley 6
Bohemian Caverns 15
Bourbon 2
Brickskeller 8
Busboys and Poets 13
Café Japoné 9
Café Milano 5
Café Saint-Ex 17
The Capital Grille Lounge 34
Charlie Palmer Steak 38
Eighteenth Street Lounge 24
ESPN Zone 30
Fado Irish Pub 31
Halo 21
Helix Lounge 22
HR-57 20

IndeBleu 32
International Bar 29
Lauriol Plaza 10
Local 16 12
Lounge 201 35
Martin's Tavern 3
Mendocino Grille & Wine Bar 7
Metropolitan Club 25
Off the Record Bar 26
The Park at 14th 27
Play Lounge 23
Post Pub 28
Proof 33
Sonoma 37
Stetson's Famous Bar & Grill 12
Stir Lounge 32
Tabaq Bistro 14
Town 17
Tryst 11

Kenyon St.
Irving St.
McMillan Reservoir
Columbia Rd.
Harvard St.
Girard St.
Fairmont St.
Euclid St.

HOWARD UNIVERSITY

Barry Pl.

13th St.
12th St.
11th St.
10th St.
9th St.
8th St.

16
15 17

U STREET-CARDOZO
14

U STREET CORRIDOR

SHAW-HOWARD UNIVERSITY

Rhode Island Ave.

7th St.
6th St.
5th St.

Logan Circle

29 1

13th St.
12th St.
11th St.
10th St.
9th St.
8th St.

N St.

New York Ave.

34 NEW YORK-FLORIDA AVE.

GALLAUDET UNIVERSITY

M St.

DOWNTOWN
Mt. Vernon Square

50 MT. VERNON SQ./CONVENTION CTR.
1

New York Ave.

1st St.

1
50 Massachusetts Ave.

K St.

I St.

New Jersey Ave.

395

H St.

North Capitol St.

CHINATOWN

GALLERY PLACE-CHINATOWN
33 32

3rd St.
2nd St.
1st St.

G St.

F St.

31

METRO CENTER
30

PENN QUARTER

Union Station

2nd St.
3rd St.
4th St.

UNION STATION

Pennsylvania Ave.

JUDICIARY SQUARE

E St.

FEDERAL TRIANGLE
34

ARCHIVES-NAVY MEMORIAL

D St.

35

C St.

Louisiana Ave.

Delaware Ave.

Stanton Square

Constitution Ave.

36

Maryland Ave.

Madison Dr.

NATIONAL MALL

U.S. Capitol

CAPITOL HILL

A St.

East Capitol St.

SMITHSONIAN

Jefferson Dr.

A St.

Independence Ave.

L'ENFANT PLAZA

FEDERAL CENTER SW

Washington Ave.

Seward Square

37

North Carolina Ave.

CAPITOL SOUTH

Capitol St.

New Jersey Ave.

South Capitol St.

Pennsylvania Ave.

EASTERN MARKET

Washington Channel

395

0   1/4 mi
0   0.25 km
N

Nightlife Best Bets

Best for **Hopheads**
★★ Brickskeller, *1523 22nd St. NW (p 147)*

Best for Watching Interns **Flirt with Elected Officials**
★ Charlie Palmer Steak, *101 Constitution Ave. NW (p 148)*

Best for Spotting **Movie Stars in Town**
★ The Park at 14th, *920 14th St. NW (p 150)*

Best for Rubbing Shoulders with **Capitol Hillers**
★ Lounge 201, *201 Massachusetts Ave. NE (p 148)*

Best for Getting **Your Groove On**
The Park at 14th, *920 14th St. NW (p 150)*

Best **Al Fresco Ambiance**
★★ Poolside at the International Bar, *Washington Plaza Hotel, 10 Thomas Circle NW (p 151)*

Best for **Wine & Romance**
★★★ 1789, *1226 36th St. NW (p 148)*

Best for Overhearing **State Secrets**
★★ Off the Record Bar, *Hay Adams Hotel, 800 16th St. NW (p 149)*

Best for **Scotch & Cigar Lovers**
★ The Capital Grille Lounge, *601 Pennsylvania Ave. NW (p 148)*

Best for **Live Jazz & Blues**
★ Blues Alley, *1073 Wisconsin Ave. NW (p 151)*

Best for Catching **Indie Acts**
★ 9:30 Club, *815 V St. NW (p 151)*

Best **Private Power Club**
★★ Metropolitan Club, *1700 H St. NW (p 148)*

Best for Spotting Post **Reporters**
★★ Post Pub, *1422 L St. NW (p 149)*

Best **Drinks** While the Kids Eat **Pizza**
★★ 2 Amys, *3715 Macomb St. NW (p 152)*

Best for Mingling with **Socialites**
★ Café Milano, *3252 Prospect St. NW (p 150)*

Best **Literary/Artsy-Fartsy Haunt**
★ Busboys and Poets, *2021 14th St. NW (p 149)*

Best for Waiting Behind the **Velvet Ropes**
★★ Play Lounge, *1219 Connecticut Ave. NW (p 150)*

Best for **Monumental Views**
★ Tabaq Bistro, *1336 U St. NW (p 149)*

Best **Rooftop Drinking**
Local 16, *1602 U St. NW (p 151)*

Best **Dive Bar**
★ Stetson's Famous Bar & Grill, *1610 U St. NW (p 147)*

Best for **Grapeheads**
★★ Proof, *775 G St., NW (p 147)*

Tip

Metro trains run until 3am on weekends, and special shuttle service also goes to Adams Morgan (home to lots of clubs, but no Metro stops). Take the Metro to the Red Line's Woodley Park–Zoo/Adams Morgan station or to the Green Line's U St.–Cardozo station, and hop on the no. 98 Adams Morgan–U Street Link Shuttle, which travels through Adams Morgan, between these two stations, after 6pm daily except Saturday, when service starts at 10am. The U Link Shuttle operates every 15 minutes and costs only 25¢.

Nightlife A to Z

Beer Lovers/Casual

★★ Brickskeller DUPONT CIRCLE   Think cramped wooden tables, a cavelike interior, greasy bar food, and a selection of more than 1,000 international beers. It's a pilgrimage site for college kids and brew lovers. *1523 22nd St. NW (at P St.).* ☎ *202/293-1885. http://www. lovethebeer.com/brickskeller.html. Metro: Dupont Circle.*

★ Fado Irish Pub PENN QUARTER   This authentic Irish watering hole has a true taste of the Emerald Isle, from vintage tables and chairs to the huge stones that make up the walls and floors, plus pints of Guinness on tap. The din here is at 10 decibels, the pub grub is savory, and the music is live. *808 7th St. NW (at H St.).* ☎ *202/789-0066. www. fadoirishpub.com. Metro: Gallery Place/Chinatown.*

★ Stetson's Famous Bar & Grill U STREET CORRIDOR   Shoot some pool with your pals over draft ale at this neighborhood pub with a respectable mix of classic rock on the jukebox, charmingly dated decor, and an outdoor patio for mellow summer nights. *1610 U St. NW (at 16th St.).* ☎ *202/667-6295. Metro: U St. Corridor.*

Wine Lovers

★★ Mendocino Grille & Wine Bar GEORGETOWN   California escapism in the heart of preppy Georgetown: light Mediterranean-style cuisine paired with 200 wines by the bottle and 35 by the glass. Great garden seating. *2917 M St. NW (at 29th St.).* ☎ *202/333-2912. www.mendocinodc.com. Metro: Foggy Bottom.*

★★ Proof PENN QUARTER   More than 1,000 different bottles, some from the owner's own collection, and an Enomatic wine system that dispenses perfect pours by the glass make this trendy spot a must-taste for oenophiles. *775 G St. NW.* ☎ *202/ 737-7663. www.proofdc.com. Metro: Gallery Place/Chinatown.*

Tabaq, in the U Street Corridor.

The chic Park at 14th, downtown.

★★★ 1789 GEORGETOWN   A new chef isn't the only attraction at this Washington mainstay. This low-lit, classic New American restaurant has a very romantic bar and one of the city's most impressive wine lists. *1226 36th St. NW (at Prospect St.). ☎ 202/965-1789. www.1789 restaurant.com. No Metro access (see box, p 93).*

★★ Sonoma CAPITOL HILL   The hottest new spot on the Hill, serving Mediterranean small plates with more than 35 well-chosen wines by the bottle. Be prepared to get friendly with strangers; the place is always packed and tables are *this-close. 223 Pennsylvania Ave. SE (at 2nd St.). ☎ 202/544-8088. www. sonomadc.com. Metro: Capitol South.*

Whiskey Lovers

★★ Bourbon GLOVER PARK   Named for the 50 Kentucky bourbons (and assorted Tennessee varieties) poured here, this casual, modern pub attracts sports fans, slumming hipsters, grad students— even neighborhood families, who dine upstairs on tasty burgers and crab cakes. *2348 Wisconsin Ave. NW (near Calvert St.). ☎ 202/625-7770. No Metro access.*

Political Intrigue

★ The Capital Grille Lounge PENN QUARTER   The premier political watering hole in town, this clubby lounge is witness to power-brokering, scandals, and plenty of cigar-tinged intrigue—plus premium whiskeys and 300 wines on its regular list. *601 Pennsylvania Ave. NW (at 6th St.). ☎ 202/737-6200. www.thecapitalgrille.com. Metro: Archives/Navy Memorial.*

★ Charlie Palmer Steak DOWNTOWN   The city's elegant outpost for this nationally acclaimed chef attracts the town's top political dogs for stiff drinks and perfectly prepared sirloins. *101 Constitution Ave. NW (at Louisiana Ave.). ☎ 202/547-8100. www. charliepalmer.com. Metro: Union Station.*

★ Lounge 201 CAPITOL HILL   Two swank bars and billiards tables attract the just-out-of-college-and-working-on-the-Hill set, who down boozy beverages as they diss their famous bosses. *201 Massachusetts Ave. NE (at 2nd St.). ☎ 202/544-5201. www.lounge201.com. Metro: Union Station.*

★ Martin's Tavern GEORGETOWN   Chris Matthews, Tucker Carlson, and every president since Harry Truman have come to this "Old Washington" pub. Saddle up to the mahogany bar for a scotch or take a seat in one of its booths, where JFK proposed to Jackie. *1264 Wisconsin Ave. NW. ☎ 202/ 333-7370. www.martins-tavern. com. No Metro access (see box, p 93).*

★★ Metropolitan Club DOWNTOWN   In a circa 1908 building listed on the National Register of Historic Places, this posh club attracts D.C.'s movers and shakers. *1700 H St. NW (at 17th St.). ☎ 202/ 835-2500. www.metroclub.org.*

Metro: Farragut North or Farragut West.

★★ Off the Record Bar DOWN-
TOWN Billed as "Washington's place to be seen and not heard," Off the Record was selected by Forbes as one of the "World's Best Hotel Bars" in July 2004. It's just steps from the White House; I wish its red-paneled walls could talk. *In the Hay-Adams Hotel: 800 16th St. NW (at H St.).* ☎ *202/638-6600. www. hayadams.com. Metro: McPherson Sq.*

★★ Post Pub DOWNTOWN If you
want to run into today's versions of Bob Woodward and Carl Bernstein, look no farther than this tiny relic of a bar. Serves draft beer and belly-filling grub to *Post* staffers, who work just around the corner. *1422 L St. NW (at Vermont Ave.).* ☎ *202/628-2111. Metro: McPherson Sq.*

Hipster Haunts
★ Busboys and Poets 14TH
STREET Local lit majors and broke fashionistas flock here for pizzas, burgers, and booze. Prices won't break the bank. *2021 14th St. NW (at U St.).* ☎ *202/387-7638.*

www.busboysandpoets.com. AE, MC, V. Metro: Cardozo/U St.

Café Saint-Ex 14TH STREET
Named for the author of *Le Petit Prince,* this Eurochic bar and bistro attracts goateed hipsters and their supercilious dates for New American fare. A DJ spins in the downstairs lounge. *1847 14th St. NW (at T St.).* ☎ *202/265-7839. Metro: Cardozo/U St.*

★★ Helix Lounge LOGAN
CIRCLE Funky, pop-centric decor plus colorful cocktails and a nice outdoor space make this retro-cool lounge in the Hotel Helix a hangout among Washington's scene-makers. *1430 Rhode Island Ave. NW (at 14th St.).* ☎ *202/462-9001. Metro: McPherson Sq. or Dupont Circle.*

★ Tabaq Bistro U STREET
CORRIDOR The decor is minimalist, with geometric shapes, sharp edges, and red tones. The glass-paneled terrace yields great views of the city. The people-watching is colorful. And, if that's not enough, come for the "hookah" menu. *1336 U St. NW (at 13th St.).* ☎ *202/265-0965. www.tabaqdc.com. Metro: Cardozo/U St.*

Helix Lounge, in 14th Street/Logan Circle.

Tryst, in Adams Morgan.

Tryst ADAMS MORGAN   Part coffee house, part playground, part gallery, part pick-up lounge, and part study hall, Tryst is all things for most Adams Morganers. Early to open and late to close, this always buzzing gathering spot is the spot to ogle original art, eat a sandwich or score a scone, groove to live music, or journal furiously while downing an English ale. *Coffee house: 2459 18th St. NW (at Columbia Rd.). Diner: 2453 18th St. NW.* ☎ *202/232-5500. www. trystdc.com. Mon–Thurs 6:30am–2am, Fri–Sat 6:30am–3am, Sun 7am–2am. Metro: Woodley Park–Zoo/ Adams Morgan.*

VIP Scene

★ **Café Milano** GEORGETOWN
Rub shoulders with Botoxed socialites, back-slapping senators, and European playboys at the lively bar scene, or sit down for a meal of middling-to-good Italian fare—if you can get a table. *3251 Prospect St. NW (at Potomac).* ☎ *202/333-6183. Metro: Foggy Bottom or Roslyn.*

Eighteenth Street Lounge
DUPONT CIRCLE   Some would say this multilevel meeting place has seen its heyday. But it continues to draw crowds and beautiful people through its unmarked front door, to mingle on salon-style sofas and groove to live

music. *1212 18th St. NW (at Connecticut Ave.).* ☎ *202/466-3922. Cover: $5–$20 Tues–Sat. Metro: Dupont Circle.*

★ **The Park at 14th** DOWNTOWN   Come dressed to kill for this velvet-roped multilevel lounge that attracts Hollywood starlets, famous athletes, and limo-riding beautiful people to its pulsing music, chic digs, and Dale Chihuly–esque chandeliers. *920 14th St. NW.* ☎ *202/737-7275. www.theparkat fourteenth.com. No cover. Metro: McPherson Square.*

★★ **Play Lounge** DUPONT CIRCLE   This hopping nightclub is packed with young people downing shots, getting their groove on, and taking twirls around the stripper's pole—to the delight of onlookers. *1219 Connecticut Ave. NW (at M St.).* ☎ *202/466-7529. www. playloungedc.com. Cover $10 Tues and Thurs–Sat. Metro: Dupont Circle.*

Stir Lounge PENN QUARTER
Well-dressed hipsters jive to thumping dance grooves with special DJs featured weekly and a large menu of fancy martinis to pick from. *705 G St. NW (at 7th St.).* ☎ *202/ 333-2538. Metro: Gallery Place/ Chinatown.*

Karaoke
★★ Café Japoné DUPONT CIRCLE If you like singing for your supper or just belting out a Broadway tune, look no farther than this local institution for sushi-loving *American Idol* rejects and pitch-perfect exhibitionists. *2032 P St. NW (at 21st St.).* ☎ *202/223-1573. Metro: Dupont Circle.*

Live Music
★★ Black Cat 14TH STREET Faded punk rockers, still riding on the Sex Pistols' glory days, gather here to vet a new generation of mohawked wonders, and to check out other national and international alternative acts. *1811 14th St. NW (between S and T sts.).* ☎ *202/667-7960. www. blackcatdc.com. Cover $5–$20 for concerts; no cover in Red Room Bar. Metro: Cardozo/U St.*

★ Blues Alley GEORGETOWN The *New York Times* once called this place "the nation's finest jazz and supper club." Indeed, its reputation is deserved, for its Cajun-infused fare and performances by legends like Eartha Kitt and Mary Wilson. *1073 Wisconsin Ave. NW (at M St.).* ☎ *202/337-4141. www.bluesalley. com. Cover $16–$75, plus $10 food and drink minimum, plus $2.25 surcharge. Metro: Foggy Bottom then Georgetown Metro Connection Shuttle.*

★★ Bohemian Caverns U STREET CORRIDOR Calling itself the "sole home of soul jazz," this legendary joint has attracted A-list artists (Duke Ellington and Miles Davis among them) for decades. Its keyboard awning greets you, and its creative cavelike interior is like no other. *2001 11th St. NW (at U St.).* ☎ *202/299-0801. www.bohemian caverns.com. $10 cover Fri–Sat; no*

food and drink minimum. Entrees $7.95–$19. Metro: Cardozo/U St.*

HR-57 LOGAN CIRCLE This tiny jazzhouse that doubles as a nonprofit for music preservation is the real deal. Grab a shabby chair in the brick-walled club to listen to amateur and professional artists jam into the night. You can BYOB for a $3 corking fee, or purchase wine and beer by the glass. *1610 14th St. NW.* ☎ *202/ 667-3700. www.hr57.org. Metro: Dupont Circle.*

★ 9:30 Club U STREET CORRIDOR Fans of '80s warblers Bob Mould and 'Ments frontman Paul Westerberg will love this intimate, smoky den for independent music. The best acoustic and low-fi sets on the East Coast. *815 V St. NW (at Vermont Ave.).* ☎ *202/265-0930. www.930.com. Tickets $10–$50 in advance. Metro: Cardozo/U St.*

Outdoor/Rooftop
★★ International Bar LOGAN CIRLCE Rich and famous hipsters who might otherwise be in Miami flock here for the exclusive outdoor pool and the buzzing scene at the rooftop bar. *In the Washington Plaza Hotel: 10 Thomas Circle NW (at M St.).* ☎ *800/424-1140 or 202/842-1300. www.washingtonplazahotel.com. Metro: McPherson Sq.*

Local 16 U STREET CORRIDOR You might feel you're at a crowded house party in this renovated townhouse turned bar that also happens to have one of the best rooftops for happy-hour mingling, dining, and drinking. *1602 U St. NW.* ☎ *202/265-2828. www.localsixteen.com. Metro: U Street/Cardozo.*

Sports
★★ ESPN Zone PENN QUARTER Gilbert Arenas fans, this is your hotspot for catching NBA hoops on

National Harbor

If you're willing to make a day and night of it, hop a cab to **National Harbor,** the newest entertainment outpost, just a few miles from downtown D.C. Here, you'll find shops, nearly 20 restaurants, and a dueling piano bar along the newly constructed streets. The immense Gaylord National Hotel is still the centerpiece, and features a top seafood eatery, an acclaimed steak restaurant, more stores, and a Bellagio-type fountain that shoots 60-feet (18m) in the air. At press time, it's still under development but more nightlife venues are expected to open soon. Call ☎ 301/749-1582 or visit www.nationalharbor.com for details.

big-screen TVs, as well as all major sporting events, from Wimbledon to the Super Bowl. *555 12th St. NW (at F St.).* ☎ *202/783-3776. www. espnzone.com/washingtondc. Metro: Gallery Place/Chinatown.*

Family Spirits
★★ **2 Amys** GLOVER PARK Mom and Dad, you need a drink, and the rug rats are hungry. So take them out for authentic Neapolitan pizza while you savor a lovely glass of Italian red wine. *3715 Macomb St. NW (at Wisconsin Ave.).* ☎ *202/885-5700. www.2amyspizza.com. Metro: Tenleytown/AU.*

Gay & Lesbian
★ **Town** U STREET CORRIDOR Wild nights are the norm at this high-energy dance club that has an outside smoking area, two levels, and video screens, and stays open until 4am. *2009 8th St. NW.* ☎ *202/ 234-TOWN. www.towndc.com. Cover $12–$20. Metro: U Street/Cardozo.*

Halo LOGAN CIRCLE Formerly an auto repair shop, this swank lounge attracts a mixture of old and young who come here to sip trend-setting cocktails. *1435 P St. NW (at 14th St.).* ☎ *202/797-9730. No cover. MC, V. Metro: Dupont Circle or McPherson Sq.* ●

Day trip to National Harbor, D.C.'s newest entertainment emporium.

D.C. **Arts & Entertainment**

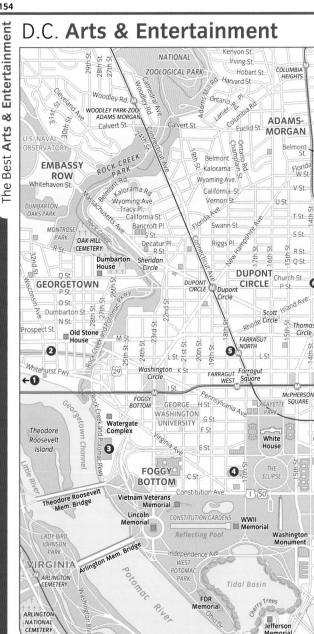

Previous page: Historic Ford's Theatre is still a vital performance venue downtown.

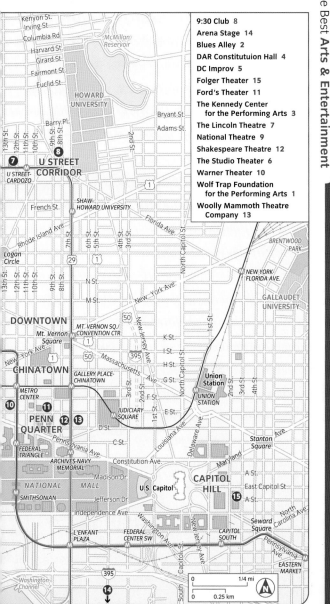

9:30 Club 8
Arena Stage 14
Blues Alley 2
DAR Constitutuion Hall 4
DC Improv 5
Folger Theater 15
Ford's Theater 11
The Kennedy Center
  for the Performing Arts 3
The Lincoln Theatre 7
National Theatre 9
Shakespeare Theatre 12
The Studio Theater 6
Warner Theater 10
Wolf Trap Foundation
  for the Performing Arts 1
Woolly Mammoth Theatre
  Company 13

Arts & Entertainment **Best Bets**

Best **Restored Theater**
★ The Lincoln Theatre, *1215 U St. NW (p 157)*

Best for **History Buffs**
★★ Ford's Theatre, *511 10th St. NW (p 157)*

Best for **High-Brow Performance**
★★★ The Kennedy Center, *2700 F St. NW (p 157)*

Best for **Avant-Garde Acts**
Woolly Mammoth, *641 D St. NW (p 158)*

Best Place to **Laugh So Hard You Cry**
DC Improv, *1140 Connecticut Ave. NW (p 157)*

Best of the **Bard**
★★ Shakespeare Theatre Company, *450 7th St. NW (p 157)*

Best for **Touring Broadway Shows**
★★ National Theatre, *1321 Pennsylvania Ave. NW (p 157)*

The edgy Studio Theatre, in 14th Street/ Logan Circle.

Best for **Edgy Playwrights**
★★ The Studio Theatre, *1501 14th St. NW (p 158)*

Best **Outdoor Theater**
★ Wolf Trap Foundation for the Performing Arts, *1645 Trap Rd., Vienna, Virginia (p 158)*

The Wooly Mammoth Theatre Company.

Arts & Entertainment A to Z

★★ Arena Stage SW WATER-FRONT   Artistic Director Molly Smith is known for staging first-rate classical and contemporary productions, attracting leading first men and women from New York and Hollywood. *1101 6th St. SW (at Maine Ave.). During renovations through Fall 2010, operating out of a temporary theater in Crystal City (1100 S. Bell St., Arlington Va.) and the Lincoln Theatre (below).* ☎ *202/488-3300. www.arenastage.org. Tickets $25–$75. Metro: Waterfront–SEU.*

★★★ DAR Constitution Hall DOWNTOWN   Everyone from Aretha Franklin to the Smashing Pumpkins has played this popular venue for household-name musicians, comedians, and lecturers. *17th Street between C and D sts., NW.* ☎ *202/628-1776. www.dar.org. Ticket prices vary. Metro: Farragut West.*

★★ DC Improv DOWNTOWN   Before they hit big, Ellen DeGeneres and Dave Chappelle performed at this underground comedy club that still draws top-notch artists weekly from across the country. *1140 Connecticut Ave. NW.* ☎ *202/296-7008. www.dcimprov.com. Tickets are $15–$20. Metro: Farragut North.*

★★ Folger Theatre CAPITOL HILL   Buy tickets here for Shakespearean plays, concerts, and literary readings, as well as fun family activities with a historical twist. *201 E. Capitol St. SE (between 2nd and 3rd sts.).* ☎ *202/544-7077. www.folger.edu. Tickets $25–$49. Metro: Capitol South.*

★★ Ford's Theatre DOWNTOWN   This theater, where John Wilkes Booth shot President Lincoln in 1865, as he watched the comedy *Our American Cousin,* is still staging compelling productions today. *511 10th St. NW (between E and F sts.).* ☎ *202/347-*

4833. www.fordstheatre.org. Tickets $25–$55. Metro: Metro Center.

★★★ The Kennedy Center for the Performing Arts FOGGY BOTTOM   Named for the late president, this Washington landmark is both a living memorial and a first-class venue for symphonies, operas, ballets, and touring theatrical and dance productions—not to mention their annual awards. *2700 F St. NW (between New Hampshire Ave. and Rock Creek Pkwy.). Tours* ☎ *202/416-8340; box office* ☎ *202/467-4600. www.kennedy-center.org. Tickets $14–$290. Metro: Foggy Bottom.*

★ The Lincoln Theatre U STREET CORRIDOR   Restored to its original splendor, this historic venue has welcomed a heavenly host of African-American musicians, from Duke Ellington and Billie Holliday to modern entertainers such as Dick Gregory. *1215 U St. NW (between 12th and 13th sts.).* ☎ *202/397-SEAT. www.the lincolntheatre.org. Tickets $20–$200. Metro: Cardozo/U St.*

Legendary Blues Alley, in Georgetown.

Performance at Arena Stage.

★★ National Theatre DOWNTOWN

Everyone from Dame Edna to Earth, Wind & Fire plays this historic "theater of Presidents," open since 1835. *1321 Pennsylvania Ave., NW (between 13th and 14th sts.).* ☎ *202/628-6161. www.national theatre.org. Tickets $37–$86. Metro: Federal Triangle or Metro Center.*

★★ Shakespeare Theatre Company PENN QUARTER

Catch the Bard's best, from *A Midsummer Night's Dream* to *Othello*, in productions with astounding sets and nationally known actors. *450 7th St. NW (between D and E sts.).* ☎ *202/ 547-1122. www.shakespearetheatre. org. Tickets $23–$68. Metro: Gallery Place/Chinatown or Archives/Navy Memorial/Penn Quarter.*

★★ The Studio Theatre 14TH STREET

This theater has earned a stellar reputation for edgy, contemporary productions by playwrights such as Neil LaBute. Its newly renovated space is the crown jewel of the recently revived 14th Street/ Logan Circle area. *1501 14th St. NW (at P St.).* ☎ *202/332-3300. www. studiotheatre.org. Tickets $32–$62. Metro: Cardozo/U St., Dupont Circle, or McPherson Sq.*

★★ Warner Theatre CAPITOL HILL

This big theater stages a range of performances, from international recording artists (Bob Weir, Hall & Oates) to touring plays (*Golda's Balcony, Cheaters*), to comedic one-man shows (Jim Gaffigan, Lewis Black). *513 13th St. NW (between E and F sts.).* ☎ *202/783-4000. www. warnertheatre.com. Ticket prices vary. Metro: Metro Center.*

★ Wolf Trap Foundation for the Performing Arts NORTHERN VIRGINIA

Year-round, enjoy touring pop, country, folk, and blues artists, plus dance, theater, opera, and orchestra performances—with outdoor plays and concerts in summer. *1645 Trap Rd. (off Rte. 7), Vienna, Virginia.* ☎ *877/WOLF-TRAP [9653-8727]. www.wolf-trap.org. Tickets $10–$70. No Metro access.*

★★ Woolly Mammoth Theatre Company PENN QUARTER

This company aims to break new ground, showcasing new works by emerging artists. Provocative, experimental, never boring. *641 D St. NW (at 7th St.).* ☎ *202/289-2443. www.woollymammoth.net. Tickets $22–$52. Metro: Gallery Place/ Chinatown.* ●

D.C. **Hotels**

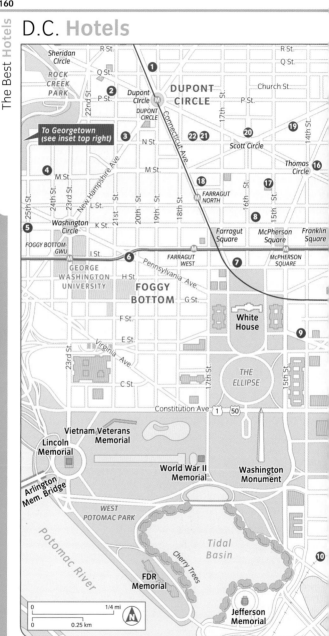

Previous page: Hotel Helix, in Logan Circle.

Georgetown

GEORGETOWN UNIVERSITY

The Dupont at the Circle 1
The Fairmont Washington 4
Four Points Sheraton 15
Hay-Adams 7
Holiday Inn on the Hill 12
Hotel George 14
Hotel Helix 19
Hotel Lombardy 6
Hotel Madera 3
Hotel Monaco 11
Hotel Palomar Dupont 2

The Liason Capitol Hill 11
The Madison Hotel 17
Mandarin Oriental 10
Mayflower Hotel 18
The River Inn 5
Hotel Rouge 20
Hotel Tabard Inn 22
St. Regis Hotel 7
Topaz Hotel 17
Washington Plaza Hotel 16
Willard InterContinental Hotel 9

Georgetown
(see inset above right)
Four Seasons Georgetown 24
Georgetown Inn 23
Ritz-Carlton Georgetown 25

Hotel Best Bets

Where **Activist Hollywood A-Listers Hold Court**
★★ Mandarin Oriental $$$ *1330 Maryland Ave. SW (p 165)*

Where **Hollywood A-Listers Get Some Sleep**
★★ Gold Floor at The Fairmont Washington $$$ *2401 M St. NW (p 163)*

Where Washington's **Young Bucks Mingle**
★★ Hotel George $$ *15 E St. NW (p 163)*

Most Romantic **Bathtub with the Best View**
★★ Willard InterContinental $$$ *1401 Pennsylvania Ave. NW (p 166)*

For Some **Shabby with Your Chic**
★★ Hotel Tabard Inn $$ *1739 N St. NW (p 165)*

Where to **Make a Great Splash**
★★ Washington Plaza (and its rooftop pool) $$ *10 Thomas Circle NW (p 166)*

Best for **Fashionistas**
★★★ Four Seasons Georgetown $$$$ *2800 Pennsylvania Ave. NW (p 163)*

Best for **Warehouse Luxe**
★★★ Ritz-Carlton Georgetown $$$$ *3100 S St. NW (p 165)*

Where to Meet an **NBA Player**
★★ Hotel Monaco $$ *700 F St. NW (p 164)*

Best for the **Entitled**
★★ The Madison Hotel $$$ *1177 15th St. NW (p 165)*

Best for **Dog Lovers**
★★ Hotel Madera $$ *1310 New Hampshire Ave. NW (p 164)*

Best for **History Buffs**
★★ Morrison House $$$ *116 S. Alfred St., Alexandria, Virginia (p 165)*

Best for **Astrology Fanatics**
★★ Topaz Hotel $$$ *733 N St. NW (p 166)*

Best for **Fans of All Things Red**
★★ Hotel Rouge $$ *1315 16th St. NW (p 164)*

Best for **Pop Culture Purists** (Who Don't Have Lots of Cash)
★★ Hotel Helix $$ *1430 Rhode Island Ave. NW (p 164)*

A room with a view at the Hay-Adams.

Hotels A to Z

★★★ The Dupont at the Circle

DUPONT CIRCLE   This charming, centrally located inn has six guest rooms, two suites, and one apartment—all with antiques, immaculate bedding, private bathrooms, and Wi-Fi access. *1604 19th St. NW (at Q St. NW). ☎ 888/412-0100 or 202/332-5251. www.dupontatthecircle.com. 9 units. Doubles from $160. AE, DISC, MC, V. Metro: Dupont Circle.*

★★ The Fairmont Washington

WEST END   Lush atrium gardens set the tone for this elegant, clubby luxury hotel. Its Gold Floor caters to A-listers with free car service, chocolates, and even a pillow menu. *2401 M St. NW (at 24th St. NW). ☎ 800/257-7544 or 202/429-2400. www.fairmont.com/washington. 415 units. Doubles from $279. AE, DISC, MC, V. Metro: Farragut North.*

★★ kids Four Points Sheraton

PENN QUARTER   In town for a conference at the Convention Center? This clean, safe, and contemporary hotel is ideally located. While its suites are designed for work—with big desks and Internet access—guests can still play in the rooftop pool. *1201 K St. NW (at 12th St. NW). ☎ 202/289-7600. www.fourpoints.com. 265 units. Doubles from $153. AE, DISC, MC, V. Metro: Gallery Place/Chinatown.*

★★★ Four Seasons Georgetown

GEORGETOWN   Travel editors, fashionistas, and movie stars in town to film political thrillers book here for the unparalleled quality and service. The lower-level spa is the capital's best, and M Street shopping is steps away. *2800 Pennsylvania Ave. NW (at M St. NW). ☎ 202/342-0444. www.fourseasons.com/*

The lobby of the pet-friendly Hay-Adams.

washington. 211 units. Doubles from $299. AE, DC, DISC, MC, V. Metro: Foggy Bottom.

★★ kids Georgetown Inn

GEORGETOWN   If you want to be in the heart of Georgetown, this decent (if unspectacular) hotel is the place to stay. Its clubby, dark-wooded interior recently underwent renovations, and the Daily Grill downstairs is family-friendly. *1310 Wisconsin Ave. NW (at N St. NW). ☎ 888/587-2388 or 202/333-8900. www.georgetowninn.com. 96 units. Doubles $195–$245. AE, DC, DISC, MC, V. No Metro access. Bus: 30, 32, or 34.*

★★★ Hay-Adams

DOWNTOWN   Steps from the White House, this luxury boutique hotel has great views of Lafayette Park and marries European elegance with a buzzy, D.C. insider's bar, Off the Record. *1 Lafayette Sq. (between 16th and H sts.). ☎ 202/638-6600. www.hayadams.com. 145 units. Doubles from $199. AE, DC, DISC, MC, V. Metro: Farragut West or McPherson Sq.*

Hotel George

CAPITOL HILL   Modern, minimalist, chic. Hill staffers flock to the hotel bar, at Bistro

Bis, and the first president himself welcomes travelers to the capital, in the silk-screen dollar-bill prints that hang in every guest room. *15 E St. NW (at N. Capitol NW).* ☎ *800/576-8331 or 202/347-4200. www.hotel george.com. 139 units. Doubles from $159. AE, DC, DISC, MC, V. Metro: Capitol Hill.*

★★ **Hotel Helix** LOGAN CIRCLE Fans of Andy Warhol, Marilyn Monroe, even PEZ, will adore this boutique hotel with a mission to celebrate all things pop. Interiors are retro, and the funky lounge draws local scene-makers. *1430 Rhode Island Ave. NW (between 14th and 15th sts. NW).* ☎ *800/706-1202 or 202/462-9001. www.hotel helix.com. 178 units. Doubles from $149. AE, DC, DISC, MC, V. Metro: McPherson Sq.*

★ **Hotel Lombardy** FOGGY BOTTOM An easy walk from The Mall, this old-time hotel is replete with friendly bellhops, an elevator operator, complimentary shoe shines, and suites that remind you of your grandmother's fanciest guest room—if she were Italian, of course. *2019 Pennsylvania Ave. NW (at I St. NW).* ☎ *202/828-2600. www.hotel lombardy.com. 140 units. Doubles from $109. AE, DC, DISC, MC, V. Metro: Foggy Bottom.*

★★ **Hotel Madera** DUPONT CIRCLE A boutique hotel for the business traveler: warm-toned yet high-tech guest rooms, with nice touches such as animal-print pillows, a complimentary wine hour, and the option to stow away personal items (such as running shoes) for return guests. Pet friendly, too. *1310 New Hampshire Ave. NW (between N and O sts. NW).* ☎ *800/430-1202 or 202/296-7600. www.hotelmadera.com. 82 units. Doubles from $179. AE, DC, DISC, MC, V. Metro: Dupont Circle.*

A room at the Hotel Helix.

★★ **Hotel Monaco** PENN QUARTER Housed in a landmark former post office, this temple to modern cool juxtaposes historic marble and sky-high ceilings with sleek, inviting, vibrantly colored guest rooms. Poste, the swank bar downstairs, attracts visiting NBA stars (from the Verizon Center down the block), who "hoop" it up in style. *700 F St. NW (at 7th St. NW).* ☎ *877/202-5411 or 202/628-7177. www.monaco-dc. com. 84 units. Doubles from $179. AE, DC, DISC, MC, V. Metro: Gallery Place/Chinatown.*

★★ **Hotel Palomar** DUPONT CIRCLE Art takes center stage at this luxury boutique hotel that offers comfortably appointed rooms with crisp Frette linens and faux lynx throws, plus a stylish restaurant. Pet friendly, too. *2121 P St. NW.* ☎ *877/866-3070 or 202/448-1800. www. hotelpalomar-dc.com. 335 units. Doubles from $149–$359 Metro: Dupont Circle.*

★★ **Hotel Rouge** DUPONT CIRCLE Young renegades into high-tech hotels will love the red-hot accommodations at this racy boutique inn. Specialty rooms feature flatpanel computer monitors, Sony Wega flatscreen TVs, PlayStation 2, and a video game library. *1315 16th St. NW (between Massachusetts Ave. and Scott Circle).* ☎ *202/232-8000. www.rougehotel.com. 137 units. Doubles from $179. AE, DC, DISC, MC, V. Metro: Dupont Circle.*

★★ **Hotel Tabard Inn** DUPONT CIRCLE Eclectic at its best: Every room is a romantic mix of original art and fine early-20th-century antiques. The excellent restaurant has a lovely summer garden, cozy divans, and a fireplace for cold nights. *1739 N St. NW (between 17th and 18th sts.).* ☎ *202/785-1277. www.tabardinn.com. 40 units. Doubles with bathroom from $140. AE, DC, DISC, MC, V. Metro: Dupont Circle or Farragut North.*

★★ **The Liaison** CAPITOL HILL Picky about your pillow? Choose from six different styles in this modernly-appointed hotel, where Hill staffers flock to its upscale-Southern Art and Soul restaurant. *415 New Jersey Ave. NW.* ☎ *202/638-1616. www.affinia.com. 343 units. Doubles from $179–$350. Metro: Union Station.*

★★ **The Madison Hotel** DOWNTOWN Famed for fawning over foreign dignitaries, The Madison is exactly how you'd imagine a small Washington hotel to be: traditional, quiet, well kept, and, yes, dignified. Spice things up by dining or drinking at trendy Palette Restaurant downstairs. *1177 15th St. NW (at M St. NW).* ☎ *800/424-8577 or 202/862-1600. www.loewshotels.com. 353 units. Doubles from $229. AE, DC, DISC, MC, V. Metro: Farragut North.*

★★ **Mandarin Oriental** SOUTHWEST A feng shui expert designed the rooms here—some with spectacular views of the Southwest Marina and the Jefferson Memorial. East meets West luxury in the beautifully balanced silk wall coverings, bamboo embellishments, and marble bathrooms. *1330 Maryland Ave. SW (at 12th St. SW).* ☎ *888/888-1778 or 202/554-8588. www.mandarin-oriental.com. 400 units. Doubles from $255. AE, DC, DISC, MC, V. Metro: Smithsonian.*

★★ **Morrison House** NORTHERN VIRGINIA The Federal-style facade here represents the historic, ornate feel within: guest rooms with fireplaces and chandeliers, a piano bar, and lots of red upholstery. *116 S. Alfred St. (at King St.), Alexandria, Virginia.* ☎ *703/838-8000. www.morrisonhouse.com. 45 units. Doubles from $199. AE, DC, DISC, MC, V. Metro: King St.*

★★★ **Ritz-Carlton Georgetown** GEORGETOWN Historic architecture meets modern elegance in this upscale hotel, once the site of a 19th-century brick-and-steel incinerator. If the guest rooms' marble bathrooms and goose-down pillows don't soothe your soul, book a treatment at the

The lobby at the Hotel Monaco, in Penn Quarter.

A room at the Hotel Monaco.

pampering spa. *3100 South St. NW (at 31st St. NW).* ☎ *800/241-3333 or 202/912-4100. www.ritzcarlton.com/ hotels/georgetown. 86 units. Doubles from $349. AE, DC, DISC, MC, V. No Metro access (see box, p 93).*

★ **kids The River Inn** FOGGY BOT-TOM   If you love to travel but hate to blow so much cash dining out, book at this centrally located, modern boutique hotel; each spacious guest room has a full kitchenette. *924 25th St. NW (at K St. NW).* ☎ *888/874-0100. www. theriverinn.com. 126 units. Doubles from $99. AE, DC, DISC, MC, V. Metro: Foggy Bottom.*

★★★ **St. Regis Hotel** DOWN-TOWN   This stately hotel a mere few blocks from the White House recently underwent a massive makeover to restore it to its original 1926 glamour. *923 16th and K sts. NW.* ☎ *202/638-2626. www.stregis. com. 175 units. Doubles from $190– $460. Metro: Farragut North.*

★★ **Topaz Hotel** DUPONT CIRCLE   This ambient palace is dedicated to free tarot card readings, horoscopes, exotic interior textures, and healing in-room spa services. *1733 N St. NW (between 17th and 18th sts.).* ☎ *202/393-3000. www. topazhotel.com. 99 units. Doubles from $199. AE, DC, DISC, MC, V. Metro: Dupont Circle or Farragut North.*

★★ **Washington Plaza Hotel** LOGAN CIRCLE   Rich and famous hipsters who might otherwise be in Miami flock here for the exclusive outdoor pool and buzzing scene at the International Bar. *10 Thomas Circle NW (at 14th St. NW).* ☎ *800/ 424-1140 or 202/842-1300. www. washingtonplazahotel.com. 340 units. Doubles from $189. AE, DC, DISC, MC, V. Metro: McPherson Sq.*

★★ **Willard InterContinental Hotel** DOWNTOWN   Beaux-Arts architecture meets history here— where Martin Luther King, Jr., wrote his "I Have a Dream" speech, and every president from Grant to "W" has bunked at least once for the night. Ask about the romantic tub in the honeymoon suite. *1401 Pennsylvania Ave. NW (at 14th St. NW).* ☎ *800/827-1747 or 202/628-9100. www.washington.intercontinental. com. 341 units. Doubles from $239. AE, DC, DISC, MC, V. Metro: Metro Center.*

Tip

See and be seen at the sleek **W Hotel,** 515 15th St. NW (☎ **202/ 661-2400;** www.starwoodhotels. com). Newly opened next to the White House as we went to press, the hip hotel features an expansive rooftop deck with landmark views and a stylish restaurant, J&G Steakhouse by Jean-Georges. ●

The
Savvy Traveler

Before You Go

Government Tourist Offices

The **Washington, D.C., Convention and Tourism Corporation (WCTC),** 901 7th St. NW, Washington, DC 20001-3719 (☎ **800/422-8644** or 202/789-7000; www.washington.org) Visitors Guide details hotels, restaurants, sights, shops, and more.

Also take a look at the D.C. government's website, **www.dc.gov**, and Cultural Tourism D.C., **www.culturaltourismdc.org**, for more information about the city.

For additional information about Washington's most popular tourist spots, access the National Park Service website, **www.nps.gov/nacc**, and the Smithsonian Institution's **www.si.edu**.

The Best Times to Go

The city's peak seasons generally coincide with the sessions of Congress and springtime. When Congress is "in," from about the second week in September until Thanksgiving, and again from about mid-January through June, hotels are full with guests on business.

Mid-March through June traditionally is the most frenzied season, when families and school groups descend to see the cherry blossoms. It's also a popular season for protest marches.

To avoid crowds, consider visiting at the end of August and early September or between Thanksgiving and mid-January—though the lighting of the National Christmas Tree is very popular.

The July 4th Independence Day celebration is spectacular, but the weather is very hot and humid in July and August. Many of Washington's performance stages close, although some outdoor arenas and parks host events.

For event schedules, see **www.washington.org**, **www.culturaltourismdc.org**, **www.dc.gov**, and **www.washingtonpost.com**.

Useful Numbers & Websites

- **National Park Service** (☎ 202/ **619-7222;** www.nps.gov/ncro). You reach a real person and not a recording when you phone this number with questions about the monuments, The Mall, national park lands, and events taking place at these locations.

- **Dial-A-Park** (☎ **202/619-7275**). This is a recording of information regarding Park Service events and attractions.

- **Dial-A-Museum** (☎ 202/357- **2020;** www.si.edu). This recording offers the locations of the 16 Washington Smithsonian museums and their daily activities.

- The **Washington, D.C., Visitor Information Center** (☎ **866/ 324-7386** or 202/289-8317; www.itcdc.com) is a small visitors center in the immense Ronald Reagan International Trade Center Building (1300 Pennsylvania Ave. NW).

- The **Smithsonian Information Center,** in the "Castle," 1000 Jefferson Dr. SW

Previous page: Ronald Reagan International Airport.

AVERAGE TEMPERATURES & RAINFALL IN WASHINGTON, D.C.

	JAN	FEB	MAR	APR	MAY	JUNE
AVG. HIGH (°F/°C)	44/5	46/8 5	4/12	66/19	76/25	83/29
AVG. LOW (°F/°C)	30/-1	29/-1	36/2	46/8	56/14	65/19
RAINFALL (IN.)	3.21	2.63	3.6	2.71	3.82	3.13

	JULY	AUG	SEPT	OCT	NOV	DEC
AVG. HIGH (°F/°C)	87/31	85/30	79/26	68/20	57/14	46/8
AVG. LOW (°F/°C)	69/20	68/20	61/16	50/10	39/4	32/0
RAINFALL (IN.)	3.66	3.44	3.79	3.22	3.03	3.05

(☎ **202/633-1000,** or TTY 202/633-5285; www.si.edu), is open every day but Christmas from 9am to 5:30pm.

• The **American Automobile Association (AAA)** has a large central office near the White House, at 1405 G St. NW, between G Street and New York Avenue NW, Washington, DC 20005-2111 (☎ **202/331-3000**).

Getting **There**

By Plane

Domestic airlines with scheduled flights into all three of Washington, D.C.'s, airports, Washington Dulles International **(Dulles),** Ronald Reagan Washington National **(National),** and Baltimore–Washington International **(BWI),** include **American** (☎ 800/433-7300; www.aa.com), **Continental** (☎ 800/523-3273; www.continental.com), **Delta** (☎ 800/221-1212; www.delta.com), **Northwest** (☎ 800/225-2525; www.nwa.com), **United** (☎ 800/864-8331; www.united.com), and **US Airways** (☎ 800/428-4322; www.usairways.com).

Quite a few low-fare airlines serve all three D.C. airports. **Southwest Airlines** (☎ 800/435-9792; www.southwest.com), at BWI Airport, has 162 daily flights to more than 35 cities. Another bargain airline at BWI is **AirTran** (☎ 800/247-8726; www.airtran.com).

Discount airlines that serve Dulles are **Virgin Atlantic** (☎ 877/359-8474; www.virgin-atlantic.com) United Airlines' subsidiary **Ted Airlines** (☎ 800/225-5833; www.flyted.com), **America West** (now operating as part of USAirways), **AirTran, Southwest, JetBlue** (☎ 800/538-2583; www.jetblue.com), and **Frontier** (☎ 800/432-1359; www.frontierairlines.com).

Two discount airlines use National Airport: **Frontier** and **Spirit** (☎ 800/772-7177; www.spiritair.com).

Shuttle Service from New York, Boston & Chicago

Delta and US Airways continue to dominate the D.C.–East Coast shuttle service. Between the two of them, hourly or almost-hourly shuttle service runs between Boston's Logan Airport and Washington, and New York's La Guardia Airport and Washington. The **Delta Shuttle** (☎ **800/933-5935**) travels daily between New York and Washington, while the **US Airways Shuttle** (☎ **800/428-4322**) operates daily between Boston and Washington and New York and Washington. **Southwest** (see details above) offers nearly hourly service daily between BWI and Chicago's Midway Airport, Providence, Hartford, Long Island, Manchester (New Hampshire), Orlando, and Nashville.

Getting into Town from the Airport

All three airports offer the following options for getting into the city.

TAXI SERVICE For a trip downtown, expect a taxi to cost anywhere from $10 to $20 for the 10- to 15-minute ride from National Airport; $44 to $50 for the 30- to 40-minute ride from Dulles Airport; and $63 for the 45-minute ride from BWI.

SUPERSHUTTLE Vans (☎ **800/ 258-3826;** www.supershuttle.com) offer shared-ride, door-to-door service. You can't reserve space on the van for a ride from the airport, so you'll likely have to wait 15 to 30 minutes to board and then make other stops before reaching your destination. If you arrive after midnight, call the 24-hour toll-free number above from National Airport or ☎ **703/416-7884** from both Dulles and BWI. To reach downtown, expect to pay about $12, plus $8 for each additional person from National; $22, plus $10 per additional person from Dulles; and $26 to $32, plus $10 per additional person from BWI. If you're calling SuperShuttle for a ride from D.C. to an airport, reserve at least 24 hours in advance.

LIMOUSINES Prices start at $25 at National, $42 at Dulles, and $95 at BWI, for private car transportation downtown. For pickup from BWI, reserve passage by calling ☎ **800/ 878-7743** or 301/912-0000; for pickup from National or Dulles, try **Red Top Executive Sedan** (☎ **703/522-3333**) or consult the Yellow Pages.

Free hotel/motel shuttles operate from all three airports to certain nearby properties. Ask about such transportation when you book a room at your hotel.

Individual transportation options at each airport are as follows:

FROM RONALD REAGAN WASHINGTON NATIONAL AIRPORT Metrorail's (☎ **202/637-7000**) Yellow and Blue lines stop at the airport and connect via an enclosed walkway to level two, the concourse level, of the main terminal, adjacent to terminals B and C. The ride downtown takes 15 to 20 minutes (longer at rush hour). It is safe, convenient, and cheap, from $1.35 and up (fares increase during rush hours).

Metrobuses (☎ **202/637-7000**) also serve the area, should you be going somewhere off the Metro route, but Metrorail is faster.

If you're renting a car from on-site **car-rental** agencies **Alamo** (☎ 703/419-2073), **Avis** (☎ 703/419-5815), **Budget** (☎ 703/419-1021), **Dollar** (☎ 866/434-2226), **Hertz** (☎ 703/419-6300), **National** (☎ 703/ 419-1032) or **Thrifty** (☎ 703/519-8701), go to level two, the concourse level, follow the pedestrian walkway to the parking garage, find garage A, and descend one flight. You can also take the free Airport Shuttle (look for the sign on the curb outside the terminal) to parking garage A. If you've rented from off-premises agencies such as **Enterprise** (☎ 703/553-7744), head outside the baggage claim area of your terminal, and catch the shuttle bus marked for your agency.

To get downtown by car, follow the signs for the George Washington Parkway. Then take I-395 North to Washington. Take the I-395 North exit, which takes you across the 14th Street Bridge. Stay in the left lane crossing the bridge and follow the signs for Route 1, which will put you on 14th Street NW. Ask your hotel for directions from 14th Street and Constitution Avenue NW.

A more scenic route runs to the left of the GW Parkway as you follow the signs for Memorial Bridge. You'll be driving alongside the Potomac River, with the monuments in view; then, as you cross over Memorial Bridge, the Lincoln Memorial greets you. Stay left coming over the bridge, swoop around left of the Memorial, turn left on 23rd Street NW, right on Constitution Avenue, and then left again on 15th Street NW (the Washington Monument will be to your right), into the heart of downtown.

FROM WASHINGTON DULLES INTERNATIONAL AIRPORT   The **Washington Flyer Express Bus** runs between Dulles and the West Falls Church Metro station, where you can board a train for D.C. In the airport, look for signs for the "Dulles Airport Shuttle." Buses to the West Falls Church Metro station run daily, every 30 minutes, and cost $10 one-way.

More convenient is the **Metrobus** that runs between Dulles and the L'Enfant Plaza Metro station, within walking distance of the National Mall and Smithsonian museums. The bus departs hourly, costs only $3, and takes 45 to 60 minutes. SmartTrip card (see below) riders are eligible for a discount.

For rental car pick-up at Dulles, head down the ramp near your baggage claim area, and walk outside to the curb to look for your rental car's shuttle bus stop. The buses come by every 5 minutes or so en route to nearby rental lots. These include

Alamo (☎ 703/260-0182), **Avis** (☎ 703/661-3500), **Budget** (☎ 703/437-9559), **Dollar** (☎ 703/661-8823), **Enterprise** (☎ 703/661-8800), **Hertz** (☎ 703/471-6020), **National** (☎ 703/471-5278), and **Thrifty** (☎ 877/283-0898).

To reach downtown from Dulles by car, exit the airport and stay on the Dulles Access Road, which leads right into I-66 east. Follow I-66 east, which takes you across the Theodore Roosevelt Memorial Bridge; be sure to stay in the center lane as you cross the bridge, and this will put you on Constitution Avenue. Ask your hotel for directions from this point.

FROM BALTIMORE–WASHINGTON INTERNATIONAL AIRPORT
Washington's Metro service runs an Express Metro Bus ("B30") between its Metrorail Green Line Greenbelt station and BWI Airport. In the airport, head to the lower level and look for "Public Transit" signs to find the bus, which runs daily every 40 minutes, takes about 30 minutes, and costs $3. At the Greenbelt Metro station, you purchase a Metro fare card and board a Metro train, which will take you into the city. Depending on where you want to go, you can either stay on the Green Line train to your designated stop or get off at the Fort Totten Station to transfer to a Red Line train, whose stops include Union Station (near Capitol Hill) and various downtown locations.

Amtrak (☎ 800/872-7245) and **Maryland Rural Commuter** (MARC; ☎ 800/325-7245) trains also run into the city. Both travel between the BWI Railway Station (☎ 410/672-6169) and Washington's Union Station (☎ 202/484-7540), about a 30-minute ride. Amtrak's service is daily (ticket prices range $13–$38 per person, one-way, depending on time and train type); while MARC's is weekdays only ($6 per person, one-way). A courtesy shuttle runs every 10 minutes or so between the airport and the train station; stop at the desk near the baggage-claim area to check for train or bus departure times. Trains depart about every hour.

BWI operates a large, off-site, car-rental facility. From the ground transportation area, a shuttle bus transports you to the lot. Rental agencies include **Avis** (☎ 410/859-1680), **Alamo** (☎ 410/859-8092), **Budget** (☎ 410/850-0850), **Dollar** (☎ 410/850-7025), **Enterprise** (☎ 410/684-3295), **Hertz** (☎ 410/850-7400), **National** (☎ 410/859-8860), and **Thrifty** (☎ 410/850-7139).

To reach Washington: Look for signs for I-195 and follow I-195 west until you see signs for Washington and the Baltimore-Washington Parkway (I-295); head south on I-295. Get off I-295 when you see the signs for Route 50/New York Avenue, which leads into the District, via New York Avenue. Ask your hotel for specific directions from New York Avenue NE.

By Car

If you are like most visitors to Washington, you're planning to drive here via one of the following major highways: I-270, I-95, and I-295 from the north; I-95 and I-395, Route 1, and Route 301 from the south; Route 50/301 and Route 450 from the east; and Route 7, Route 50, I-66, and Route 29/211 from the west.

No matter which road you take, you will likely have to navigate part of the **Capital Beltway** (I-495 and I-95). The Beltway girds the city, about 66 miles (106km) around, with more than 56 interchanges or exits, and is nearly always congested, especially during weekday morning and evening rush hours (roughly 6–9:30am and 3–7pm). Commuter traffic on the Beltway rivals or surpasses that of L.A.'s major freeways, and drivers can get crazy, weaving in and out of traffic.

By Train

Amtrak (☎ 800/USA-RAIL; www.amtrak.com) offers daily service to Washington from New York, Boston, Chicago, and Los Angeles (you change trains in Chicago). Amtrak also travels daily from points south of Washington, including Raleigh, Charlotte, Atlanta, cities in Florida, and New Orleans.

Metroliner service—which costs a little more but provides faster transit and roomier, more comfortable seating than regular trains—is available between New York and Washington, D.C., and points in between. Even faster, roomier, and more expensive are Amtrak's high-speed **Acela Express** trains. The trains travel 150 mph (242kmph), linking Boston, New York, and Washington.

Acela Express trains travel between New York and Washington in 2 hours and 50 minutes (about 20 min. faster than the Metroliner), and between Boston and Washington in about 6½ hours.

Amtrak trains arrive at historic **Union Station,** 50 Massachusetts Ave. NE (☎ 202/371-9441; www.unionstationdc.com).

By Bus

Coming from New York? **Bolt Bus** (www.boltbus.com) now provides daily express service from Manhattan to Washington, and vice versa. Its buses are new, and outfitted with free wireless access and plug-ins for charging laptops and cell phones. The Bolt Bus picks up and drops off in a prime downtown location too, at H Street between 9th and 10th streets. (A red Bolt Bus sign marks the spot.) Fares can range up to $20.

Another option is the well-known **Chinatown Bus** (www.chinatown-bus.com) that makes frequent runs between New York and Washington. Its buses are older and can be crowded, though. Fares range from $1 to $20.

Vamoose (☎ **877/393-2828;** www.vamoosebus.com) offers service for $25 each way from New York City (near Penn Station) to Bethesda, MD, and Arlington, VA, where you can make a connection to D.C.'s Metro system.

Getting **Around**

By Metro

Metrorail's (www.wmta.com) system of 86 stations and 106 miles (171km) of track includes stops near most sightseeing attractions and extends to suburban Maryland and northern Virginia. Five lines—Red, Blue, Orange, Yellow, and Green—connect at several points, making transfers easy. All but Yellow and Green Line trains stop at Metro Center; all except Red Line trains stop at L'Enfant Plaza; all but Blue and Orange Line trains stop at Gallery Place/Chinatown.

Metro stations are identified by brown columns bearing the station's name topped by the letter M. Below the M is a colored stripe or stripes indicating the line or lines that stop there. The free **Metro System Pocket Guide** has a map and lists the closest Metro stops to points of interest. You can download a copy from the website, www. wmta.com.

To enter or exit a Metro station, you need a computerized **fare card,** available at vending machines near the entrance. The machines take credit cards or nickels, dimes, quarters, and bills from $1 to $20; they can return up to $4.95 in change (coins only). At this time, the minimum fare to enter the system is $1.35, which pays for rides to and from any point within 7 miles (11km) of boarding during nonpeak hours; during peak hours (Mon–Fri 5–9:30am and 3–7pm), $1.35 takes you only 3 miles (5km). The maximum you will pay to the furthest destination is $4.50. Metro Authority is always contemplating a fare hike, though.

If you plan to take several Metrorail trips during your stay, put more value on the fare card to avoid having to purchase a new card each time you ride. For stays of more than a few days, your best value is the **7-Day Fast Pass,** $39 per person for unlimited travel; **1-Day Rail Passes,** $7.80 per person for unlimited passage that day, after 9:30am weekdays, and all day on Saturday, Sunday, and holidays. You can buy these passes online now or use the passes/fare cards machine in the station. Giant, Safeway, and other grocery stores also sell fare cards.

Metrorail opens at 5am weekdays and 7am Saturday and Sunday, operating until midnight Sunday through Thursday, and until 3am Friday and Saturday. Call ☎ **202/637-7000,** or visit www.wmata.com, for holiday hours and information on Metro routes.

By Bus

The **Metrobus** system operates 12,435 stops on its 1,489-square-mile (2,397-sq.-km) route, extending into the Virginia and Maryland suburbs. Stops have red, white, and blue signs that tell you what buses pull into a stop, but not where they go. **Warning:** Don't rely on the bus schedules posted at bus stops—they're often out of date. For more information, call ☎ **202/637-7000.**

Base fare in the District is $1.35 for those using cash, and $1.25 if you use a SmarTrip; transfers are free and valid for 2 hours from boarding. If you'll be in Washington for a while and plan to use the buses a lot, consider a 1-week pass ($11), available online and at the Metro Center station and other outlets. Buy tokens at the Metro Center Sales Office, at 12th and F streets, the 12th Street entrance.

Most buses operate daily almost around the clock. Service is frequent on weekdays, especially during peak hours. On weekends and late at night, service is less frequent.

Up to two children 4 and under ride free with a paying passenger on Metrobus. Reduced fares are available for seniors (☎ **202/637-7000**) and people with disabilities (☎ **202/962-1100**). If you leave something on a bus, a train, or in a station, call Lost and Found at ☎ **202/962-1195.**

By Car
More than half of all visitors arrive by car. Once you get here, though, my advice is to park it and walk or use the Metrorail. Traffic is always thick during the week, parking spots are scarce, and parking lots are pricey.

Watch out for **traffic circles.** Cars in the circle have the right of way, but no one heeds this rule. Cars zoom in without a glance at the cars already there.

Sections of certain streets become **one-way** at rush hour: Rock Creek Parkway, Canal Road, and 17th Street NW are three examples. Other streets during rush hour change the direction of some of their traffic lanes: Connecticut Avenue NW is the main one. Lit-up traffic signs alert you to what's going on, but pay attention. You can make a right on a red light, unless a sign is posted prohibiting it.

Car Rentals/Shares
All the major car-rental companies are represented here. See area airports at the beginning of this chapter for phone numbers for each company's airport locations. Within the District, car-rental locations include **Avis,** 1722 M St. NW (☎ 202/467-6585) and 4215 Connecticut Ave. NW (☎ 202/686-5149); **Budget,** Union Station (☎ 202/289-5373); **Enterprise,** 3307 M St. NW (☎ 202/872-5790); **Hertz,** Union Station (☎ 202/289-5366); **Alamo,** Union Station (☎ 202/842-7454); and **Thrifty,** 12th and K streets NW (☎ 202/783-0400).

Whether you need a car for an hour or a month, **Zipcar** (☎ 866/494-7227 or ☎ 202/737-4900; www.zipcar.com) offers its "members"—anyone can join for $75— flexible car-use arrangements, with gas, insurance, and other services included. Zipcar charges $9.25 an hour; its daily rate is $69. Given that hotels charge about $26 for overnight parking, the Zipcar deal, which includes parking, could still be cost-effective.

Travelers with Limited Mobility
Washington, D.C., is one of the most accessible cities in the world for travelers with limited mobility. The best overall source of information about accessibility at specific Washington hotels, restaurants, shopping malls, and attractions is available from the nonprofit organization **Access Information.** You can read the information (including restaurant reviews) online at **www.disabilityguide.org,** or order a free copy of the *Washington, DC, Access Guide* by calling ☎ **301/528-8664,** or by writing to Access Information, 21618 Slidell Rd., Boyds, MD 20841.

The **Washington Metropolitan Transit Authority** publishes accessibility information on its website **www.wmata.com,** or you can call ☎ **202/962-1100** with questions about Metro services for travelers with disabilities, including how to obtain an ID card that entitles you to discounted fares. (Make sure that you call at least 3 weeks ahead to allow enough time to obtain an ID card.) For up-to-date information about how Metro is running the day you're using it, call ☎ **202/962-1212.**

Each station has an elevator with Braille number plates and wide fare gates for wheelchair users; rail cars are fully accessible. Metro has installed punctuated rubber tiles to warn visually impaired riders that they're nearing the tracks; barriers between rail cars prevent the blind from mistaking the gap for entry to a car. For the hearing impaired, flashing lights indicate arriving trains; for the visually impaired, door chimes let you know when doors are closing. Train operators make station and on-board announcements of train destinations and stops. Nearly all Metrobuses have wheelchair lifts and kneel at the curb. The TTY number for Metro information is ☎ **202/638-3780.**

Tourmobile trams (p 9) are accessible to visitors with disabilities. The company also operates special vans for immobile travelers, complete with wheelchair lifts. Call a day ahead to ensure that the van is available for you when you arrive (☎ **202/554-5100**) or go to www.tourmobile.com.

Major Washington museums, including all Smithsonian museum buildings, are accessible to wheelchair visitors. A comprehensive free publication called *Smithsonian Access* lists all services available to visitors with mobility issues. Call ☎ **202/633-2921** or TTY 202/633-4353, or find the information online at http://www.si.edu/visit/visitors_with_disabilities.htm.

Likewise, theaters and all of the memorials are equipped to accommodate visitors with disabilities. There's limited parking for visitors with disabilities at some of these locations. Call ahead for accessibility information and special services.

Fast **Facts**

AREA CODES In the District of Columbia, it's ☎ 202; in suburban Virginia, ☎ 703; in suburban Maryland, ☎ 301. You must use the area code when dialing any number, even local calls within the District or to nearby Maryland or Virginia suburbs.

ATMS Automated teller machines (ATMs) are on most every block. Most accept Visa, MasterCard, American Express, and ATM cards from other U.S. banks. Expect to pay up to $3 per transaction if you're not using your own bank's ATM.

BUSINESS HOURS Offices are usually open weekdays from 9am to 5pm. Banks are open Monday through Thursday from 9am to 3pm, 9am to 5pm on Friday, and sometimes Saturday mornings. Stores typically open between 9 and 10am and close between 5 and 6pm from Monday through Saturday. Stores in shopping complexes or malls tend to stay open late: until about 9pm on weekdays and weekends, and many malls and larger department stores are open on Sunday.

CAR RENTALS See "Getting Around," earlier in this chapter.

DRUGSTORES CVS, Washington's major drugstore chain (with more than 40 stores), has two convenient 24-hour locations: in the West End, at 2200 M St. NW (☎ **202/296-9877**), and at Dupont Circle (☎ **202/785-1466**), both with round-the-clock pharmacies. Check your phone book for other convenient locations.

ELECTRICITY   Like Canada, the United States uses 110 to 120 volts AC (60 cycles), compared to 220 to 240 volts AC (50 cycles) in most of Europe, Australia, and New Zealand. If your small appliances use 220 to 240 volts, you'll need a 110-volt transformer and a plug adapter with two flat parallel pins to operate them here. Downward converters that change 220 to 240 volts to 110 to 120 volts are difficult to find in the United States, so bring one with you.

EMBASSIES & CONSULATES   All embassies are in D.C., the nation's capital. Online, you will find a complete listing, with links to each embassy, at www.embassy.org/embassies/index.html.

Here are the addresses of several: **Australia,** 1601 Massachusetts Ave. NW (☎ 202/797-3000; www.austemb.org); **Canada,** 501 Pennsylvania Ave. NW (☎ 202/682-1740; www.canadianembassy.org); **Ireland,** 2234 Massachusetts Ave. NW (☎ 202/462-3939; www.irelandemb.org); **New Zealand,** 37 Observatory Circle NW (☎ 202/328-4800; www.nzembassy.org); and the **United Kingdom,** 3100 Massachusetts Ave. NW (☎ 202/588-6500; www.britainusa.com/consular/embassy).

EMERGENCIES   In any emergency, call ☎ **911.**

HOLIDAYS   Banks, government offices, post offices, and many stores, restaurants, and museums are closed on the following legal national holidays: January 1 (New Year's Day), the third Monday in January (Martin Luther King, Jr., Day), January 20 (Inauguration Day), the third Monday in February (Presidents' Day, Washington's Birthday), the last Monday in May (Memorial Day), July 4 (Independence Day), the first Monday in September (Labor Day), the second Monday in October (Columbus Day), November 11 (Veterans' Day/Armistice Day), the fourth Thursday in November (Thanksgiving Day), and December 25 (Christmas).

HOSPITALS   If you don't require immediate ambulance transportation but still need emergency-room treatment, call one of the following hospitals (and get directions): **Children's Hospital National Medical Center,** 111 Michigan Ave. NW (☎ 202/884-5000); **George Washington University Hospital,** 900 23rd St. NW at Washington Circle (☎ 202/715-4000); **Georgetown University Medical Center,** 4000 Reservoir Rd. NW (☎ 202/687-5100); or **Howard University Hospital,** 2042 Georgia Ave. NW (☎ 202/865-6100).

INTERNET ACCESS   Your hotel is your best bet since many hotels now offer free Internet access. **Kramerbooks & Afterwords Café,** 1517 Connecticut Ave., NW (☎ **202/387-1400**) in Dupont Circle has one computer available for free Internet access (15-min. limit). **Tryst,** 2459 18th St., NW, (☎ **202/232-5500**) is also a good stop for free wireless access. Most **Starbucks, Caribou Coffees,** and **Cosi** coffee shops also offer free Internet access.

LIQUOR LAWS   The legal age for purchase and consumption of alcoholic beverages is 21; proof of age is required, so bring an ID when you go out. Liquor stores are closed on Sunday. Gourmet grocery stores, mom-and-pop grocery stores, and 7-Eleven convenience stores often sell beer and wine, even on Sunday.

Do not carry open containers of alcohol in your car or any public area that isn't zoned for alcohol consumption. The police can fine you on the spot. And nothing will ruin your trip faster than getting a citation for DUI (driving under the influence), so don't even think about driving while intoxicated.

MAIL The main post office in the capital is the **National Capitol Station,** 2 Massachusetts Ave. NE (☎ **202/523-2368;** www.usps.com). Mailboxes are blue with a red-and-white stripe and carry the inscription U.S. MAIL. All U.S. addresses have a five-digit postal code (or zip code), after the two-letter state abbreviation. This code is essential for prompt delivery.

At press time, domestic postage rates were 28¢ for a postcard and 44¢ for a letter. For international mail, a first-class letter of up to 1 ounce costs 98¢ (75¢ to Canada and 79¢ to Mexico), a first-class postcard costs 98¢ (75¢ to Canada and 79¢ to Mexico), and a preprinted postal aerogramme costs 75¢.

NEWSPAPERS & MAGAZINES At the airport, pick up a free copy of **Washington Flyer magazine** (www.washingtonflyer.com), which is handy as a planning tool.

Washington has two daily newspapers: the **Washington Post** (www.washingtonpost.com) and the **Washington Times** (www.washingtontimes.com). The Friday "Weekend" section of the *Post* is essential for finding out what's going on, recreation-wise. *City Paper,* published every Thursday and available free at downtown shops and restaurants, covers some of the same material but is a better guide to the club and art-gallery scene.

Also on newsstands is **Washingtonian,** a monthly magazine with features, often about the "100 Best" this or that (doctors, restaurants, and so on) in Washington; the magazine also offers a calendar of events, restaurant reviews, and profiles of Washingtonians.

POLICE In an emergency, dial ☎ **911.** For a nonemergency, call ☎ **202/727-1010.**

SAFETY Washington, like any urban area, has a criminal element, so it's important to stay alert and take normal safety precautions.

Ask your hotel front-desk staff or the city's tourist office if you're in doubt about which neighborhoods are safe.

SMOKING In 2006, D.C. lawmakers banned smoking in bars, restaurants, and public places, with exemptions for outdoor areas, hotel rooms, retail tobacco outlets, and cigar bars.

TAXES The U.S. has no value-added tax (VAT) or other indirect tax at the national level. The sales tax on merchandise is 5.75% in D.C. The tax on restaurant meals is 10%, and you'll pay 14.5% hotel tax. The hotel tax in Maryland varies by county from 5% to 8%. The hotel tax in Virginia also varies by county, averaging about 9.75%.

TELEPHONE & FAX Private corporations run the telephone system in the U.S., so rates—especially for long-distance service and operator-assisted calls—can vary widely. Generally, hotel surcharges on long-distance and local calls are astronomical, so you're usually better off using a **public pay telephone,** which you'll find clearly marked in most public buildings and private establishments as well as on the street. Convenience grocery stores and gas stations always have them.

Many convenience groceries and packaging services sell **prepaid calling cards** in denominations up to $50; these can be the least expensive way to call home. Many public phones at airports now accept American Express, MasterCard, and Visa credit cards. **Local calls** made from public pay phones in most locales cost either 25¢ or 35¢. Pay phones do not accept pennies, and few will take anything larger than a quarter. You may want to look into leasing a cellphone for the duration of your trip.

Most long-distance and international calls can be dialed directly from any phone. **For calls within the United States and to Canada,** dial 1 followed by the area code and the seven-digit number. **For other international calls,** dial 011 followed by the country code, city code, and the telephone number of the person you are calling.

Calls to area codes **800, 888, 877,** and **866** are toll free. However, calls to numbers in area codes **700** and **900** (chat lines, bulletin boards, "dating" services, and so on) can be very expensive—usually a charge of 95¢ to $3 or more per minute, and they sometimes have minimum charges that can run as high as $15 or more.

For **reversed-charge or collect calls,** and for person-to-person calls, dial 0 (zero, not the letter o) followed by the area code and number you want; an operator will then come on the line to assist you. If you're calling abroad, ask for the overseas operator.

For **local directory assistance (information),** dial ☎ 411; for long-distance information, dial ☎ 1, then the appropriate area code and 555-1212.

TIME   Washington D.C. observes Eastern Standard Time (EST), like New York City. **Daylight saving time** is in effect from 1am on the first Sunday in April through 1am on the last Sunday in October, except in Arizona, Hawaii, part of Indiana, and Puerto Rico. Daylight saving

time moves the clock 1 hour ahead of standard time. At 1am on the last Sunday in October, clocks are set back 1 hour. For the correct time, call ☎ **202/844-2525.**

TIPPING   In hotels, tip **bellhops** at least $1 per bag, and tip the **chamber staff** $1 to $2 per day. Tip the **doorman** or **concierge** only if he or she has provided you with some specific service (for example, calling a cab for you or obtaining difficult-to-get theater tickets). Tip the **valet-parking attendant** $1 every time you get your car.

In restaurants, bars, and nightclubs, tip **service staff** 15% to 20% of the check, tip **bartenders** 10% to 15%, tip **checkroom attendants** $1 per garment, and tip **valet-parking attendants** $1 per vehicle. Tipping is not expected in cafeterias and fast-food restaurants.

Tip **cab drivers** 15% of the fare.

As for other service personnel, tip **skycaps** at airports at least $1 per bag, and tip **hairdressers** and **barbers** 15% to 20%.

Tipping ushers at movies and theaters, and gas-station attendants, is not expected.

TOILETS   You won't find public toilets or "restrooms" on the streets in D.C., but they can be found in hotel lobbies, bars, restaurants, coffee shops, museums, department stores, railway and bus stations, and service stations. Large hotels and fast-food restaurants are probably the best bet for good, clean facilities. Restaurants and bars in heavily visited areas may reserve their restrooms for patrons; purchasing a cup of coffee or soft drink will usually qualify you as a customer.

WEATHER   Call ☎ **202/936-1212** or visit www.weather.com. Also see the chart on p 169.

Recommended **Reading**

Fiction lovers might pick up books by Ward Just, including his collection of stories *The Congressman Who Loved Flaubert;* Ann Berne's *A Crime in the Neighborhood;* Marita Golden's *The Edge of Heaven;* Allen Drury's *Advise and Consent.* Or consider a mystery whose plot revolves around the capital, such as Margaret Truman's series that includes *Murder at the Smithsonian, Murder at the Kennedy Center,* and so on, or George Pelecanos's hard-core thrillers that take you to parts of Washington you'll never see as a tourist, such as in *Hell to Pay, Drama City,* and, in 2009, *The Way Home;* he also recently compiled and edited *D.C. Noir,* a collection of 16 gritty short stories, including one by Pelecanos himself.

National Book Award finalist *Lost in the City*—by Pulitzer Prize–winning novelist Edward P. Jones—is a beautifully written collection of short stories about the daily lives of African Americans in the capital.

Contenders, by Terence Winch, is a lively collection of stories about life in Washington in the 1970s and 1980s, as lived by the young and restless of that time.

History buffs shouldn't miss Arthur Schlesinger's *The Birth of the Nation;* F. Cary's *Urban Odyssey;* or David Brinkley's *Washington at War.* Paul Dickson's *On This Spot* traces the history of the city by revealing exactly what took place at specific locations—"on this spot"—in years gone by, neighborhood by neighborhood.

If you like your history leavened with humor, purchase Christopher Buckley's *Washington Schlepped Here: Walking in the Nation's Capital,* an irreverent nonfiction take on D.C.'s famous sites and characters. Buckley has also written a couple of funny, Washington-based novels, *The White House Mess* and *No Way to Treat a First Lady.* For another humorous read, put your hands on Dave Barry's *Dave Barry Hits Below the Beltway.*

Two memoirs are musts for finding out how the powerful operate in Washington: *Personal History,* by former Washington Post publisher Katharine Graham, and *Washington,* by Meg Greenfield, who was a columnist and editor at the Post for more than 30 years before her death in 1999. Katharine Graham's *Washington* is yet another good read—an anthology of more than 100 essays and articles about Washington by an eclectic bunch of people, from Will Rogers to Henry Kissinger, gathered by Graham.

Finally, to find out more about the architecture of Washington, pick up the *AIA Guide to the Architecture of Washington, D.C.,* by Christopher Weeks; for information about parks and hiking trails, look for *Natural Washington* by Richard Berman and Deborah Gerhard (I recommend these books although both need updating).

Last but not least: The perennially inspiring words of Abraham Lincoln are always worth revisiting.

Photo **Credits**

p i, left: © Chris Mellor/Lonely Planet Images/Getty Images; p i, center: © Jon Arnold Images/AGE Fotostock, Inc.; p i, right: © Richard T. Nowitz/National Geographic/Getty Images; p ii, top: © Wendell Metzen/PhotoLibrary; p ii, second from top: Courtesy Smithsonian Institution, Washington, DC; p ii, middle: © John Neubauer/Lonely Planet Images; p ii, second from bottom: © Richard Cummins/Lonely Planet Images; p ii, bottom: © Allison Dinner Photography; p iii, top: © Joe Sohm/Visions of America, LLC/Alamy Images; p iii, second from top: © Allison Dinner Photography; p iii, middle: © Nagelstock.com/Alamy Images; p iii, second from bottom: © Richard T. Nowitz/Corbis; p iii, bottom: © David Phelps/Courtesy Hotel Helix; p 1: © Ethel Davies/ImageState/Alamy Images; p 4: © Ron Sachs/Corbis/Sygma; p 5: © David Brooks/Corbis; p 6, top: © Karen Bleier/Getty Images; p 6, bottom: © William Phillips/Alamy Images; p 7: © Wendell Metzen/PhotoLibrary; p 9: © Richard T. Nowitz/AGE Fotostock; p 10, top: © Walter Bibikow/Jon Arnold Images/Alamy Images; p 10, bottom: © Joseph Sohm/Jupiterimages; p 11: © Todd Gipstein/Corbis; p 12, top: © Ken Ross/Viestiphoto.com; p 12, bottom: © National Gallery of Art, Washington, DC/Bridgeman Art Library; p 13: © Wally McNamee/Corbis; p 15, top: © Ken Ross/Viestiphoto.com; p 15, bottom: © Todd Gipstein/National Geographic/Getty Images; p 16: © Coston Stock/Alamy Images; p 17, top: © John Neubauer/Lonely Planet Images; p 17, bottom: © Jake Rajs/Getty Images; p 18, top: © Robert Harding Picture Library Ltd/Alamy Images; p 18, bottom: © Richard A. Bloom/Corbis; p 19: © Allison Dinner Photography; p 21, top: Courtesy

Photo Credits

Kramer's Books; p 21, bottom: © Rick Gerharter/Lonely Planet Images; p 22, top: © Rick Gerharter/Lonely Planet Images; p 22, bottom: © DCstockphoto.com/Alamy Images; p 23: © Richard Cummins/Lonely Planet Images; p 24: © Wim Wiskerke/Alamy Images; p 25: Courtesy Smithsonian Institution, Washington, DC; p 28: © A.T. Willett/Alamy Images; p 29: © Gail Mooney/Masterfile; p 30, top: © Chuck Pefley/Alamy Images; p 30, middle: © John Angerson/Alamy Images; p 30, bottom: Courtesy International Spy Museum; p 31, top: © Steven Widoff/Alamy Images; p 31, middle: Courtesy International Spy Museum; p 32, top: © Rough Guides/Alamy Images; p 32, bottom: © Tramonto/AGE Fotostock; p 35, top: © PCL/Alamy Images; p 35, bottom: Courtesy The Hay-Adams ; p 38: © Dean Conger/Corbis; p 39, top: © Kelly-Mooney Photography/Corbis; p 39, bottom: © Robert Shafer/Stock Connection Blue/Alamy Images; p 40: © PNC/AGE Fotostock, Inc.; p 41: © Ken Ross/Viestiphoto.com; p 42: © Ilene MacDonald/Alamy Images; p 43: © Bob Rowan/Progressive Image/Corbis; p 46: © Robert Ginn/PhotoLibrary; p 47: © Ken Ross/Viestiphoto.com; p 48: © Stephanie Maze/Corbis; p 49: © James Lemass/PhotoLibrary; p 53, top: © Rough Guides/Alamy Images; p 53, bottom: © Nina Leen/Time & Life Pictures/Getty Images; p 54: Courtesy Smithsonian Institution, Washington, DC; p 55, top: © Popperfoto/Alamy Images; p 55, bottom: © Edward Owen/Art Resource, NY; p 56, top: © Rough Guides/Alamy Images; p 56, bottom: © Rough Guides/Alamy Images; p 58: © Jeff Greenberg/AGE Fotostock; p 59: © John Neubauer/Lonely Planet Images; p 61: © National Gallery of Art, Washington, DC/SuperStock, Inc.; p 62, top: © Ken Ross/Viestiphoto.com; p 62, bottom: © National Gallery of Art, Washington, DC./SuperStock, Inc.; p 63: © National Gallery of Art, Washington, DC/Bridgeman Art Library; p 65, top: © Smithsonian Institution, Washington, DC/Bridgeman Art Library; p 65, bottom: Courtesy Smithsonian Institution, Washington, DC; p 66, top: © i2i Images/Jupiterimages; p 66, bottom: Courtesy Smithsonian Institution, Washington, DC; p 67: © Alex Segre/Alamy Images; p 69, top: Courtesy Smithsonian's National Museum of American History; p 69, bottom: © Ken Ross/Viestiphoto.com; p 70: Courtesy Smithsonian's National Museum of American History; p 71, top: © Ken Ross/Viestiphoto.com; p 71, bottom: Courtesy Smithsonian's National Museum of American History; p 73: © Phillips Collection, Washington, DC/Bridgeman Art Library; p 74: © Ken Ross/Viestiphoto.com; p 77: © Aldo Tutino/Art Resource NY; p 78: © Held Collection/Bridgeman Art Library International; p 79: © Richard Cummins/Lonely Planet Images; p 81, top: © Allison Dinner Photography; p 81, bottom: © Ken Ross/Viestiphoto.com; p 83, top: © Ken Ross/Viestiphoto.com; p 83, bottom: © Allison Dinner Photography; p 84: © Allison Dinner Photography; p 85, top: © Rick Gerharter/Lonely Planet Images; p 85, bottom: © Rough Guides/Alamy Images; p 87, top: © Rough Guides/Alamy Images; p 87, bottom: © Rick Gerharter/Lonely Planet Images; p 88, top: © Allison Dinner Photography; p 88, bottom: © Ken Ross/Viestiphoto.com; p 89: © Allison Dinner Photography; p 91, top: © Chuck Pefley/Alamy Images; p 91, bottom: © Chuck Pefley/Alamy Images; p 92: © Lee Snider/Photo Images/Corbis; p 93: © Alex Segre/Alamy Images; p 95: © Ken Ross/Viestiphoto.com; p 96, top: © Richard T. Nowitz/Corbis; p 96, bottom: Courtesy Apartment Zero; p 97: © Dan Herrick/Lonely Planet Images; p 99, top: © Kelly-Mooney Photography/Corbis; p 99, bottom: © Richard T. Nowitz/Corbis; p 101, top: © Andre Jenny/Alamy Images; p 101, bottom: © Ken Ross/Viestiphoto.com; p 102: © Ken Ross/Viestiphoto.com; p 103: © Allison Dinner Photography; p 108: © Allison Dinner Photography; p 109, top: © Allison Dinner Photography; p 109, bottom: © Allison Dinner Photography; p 110, top: © Allison Dinner Photography; p 110, bottom: © Allison Dinner Photography; p 111: © Allison Dinner Photography; p 112, top: Courtesy Leopold's Kafe; p 112, bottom: © Allison Dinner Photography; p 113: © Allison Dinner Photography; p 115: © Joe Sohm/Visions of America, LLC/Alamy Images; p 117: © Pat O'Hara/Corbis; p 118, top: © William S. Kuta/Alamy Images; p 118, bottom: © Rick Gerharter/Lonely Planet Images; p 119: © Kelly-Mooney Photography/Corbis; p 121: © Joe Sohm/Visions of America, LLC/Alamy Images; p 122: © Bill Brooks/Alamy Images; p 123, top: © William S. Kuta/Alamy Images; p 123, bottom: © Sandra Baker/Alamy Images; p 125, top: © Chuck Pefley/Alamy Images; p 125, bottom: © John Neubauer/Lonely Planet Images; p 127: © Peter Miller/eStock Photo; p 128: © DanitaDelimont.com/Alamy Images; p 129: © Allison Dinner Photography; p 135: © Allison Dinner Photography; p 136, top: © Allison Dinner Photography; p 136, bottom: © Ken Ross/Viestiphoto.com; p 137: © Allison Dinner Photography; p 138, top: © Allison Dinner Photography; p 138, bottom: © Ken Ross/Viestiphoto.com; p 139: © Allison Dinner Photography; p 140, top: © Allison Dinner Photography; p 140, bottom: © Allison Dinner Photography; p 141: © Ken Ross/Viestiphoto.com; p 142: © Ken Ross/Viestiphoto.com; p 143: © Bill Helsel/Alamy Images; p 147: © Allison Dinner Photography; p 148: © Jim Folliard & The Park at 14th; p 149: © David Phelps/Courtesy Hotel Helix; p 150: © Ken Ross/Viestiphoto.com; p 152: © Ken Ross/Viestiphoto.com; p 153: © Richard T. Nowitz/Corbis; p 156: Courtesy Studio Theater; p 157, top: © Ken Ross/Viestiphoto.com; p 157, bottom: Courtesy Blues Alley; p 158: © Scott Suchman Photography; p 159: © David Phelps/Courtesy Hotel Helix; p 162: Courtesy The Hay-Adams; p 163: Courtesy The Hay-Adams; p 164: © David Phelps/Courtesy Hotel Helix; p 165: Courtesy Hotel Monaco; p 166: © David Phelps/Courtesy Hotel Monaco; p 167: © Joe Raedle/Getty Images.